I0002277

Apache Druid
A Comprehensive Guide to Real-Time Data Analytics and Processing

Nova Trex

© 2024 by Wang Press. All rights reserved.

No part of this publication may be reproduced, distributed, or transmitted in any form or by any means, including photocopying, recording, or other electronic or mechanical methods, without the prior written permission of the publisher, except in the case of brief quotations embodied in critical reviews and certain other noncommercial uses permitted by copyright law.

Published by Wang Press

For permissions and other inquiries, write to:
P.O. Box 3132, Framingham, MA 01701, USA

Contents

3

4

Introduction

In an era where data is generated at unprecedented rates, the ability to process, analyze, and derive insights from this data in real-time has become a critical asset for organizations worldwide. "Apache Druid: A Comprehensive Guide to Real-Time Data Analytics and Processing" serves as an in-depth resource for navigating the intricacies of Apache Druid, an open-source, highly scalable database specifically designed for fast, real-time data ingestion and analytics.

Apache Druid distinguishes itself through its hybrid architecture, adept at handling both real-time and batch analytics tasks with exceptional speed. Architects and engineers prize Druid not merely for its technical capabilities but for how it empowers businesses to turn real-time data insights into strategic actions. This book is crafted to guide data practitioners—be they engineers, analysts, or IT professionals—through the nuanced capabilities of Apache Druid, thus enabling them to build and optimize robust, interactive analytics frameworks.

Kicking off with installation and configuration, this guide sets the stage by ensuring readers establish a solid foundation from which to leverage Druid's power. The intricate architecture of Apache Druid is unpacked systematically, offering readers a clear perspective on its core components, like the Middle Manager, Historical nodes, and Broker processes. Understanding these integral parts not only aids in operational efficiency but also enhances the system's scalability and flexibility in handling diverse data workloads.

One of Druid's standout features is its versatile data ingestion capabilities. Whether it's real-time streaming data from sources like Kafka or batch uploads from cloud storage, Druid is built to accommodate varied data feed types seamlessly. We delve deep into these processes, exploring techniques and methodologies that enable efficient data management and transformation, ensuring that data is readily available for querying.

Following data ingestion, the book provides comprehensive coverage of querying within Druid. Readers will engage with innovative querying techniques ranging from simple timeseries queries to more complex aggregations and joins. This section arms users with the querying prowess needed to articulate business insights from vast datasets intuitively and interactively, thus driving informed decision-making.

Performance tuning and scaling strategies are addressed meticulously, vital for businesses aiming to keep pace with growing data demands. Readers will discover how to enhance Druid's performance, ensuring the system adapts fluidly to heightened concurrency and storage needs. These insights underpin the creation of an agile analytics environment capable of supporting sustained business growth.

Transitioning from the technical to the practical, we emphasize real-world operational considerations like monitoring, troubleshooting, and blending Druid into existing data ecosystems. These discussions are designed to enable practitioners to predict, identify, and rectify issues before they impact business operations adversely.

The book concludes with an exploration of security measures and best practices within Apache Druid deployments. In a landscape increasingly defined by data privacy concerns, implementing stringent security protocols is non-negotiable. Our coverage of security strategies equips readers with knowledge needed to safeguard data integrity and maintain compliance with data protection regulations.

"Apache Druid: A Comprehensive Guide to Real-Time Data Analytics and Processing" is not just a manual for mastering a sophisticated platform; it is an invitation to partake in the transformative journey of real-time analytics. Through its pages, readers gain not only the knowledge to deploy and manage Druid but also the confidence to usher their organizations toward data-driven futures. Whether you are just beginning your journey with Druid or are looking to refine and optimize your current deployments, this book is your essential companion in mastering real-time data analytics.

Chapter 1

Introduction to Apache Druid

Apache Druid is a powerful open-source analytics data store designed for rapid data ingestion and real-time analytical queries. This chapter offers an in-depth overview of Druid, highlighting its unique capabilities and the key advantages it brings to the landscape of modern data analytics. The text further contrasts Druid with other data systems, providing a clear understanding of its application across various industries. Additionally, the chapter traces the evolution of Druid from its inception to its present state, underscoring the advancements and community-driven developments that have enhanced its features and usability.

1.1 Overview of Apache Druid

Apache Druid stands as a pivotal technology in the domain of real-time data analytics, designed to ingest vast amounts of data with a focus on high-speed querying and low-latency performance. At the core of Druid is its ability to provide sub-second query responses on aggregate data, drawing upon a blend of time-series database and distributed storage characteristics. Developed to address the shortcomings of traditional databases in processing real-time data streams, Druid excels in analytics applications where rapid query completion and high availability are paramount.

Druid's architecture is engineered to operate in a distributed and fault-tolerant manner, ensuring reliable ingestion, storage, and querying of time-based event data. Typical applications of Druid involve event data with timestamp columns, which are crucial for its efficient indexing strategy. Druid can manage data ranging from simple numerical metrics to more complex dimensional data, making it highly versatile for a wide array of use cases.

As a column-oriented, distributed data store, Druid employs a novel indexing structure known as segment files, which are immutable and allow for efficient data compression and fast access. This immutability simplifies concurrency and consistency management, a pivotal aspect of Druid's operational strength. The segment-oriented design is complemented by an advanced caching layer that facilitates query optimization and reduces latency across distributed nodes.

The system's architecture is built around several core components, each fulfilling a specific role. The components are as follows:

- **Historical Nodes:** Responsible for storing and serving queries on immutable segment files. Historical nodes ensure queries are answered with sub-second latency and form the backbone of Druid's scalability.

- **MiddleManager Nodes:** Handle data ingestion tasks and perform real-time indexing. MiddleManagers convert real-time data into immutable segments, which are eventually handed over to Historical nodes.

- **Broker Nodes:** Provide the query distribution and gathering service, acting as endpoints for incoming analytical queries and forwarding them to appropriate Historical and MiddleManager nodes.

- **Coordinator Nodes:** Oversee the assignment of segments to Historical nodes, manage data tiering strategies, and ensure data redundancy and availability.

- **Overlord Nodes:** Manage job scheduling and task management for indexing activities, coordinating with MiddleManager nodes to execute ingestion tasks.

The interaction between these components facilitates Druid's operational efficiency and scalability across a cluster of commodity hardware. The separation of duties ensures that Druid can concurrently ingest and serve data, achieving near real-time performance.

Druid supports both batch and streaming data ingestion, thus offering flexibility in data load strategies. Batch ingestion typically involves the use of ETL jobs that pre-process data before loading it into Druid. Streaming ingestion, on the other hand, uses real-time computational engines like Apache Kafka, allowing Druid to ingest data continuously as it arrives.

Here is a simple Python code example using the pydruid library to communicate with a Druid instance and execute a simple time-series query:

```python
from pydruid.client import PyDruid
from pydruid.utils.aggregators import longsum
from pydruid.utils.postaggregator import Postaggregator
from datetime import datetime

# Connect to the Druid broker
client = PyDruid('http://localhost:8888', 'druid/v2/')

# Time boundary query
topn_query_result = client.time_boundary(datasource='your_data_source')

# Print result
print("Time Boundary Query Result:")
for result in topn_query_result:
    print(result)
```

The use of Python to run queries exemplifies Druid's interoperability with various programming environments, contributing to its usability across different workflows.

Druid's high concurrency support allows it to handle thousands of queries per second, making it suitable for applications ranging from web analytics, application performance monitoring, to financial market data analysis. The system is optimized for OLAP (Online Analytical Processing) type of queries that are prevalent in these scenarios.

Furthermore, Druid is equipped with features like approximate algorithms for sketches and top aggregates which enable performance optimizations for large datasets, minimizing computational overhead. This capability is especially useful for quick, ad-hoc analysis and exploratory data analysis tasks.

Druid introduces efficient data sharding techniques, primarily based on hashing, partitioning, and range partitioning of dimension values. This sharding mechanism is fundamental for distributing data evenly across the cluster, optimizing resource utilization and load balancing.

In the context of security, Druid provides several layers of access control, including row, column, and table-level security features. Access is governed using integration with industry-standard security frameworks and protocols, offering robust security constraints for enterprise applications.

The deployment of Apache Druid can be further enhanced through integration with data visualization tools and business intelligence platforms. These integrations enable organizations to leverage Druid's rapid query responses in generating dynamic dashboards and reports, facilitating real-time insights for decision-makers.

The scalability, efficiency, and flexibility of Druid are augmented by its active open-source community, which continuously contributes to its development and enhancement. The community also drives a rich ecosystem of plugins, extensions, and connectors that expand Druid's capabilities, making it adaptable to evolving analytical needs in the data landscape.

```
SELECT
  TOPN(city, 5) AS top_cities,
  COUNT(*) AS city_count
FROM
  city_traffic
WHERE
  __time >= CURRENT_TIMESTAMP - INTERVAL '1' DAY
GROUP BY
  city
```

This SQL-like example demonstrates Druid's query language features, which offer powerful windowing functions and rollups. The query language allows users to execute complex aggregations and explorations, echoing SQL's syntax while incorporating Druid-specific features suited for high-volume analytics.

Through the various facets discussed, Apache Druid emerges as a comprehensive data store that adheres to the principles of high availability, fault tolerance, and real-time processing. It facilitates rapid data exploration and insight generation, recognized for its strategic role in large scale data systems and analytics solutions.

1.2   Key Features and Benefits of Druid

Apache Druid is endowed with a robust set of features specifically designed to tackle the challenges associated with fast analytics on large volumes of data. Its unique abilities make it an attractive platform for numerous data-intensive applications. This section delves into the key features that define Druid's utility and highlights the substantial benefits it offers to businesses and data processing applications.

One of the cardinal features of Druid is its architectural design that revolves around real-time ingestion, columnar storage, and a distributed database environment. This triad of capabilities enables Druid to process and query data within milliseconds, thus supporting real-time analytics and decision-making processes.

- **Real-time Data Ingestion.** Druid allows for both batch and streaming ingestion modes, enabling seamless data processing from various sources. Its real-time ingestion capability is a crucial feature, permitting data to flow from streaming platforms like Apache Kafka or Amazon Kinesis and be queried almost instantaneously. These ingested data streams can be aggregated on-the-fly using roll-up techniques, thereby significantly reducing the storage footprint. This real-time capability is especially beneficial in dynamic environments where data changes rapidly, and prompt responses are essential.

- **Columnar Storage.** Data in Druid is organized in a column-oriented format, optimizing both storage and query speed. This format is known to offer better compression ratios and faster scan speeds as compared to the traditional row-oriented storage. Each column in Druid's architecture is stored independently, allowing for selective access of only the required columns during query execution, reducing I/O operations and speeding up query

13

responses. Moreover, columnar storage synergizes with Druid's segment-based sharding, ensuring efficient data distribution and load balancing across the cluster.

- **Distributed Architecture.** The distributed nature of Druid ensures fault tolerance and horizontal scalability. By segmenting data and distributing it across numerous Historical and Real-time nodes, Druid achieves high availability and can process queries against massive datasets without compromising on speed or accuracy. The system is designed to scale linearly, allowing resources to be expanded or contracted according to the load, thus optimizing infrastructure costs and performance.

- **Advanced Indexing.** Druid employs a diverse array of indexing mechanisms, including bitmap and inverted indexes, to facilitate rapid and efficient query processing. Bitmap indexes are particularly advantageous for high-cardinality columns as they provide compact and fast search capabilities. Additionally, Druid supports dictionaries for string columns, which map unique string values to integer identifiers, further enhancing the performance of lookups and joins.

- **Flexible Schemas.** Druid's flexible schema support means users can ingest data without predefining the schema. This feature allows Druid to handle schema-on-read capabilities, adapting to changes in data structure dynamically, which is critical for business intelligence applications requiring rapid adaptation to evolving data landscapes.

- **Query Capabilities.** Druid supports an array of query types including time-series, top-n, group by, and search queries. Its SQL-like query language is intuitive for users familiar with relational databases, ensuring a gentle learning curve. The query engine is optimized for running OLAP-style queries, which are central to numerous statistical and exploratory data analysis operations. Druid's approximate query algorithms, such as sketches and hyperloglog, provide fast estimations for significant-scale analytics without needing exact computations, which might be computationally expensive.

14

Consider the following example using Druid's SQL-like interface to perform a top-n query, illustrating its simplified yet powerful querying capability:

```
SELECT
  city,
  SUM(events) AS total_events
FROM
  website_traffic
WHERE
  ___time >= CURRENT_TIMESTAMP - INTERVAL '7 DAY'
GROUP BY
  city
ORDER BY
  total_events DESC
LIMIT 5
```

The superior query flexibility, combined with an enhanced caching layer, substantially reduces response time, thus reinforcing real-time decision capabilities in fast-paced data environments.

- **Strong Community and Ecosystem.** Druid is backed by a vibrant open-source community that continually enhances its core functionalities and extends its ecosystem with a rich array of plugins and extensions. This community-driven development ensures the platform remains at the forefront of innovation, responding to emergent user needs and technology trends proficiently.

- **Business Benefits.** The strategic application of Druid derives immense business value. By leveraging real-time analytics, businesses can improve operational efficiencies, embark on data-driven strategies, and optimize customer experiences. For instance, in a retail scenario, Druid enables real-time monitoring of sales data, allowing stakeholders to make informed stock replenishment decisions, refine marketing strategies, and enhance customer satisfaction through personalized service offerings.

The deployment of Druid also significantly aids in cost efficiency. Its open-source nature eliminates licensing costs, and its capability to run on commodity hardware reduces the need for expensive specialized systems. The technology's operational advantages translate into tangible financial savings and improved return on investment for organizations leveraging its capabilities.

- **Enhanced Security.** Organizations managing sensitive data require robust security. Druid incorporates comprehensive authorization and authentication mechanisms, ensuring secure access to data. These include integration with standard protocols like LDAP and Kerberos, offering fine-grained access controls at row, column, or data source levels.

- **Operational Intelligence.** Druid enables businesses to derive operational intelligence from large data streams. Real-time analytics facilitated by Druid empowers businesses with the capability to detect anomalies, monitor performance trends, and identify action points – all critical for maintaining a competitive edge in today's rapid-paced market environments.

```
from pydruid.client import PyDruid
from pydruid.utils.aggregators import count

client = PyDruid('http://localhost:8888', 'druid/v2/')

city_events_query = client.timeseries(
    datasource='website_traffic',
    granularity='day',
    intervals='2023-10-01/2023-10-07',
    aggregations={'event_count': count('events')},
    filter=('', 'city', '==', 'New York')
)

print("Timeseries Query Result for New York:")
for entry in city_events_query:
    print(entry)
```

Druid's utility extends across various sectors, from banking, where it supports fraud detection and risk management, to telecommunications, where it facilitates network performance monitoring and optimization. These diverse applications underscore its adaptability and integral role in enabling data-centric operations.

In essence, Apache Druid captures the intersection of performance, scalability, and analytical profundity, rendering it indispensable for modern enterprises that thrive on speed and insight. The key features encapsulated in Druid deliver acceleration in data processing, support for comprehensive data strategies, and the capability to unleash new innovations in data-driven domains.

1.3 Compare Druid with Other Data Systems

Apache Druid's innovative approach to real-time analytics sets it apart in the landscape of modern data systems. To gain a deeper appreciation of Druid's unique capabilities, it is essential to examine how it compares with other prevalent data systems and analytics platforms, such as Hadoop, Cassandra, and traditional data warehouses. This section will provide a detailed analysis of these systems, exploring their architectures, use cases, and specific advantages over Druid or vice versa.

Comparison with Hadoop. Hadoop is a well-established data processing framework that utilizes a distributed architecture for handling and processing large-scale batch and real-time data across clusters of computers. It primarily comprises Hadoop Distributed File System (HDFS) and MapReduce for storage and processing, respectively, alongside other ecosystem components such as Hive and HBase.

Hadoop excels in batch processing and is highly effective in handling large volumes of data with complex computational tasks. However, the traditional MapReduce paradigm can introduce latency for real-time analytics, as the data processing occurs in a sequential manner. In contrast, Druid's strength lies in real-time, low-latency querying capabilities, optimized through its in-memory, column-oriented storage and segment design.

Druid capitalizes on a specialized architecture that supports fast, sub-second analytical queries, positioning it as a superior choice for real-time data workloads. Apache Druid achieves scalable real-time ingestion and analytical processing seamlessly, an area where Hadoop can struggle without significant customization and additional components like Apache Storm or Apache Flink.

```
# Druid example for real-time analytics
from pydruid.client import PyDruid
from pydruid.utils.aggregators import longsum
from datetime import datetime

client = PyDruid('http://localhost:8888', 'druid/v2/')
result = client.timeseries(
    datasource='advertising_metrics',
    granularity='hour',
```

```
    intervals='2023-09-01/2023-09-07',
    aggregations={'impressions_sum': longsum('impressions')}
)

# Print the result
print("Druid Real-time Impressions per Hour:")
for entry in result:
    print(entry)
```

In terms of scalability, both systems expand horizontally; however, Druid's architecture facilitates finer granularity scaling through its decoupled query, ingestion, and storage nodes. This separation of concerns allows for differentiated scaling strategies based on workload demands.

Comparison with Cassandra. Cassandra boasts a distributed NoSQL database architecture, acclaimed for its high availability and fault tolerance across commodity hardware. It is designed to handle large volumes of writes and reads, making it suitable for applications where write scalability is crucial, such as IoT data collection or write-heavy applications.

One of the fundamental differences between Cassandra and Druid is their data model and query capabilities. Cassandra leverages a wide-column store model, optimal for writes and throughput but can deliver query latencies that are less predictable when it comes to analytical queries requiring complex aggregations or joins.

Druid, with its columnar store, bitmap indexing, and specialized query engine, offers optimized analytical capabilities with quick query response times for time-based aggregations, an area where Cassandra requires significant custom indexing or materialized views to achieve comparable performance. Furthermore, Druid's inherent support for real-time ingestion and its approximation algorithms for faster analysis on large datasets distinguish it as more suitable for high-speed analytics applications.

```
-- Example of Druid's fast aggregation
SELECT
    country,
    AVG(sales_amount) AS avg_sales
FROM
    retail_transactions
WHERE
```

```
    ___time >= CURRENT_TIMESTAMP - INTERVAL '1' MONTH
GROUP BY
    country
```

Cassandra provides a more robust model for consistency and high write availability with tunable consistency levels, outperforming Druid in scenarios necessitating highly durable and consistent write workloads.

Comparison with Traditional Data Warehouses. Traditional data warehouses such as Oracle, Teradata, and Amazon Redshift have long been the backbone of enterprise-level data analysis, offering structured data storage, robust OLAP query handling, and comprehensive data management tools.

These systems excel in structured query capabilities and integration with ETL processes for batch-oriented analysis. However, their architecture typically involves significant latency when dealing with streaming or rapidly changing real-time data, an area where Druid excels. Traditional warehouses often require pre-aggregated data to ensure quick response times for complex queries, adding overhead to data processing pipelines.

Druid offers a unique advantage in environments where data freshness and low-latency query performance are prioritized, as is often the case in operational intelligence use cases. It supports immediate data visibility upon ingestion, something classical data warehousing struggles to achieve without significantly compromising on performance or relying on supplementary tools for near real-time insights.

Use Cases and Application Domains. The application domains of Druid differ significantly from traditional systems given its design primarily for real-time analytics. Druid fits exceptionally well in use cases such as:

- **Digital Advertising:** Real-time bidding and advertisement performance tracking, enabling marketers to optimize campaigns with up-to-the-minute data.

19

- **Network Monitoring:** Monitoring system logs and network data to detect anomalies and ensure uptime, where quick visibility into current metrics is paramount.

- **E-commerce Analytics:** Real-time dashboards track sales and customer behavior, adapting marketing strategies on the fly.

Meanwhile, other systems such as Hadoop are extensively utilized in domains where extensive historical data processing is critical, like genomic data analysis or extended log file processing.

Druid's Integration and Interoperability. Another point of comparison for Druid against traditional and contemporary systems is its ability to integrate with existing data ecosystems. Druid often acts as a complementary component within existing architectures, streaming from platforms like Kafka to enhance its ingestion pipeline or serving as a back-end for real-time data visualization tools.

```
// JavaScript integration example for real-time dashboards
fetch('http://localhost:8888/druid/v2/?query=your_query')
  .then(response => response.json())
  .then(data => {
    // Render real-time data on a web page
    console.table(data);
  });
```

This interoperable nature affords Druid flexibility, allowing it to serve both as a real-time analytical engine and a complementary node in larger data workflows, thereby expanding its practical utility and adoption potential.

While Druid, Hadoop, Cassandra, and traditional warehouses each present powerful options with distinct strengths, Druid caters to unique needs in high-speed, real-time analytics. Its capacity for rapid data insights without extensive preprocessing, combined with its ability to seamlessly integrate into broader data architectures, renders it indispensable in scenarios demanding immediate data actionability and dynamic query workloads.

1.4   Use Cases and Applications

Apache Druid stands out for its powerful real-time data ingestion and fast analytical querying capabilities, making it well-suited for a myriad of industrial applications. Its flexibility and performance are central to the modern data landscape, enabling businesses and organizations to leverage data for significant strategic advantages and sense-making. This section examines a range of industries and scenarios where Druid is most commonly deployed, elucidating its diverse applications and impact.

- **Digital Marketing and Advertising.** In the digital marketing and advertising sphere, data-driven strategies are critical for optimizing campaign performance and ensuring maximum return on investment (ROI). Apache Druid plays a crucial role in this domain by providing real-time insights into consumer behavior, clickstreams, and advertisement performance. Marketers can monitor continuous streams of click and impression data, enabling rapid adjustments to campaigns, audience segmentation, and bid strategies.

  For instance, a marketing platform can use Druid to aggregate user interaction data from a series of advertisements, allowing campaign managers to visualize performance and derive actionable insights into which creatives or channels yield the highest engagement. By integrating with message brokers such as Apache Kafka, Druid can ingest events as they occur, offering metrics like impressions, clicks, and conversions in real-time dashboards.

```
from pydruid.client import PyDruid
from pydruid.utils.aggregators import longsum, doublesum
from pydruid.utils.filters import Dimension, Filter

client = PyDruid('http://localhost:8888', 'druid/v2/')

# Fetch data for ad campaigns
result = client.timeseries(
    datasource='ad_impressions',
    granularity='hour',
    intervals='2023-10-01/2023-10-07',
    aggregations={
        'total_clicks': longsum('clicks'),
        'total_impressions': longsum('impressions'),
        'revenue': doublesum('revenue')
    },
```

```
    filter=Filter('state', '=', 'active')
)

# Print campaign metrics
print("Real-Time Ad Campaign Metrics:")
for entry in result:
    print(entry)
```

- **Telecommunications and Network Monitoring.** Telecommunications firms require robust systems for network traffic data analysis and real-time optimization. Druid's ability to ingest and analyze large quantities of log data from network devices enables operators to track system utilization, identify bottlenecks, detect anomalies, and anticipate capacity issues.

  A telecommunications company could employ Druid to gather metrics on data packets, error rates, and throughput, providing network administrators with an instant view of network health. Such real-time monitoring helps in proactive maintenance and optimization efforts, ensuring consistent service delivery.

  One practical application is monitoring call detail records (CDR), which log information about voice and data transactions across networks. Druid enables high-speed aggregations and visualizations of CDR, facilitating real-time anomaly detection and fraud prevention mechanisms.

- **Financial Services and Risk Management.** In the financial industry, high-frequency trading and risk management necessitate rapid access to time-sensitive data. Apache Druid's architecture supports the ingestion and analysis of streams of market data, making it indispensable for trading platforms and financial services that rely on intricate market models.

  Financial institutions leverage Druid to develop dashboards that showcase key performance indicators (KPIs), visualize trading patterns, and expose fraud through real-time anomaly detection. Its ability to handle high-cardinality datasets with precision allows for multifaceted reporting and analytics. For instance, tracking trading volume, price fluctuations, and trader behavior in the stock market, financial analysts can provide real-time recommendations and alerts to traders.

  Consider the case of a risk management application using Druid to respond to market sentiments and transaction anomalies. By scanning live datasets for irregular patterns, Druid helps mitigate risks associated with trading activities.

- **Retail and E-commerce.** Retail and e-commerce enterprises benefit considerably from timely data insights derived from customer interactions and sales transactions. Apache Druid enables real-time analytics on sales data, customer preferences, and inventory levels, assisting retailers in making informed decisions.

  Retailers use Druid to power features like dynamic pricing, recommendation engines, and customer segmentation by analyzing historical and current purchase data. Additionally, it is instrumental in providing personalized shopping experiences based on real-time customer journey mapping.

  An e-commerce platform, for example, can leverage Druid's data engine to integrate with existing CRM and inventory systems, maintaining up-to-the-minute snapshots of product performance and customer engagement. This integration permits proactive stock maintenance and promotional campaigns aligned with current trends.

```sql
-- Example query for analyzing sales in real-time using Druid
SELECT
  product_id,
  COUNT(*) AS purchase_count,
  SUM(purchase_amount) AS total_revenue
FROM
  online_sales
WHERE
  __time >= CURRENT_TIMESTAMP - INTERVAL '1 DAY'
GROUP BY
  product_id
ORDER BY
  total_revenue DESC
LIMIT 10
```

- **Internet of Things (IoT) and Sensor Analytics.** The proliferation of IoT devices has led to an immense surge in data generation, necessitating robust systems for ingesting, storing, and analyzing sensor data efficiently. Apache Druid is well-suited for IoT analytics, offering high ingestion rates alongside the capability to perform real-time aggregations on time-series data.

  Druid's ability to manage high-cardinality data effortlessly makes

23

it ideal for scenarios involving sensor data ingested from numerous diverse sources. Real-time processing of IoT data streams empowers applications in manufacturing, smart city infrastructure, and health monitoring.

In smart city projects, for example, Druid can be used to monitor sensor data related to traffic signals, energy usage, and public transportation systems, facilitating sustainable urban management and enhancing the quality of life for citizens.

- **Log and Security Analytics.** Enterprises often manage expansive volumes of system logs and security feeds as part of their operational and compliance strategies. Apache Druid effectively processes and analyzes these log records, providing security teams with quick access to actionable insights. This application is key for system administrators and security analysts seeking to improve their incident response times and monitoring capabilities.

  By ingesting logs in real-time, organizations can swiftly identify suspicious activities, operational anomalies, and resource misconfigurations, supporting comprehensive security intelligence and automated response systems.

  For example, a security team can build a Druid-based dashboard to visualize access logs and track user activity, highlighting potential security threats and facilitating investigation workflows.

In summary, the adoption of Apache Druid across various domains highlights its versatility and capability to drive business value through real-time analytics and insights. Druid excels in delivering high-speed data processing, complex event handling, and providing a foundation for operational intelligence that advances strategic initiatives. The aforementioned applications outline Druid's impact on transforming data into actionable intelligence, illuminating its strategic importance in modern analytical environments.

1.5 History and Evolution of Druid

Apache Druid's journey from its inception to its current standing in the world of data systems is a compelling story of innovation, community engagement, and technical advancement. Tracking Druid's history involves understanding the motivations behind its creation, key milestones that have punctuated its evolution, and the role of community contributions in steering its trajectory.

Origins and Motivation.

Druid was conceived in 2011 by the Founder and CTO of Metamarkets, Eric Tschetter, and his team. The initial motivations for creating Druid emerged from Metamarkets' need for a real-time analytics platform capable of providing rapid insights into large streams of data. Traditional databases and data warehouses were prohibitively slow for the sub-second query response times they required. The existing solutions couldn't meet the scalability, speed, or real-time requirements demanded by applications focused on live data.

The team at Metamarkets sought to overcome these limitations with a system that would combine the best of both OLAP capacities with real-time data processing. Thus, Druid was developed to handle high concurrency with low latency on complex queries over vast datasets, tailored specifically for streaming data environments.

Initial Development and Open Source Contribution.

Druid was officially open-sourced in October 2012 under the GPL license, marking a significant milestone in its development timeline. By contributing Druid to the open-source community, Metamarkets aimed to foster collaboration, innovation, and widespread adoption of a technology that could drive real-time analytics forward.

The initial release included fundamental features such as column-oriented storage, core ingestion capabilities, and a multi-node architecture that provided horizontal scalability and fault tolerance.

```
# Example of Druid's initial configuration file
druid:
  processing:
    buffer:
      sizeBytes: 10485760
      numThreads: 2
```

25

```
segmentCache:
  locations:
    - { path: "/tmp/druid/segments", maxSize: 100000000000 }
server:
  maxSize: 20480000000
```

Key Milestones and Technical Advancements.

Over the years, Druid has witnessed numerous technical advancements, with each iteration enhancing its core capabilities and extending its reach into new application domains. Several key milestones
highlight its evolutionary path:

- **2013—Real-time Ingestion:** Druid introduced real-time ingestion capabilities, allowing it to consume data streams via integration with message brokers like Apache Kafka. This feature
  fundamentally transformed how data could be ingested and processed in Druid, enabling continuous ingestion rather than relying solely on batch-processing models.

- **2015—Pluggable Storage and Indexing:** The introduction
  of a pluggable storage system greatly expanded Druid's flexibility, facilitating various storage configurations and indexes. This
  advancement enabled Druid to support more complex query patterns and optimize performance across different data scales and
  structures.

- **2017—Native SQL Support:** With the addition of SQL support, Druid democratized access to its analytical engine, providing users the ability to execute queries using familiar SQL syntax.
  This feature widened Druid's accessibility significantly, enabling
  analysts and developers alike to interact with the data effectively.

- **2019—Joining Apache Foundation:** The acceptance into
  the Apache Software Foundation as an incubating project
  marked another pivotal moment for Druid. This development
  signaled its maturity as an open-source product and opened
  avenues for growth, transparency, and rigorous community
  governance.

Evolution of Community and Ecosystem.

The evolution of Druid's community has been instrumental in its growth, with numerous organizations and independent contributors actively participating in development, bug fixing, and feature enhancements. The Apache Druid community has cultivated a diverse ecosystem encompassing varied plugins, extensions, and integrations, enriching its core architecture and enabling customizable deployments across different industries.

The contribution models within the community encourage open collaboration for enhancing Druid's performance, security, and functional capabilities. Open forums, mailing lists, and collaborative platforms provide an avenue for discourse, ensuring that the roadmap aligns with emerging technological trends and user feedback.

Adoption Across Industries.

Druid's evolution has also been characterized by its adoption across a range of industries, each leveraging its distinct real-time analytical capabilities to drive competitive advantages. Its adoption in industries such as telecommunications, finance, and e-commerce underscores its versatility and efficiency in the handling of data-intensive workloads.

For instance, innovative e-commerce platforms employ Druid to harness real-time behavioral analytics, enabling the delivery of personalized shopping experiences. Similarly, financial institutions employ Druid-powered dashboards for market analysis, facilitating rapid assessments of trading activities and investment strategies.

Current State and Future Trajectories.

As Apache Druid enters its mature phase within the Apache ecosystem, it continues to develop along several promising trajectories. Key areas of ongoing development include enhanced machine learning integration, augmented real-time data handling capacities, and refined support for multi-cloud and hybrid deployments.

The potential expansion of its features into areas such as more sophisticated multi-tenancy support, deeper AI algorithm integration, and enhanced graphical query interfaces will likely propel Druid further into the pantheon of high-performance analytical data systems.

Moreover, the Apache Druid community remains vigilant in adopting cutting-edge architectural concepts and maintaining open standards compliance, ensuring Druid's compatibility and functionality remain at the forefront of real-time data analytics innovation.

In sum, the history and evolution of Apache Druid present a narrative of transformation from a specialized analytics platform to a robust, widely-adopted cornerstone in the world of open-source big data solutions. The consistent strategic focus on real-time processing, scalability, and community-driven enhancement has solidified its status as an indispensable tool for modern, complex data landscapes.

Chapter 2

Installing and Setting Up Apache Druid

This chapter provides a detailed guide on the installation and configuration of Apache Druid, suitable for diverse environments. It outlines system prerequisites and preparatory steps necessary to ensure a smooth setup process. Step-by-step instructions are provided for downloading, installing, and configuring essential Druid components. Further, the text guides readers through setting up a clustered environment and verifies successful installation through testing with sample data. Additionally, common installation issues are identified, along with practical solutions to troubleshoot and resolve these challenges effectively.

2.1 System Requirements and Preparations

The proper and efficient functioning of Apache Druid depends significantly on understanding the system requirements and conducting necessary preparations. This section elucidates the hardware and software prerequisites and provides guidance on preparatory steps to ensure a smooth setup. These include not only basic hardware and operating system considerations but also insights into specific configurations that optimize performance and reliability.

- **Hardware Requirements**

Apache Druid is designed to handle high query performance on large datasets. The fundamental hardware requirements to achieve optimal performance include:

- **CPU**: Druid nodes are heavily dependent on multi-core processors, where more cores allow for increased parallelism in data processing tasks. A recommended starting point is modern x86_-64 processors with at least 8 cores per machine for smaller installations and upwards of 16 cores for larger scales.

- **Memory (RAM)**: Memory requirements depend significantly on the types of data ingestion and query loads. A baseline for testing and small-scale deployment is 16 to 32 GB of RAM per node. In production environments, it is advisable to allocate 64 GB of RAM or more, depending on workload complexity and volume.

- **Storage**: SSDs are preferred to traditional HDDs for storage due to their faster read/write capabilities, which is crucial for Druid's performance, especially for nodes handling historical data. The storage allocations should consider the dataset size and replication factor. A starting point might be 1 TB per node, scalable with the dataset.

- **Network**: A high-throughput network is essential, with 1 Gbps minimum recommended, and 10 Gbps being ideal for robust installations, ensuring low latency and efficient cluster communication.

It is crucial to note that while these specifications support typical deployment scenarios, scaling hardware resources in line with business needs and query complexities can significantly influence Druid's performance outcomes.

- **Operating System and Software Requirements**

Druid's software efficiency partially hinges on the correct choice and configuration of the operating system and requisite software. The following are recommended:

- **Supported Operating Systems**: Apache Druid is compatible with most modern UNIX-like operating systems, with Linux (such as Ubuntu, CentOS, or Debian) being the most widely used in production deployments. It is essential to ensure the OS version supports the latest Java versions. While MacOS and Windows can be used for testing and development environments, they are not recommended for production-grade systems.

- **Java Development Kit (JDK)**: Druid requires Java 8 or later, with OpenJDK 8+ being the recommended choice for most installations. Ensure that the JAVA_HOME environment variable is correctly set to point to the JDK installation directory.

Run the following command to verify the Java version installed on your system:

```
java -version
```

On execution, the version output should be similar to:

```
openjdk version "1.8.0_252"
OpenJDK Runtime Environment (AdoptOpenJDK)(build 1.8.0_252-b09)
OpenJDK 64-Bit Server VM (AdoptOpenJDK)(build 25.252-b09, mixed mode)
```

- **Environment Configuration**

Prior to installation, setting up the environment involves configuring network parameters, setting file handle and process limits, and ensuring timezone consistency across cluster nodes.

- **Network Configuration**: Configure each server's network to handle a high number of simultaneous connections and large data volumes. It is advisable to adjust the maximum number of file descriptors. For example, you can increase these limits by editing /etc/security/limits.conf:

31

```
* soft nofile 65536
* hard nofile 65536
```

Additionally, consider configuring network interfaces for optimal performance using tools like ethtool.

- **Process Limits and Swappiness**: Disable swap space or set swappiness to 0 to prevent Druid from using slow disk swapping extensively instead of RAM. Modify in /etc/sysctl.conf:

```
vm.swappiness=0
```

Applying these changes ensures that resources are efficiently tailored to Druid's operational needs.

- **Time Synchronization**: Synchronize the system time on each node using Network Time Protocol (NTP) to maintain uniformity within the cluster. This is critical for timestamped data and for maintaining system logs consistency.

- **Dependency Installations**

Ensure that necessary dependencies such as database systems or distributed storage services are in place.

- **Metadata Storage**: Druid requires a metadata store for maintaining cluster state. PostgreSQL is a commonly used option for production systems. Install and configure PostgreSQL as follows:

```
sudo apt-get install postgresql
```

Create a database and user for Druid, setting appropriate permissions to allow Druid components to access it.

```
sudo -u postgres psql
CREATE DATABASE druid;
CREATE USER druid WITH ENCRYPTED PASSWORD 'password';
GRANT ALL PRIVILEGES ON DATABASE druid TO druid;
```

- **Deep Storage**: A reliable deep storage layer such as Amazon S3, HDFS, or Google Cloud Storage is essential for Druid. Configuration specifics for these storages will depend on the provider and are vital for archiving historical data.

32

- **Pre-installation Checks**

Upon fulfilling hardware, software, and configuration requirements, one must perform preliminary checks before installation. Verify network connectivity across nodes using ping and telnet or secure shell (ssh) commands to ensure there are no firewalls or IP restrictions that hamper communication between nodes.

Assess log directories set up with the proper permissions, ensuring Druid can write debug and operational log data for efficient troubleshooting. Also, system health checks can identify potential bottlenecks and ensure that the system is running optimally.

This methodological approach to system requirements and preparation sets a solid foundation for installing and configuring Apache Druid efficiently. By optimizing infrastructure and environmental variables from the outset, the deployment process becomes significantly streamlined, and operating stability is enhanced. As we proceed to the installation phase, these preparatory steps will mitigate potential complications, facilitating a more seamless operation as you work with Apache Druid.

2.2 Downloading and Installing Druid

This section provides comprehensive instructions for downloading and installing Apache Druid across various operating systems and environments. It encompasses both standalone setups for development and testing, as well as multi-node configurations for production deployments, while addressing potential operational prerequisites and optimizing installation processes.

Obtaining Apache Druid

Firstly, secure the latest stable version of Apache Druid, which can be retrieved via the official Druid download page at http://druid.apache.org/downloads.html. Ensure version compatibility with existing systems or databases to prevent integration issues.

For example, to download Druid using wget:

```
wget https://downloads.apache.org/druid/X.Y.Z/apache-druid-X.Y.Z-bin.tar.gz
```

Replace X.Y.Z with the desired Druid version number. Confirm the integrity of the downloaded file against the corresponding PGP signatures or MD5/SHA checksums provided on the download page.

Installation on Linux

After obtaining the package, execute the following steps to install Apache Druid on a Linux-based system:

1. Extract the Tarball: Use the tar utility to extract files:

   ```
   tar -zxvf apache-druid-X.Y.Z-bin.tar.gz
   ```

   This command will create a directory named apache-druid-X.Y.Z in your working directory.

2. Directory Structure Examination: Navigate into the Druid directory to familiarize yourself with its structure. Key subdirectories include:

   - bin: Contains startup scripts and utilities for running Druid.
   - conf: Houses configurations, including templates for various types of setups.
   - lib: Comprises libraries essential for Druid operations.

3. Configure Environment Variables: Establish environment variables to streamline Druid's operations. For instance:

   ```
   export DRUID_HOME=~/apache-druid-X.Y.Z
   export PATH=$PATH:$DRUID_HOME/bin
   ```

4. Prerequisite Installations: Depending on your use-cases, ensure other required software or components are available. Java should be configured as specified previously.

5. Starting the Druid Services: Use provided scripts to start Druid. For example, the following command boots up a micro-quickstart single-node version:

```
bin/start-micro-quickstart
```

This command bootstraps essential Druid services for exploration and basic testing. Monitor the script's console output or corresponding log files for any operational anomalies.

Configuring Druid for Windows Operating System

Running Druid on Windows is suitable primarily for development or testing purposes. Employ the Windows Subsystem for Linux (WSL) or equivalent to facilitate UNIX-like functionality. Follow similar steps as described for Linux installations once WSL is operational.

1. WSL Installation: Enable and install WSL through PowerShell:

```
wsl --install
```

2. Druid on WSL: Follow the Linux installation instructions within the WSL environment.

Launching Druid services typically involves executing scripts from the UNIX shell initialized by WSL, and it mirrors the command-line operations discussed in the Linux setup.

Installing on macOS

Druid installations on macOS are conducted similarly to those on Linux:

1. Extract Framework: Use the tar utility familiar to macOS systems:

```
tar -zxvf apache-druid-X.Y.Z-bin.tar.gz
```

2. Configure System Environment: Set essential environment variables and JAVA_HOME.

3. Service Initialization: Utilize the following script to initialize the Druid sandbox:

```
bin/start-micro-quickstart
```

This brings up core Druid services, excluding deep storage or complex cluster configuration, sufficient for exploration within the local environment.

Advanced Deployment: Multi-node Configuration

For a production-ready Druid installation, a multi-node configuration becomes necessary. This setup demands a robust understanding of each Druid component and their interplay within a networked environment.

1. Download and Extract: On each server node needed for the cluster, download and extract Druid as previously outlined.

2. Node Specialization and Configuration: Define roles for each node, such as Master (Coordinator and Overlord), MiddleManager, Broker, Historical, and others. Adjust configurations within the conf directory accordingly:

For instance, to modify common.runtime.properties for a multi-node environment:

```
druid.host=master.node.local:8081
druid.port=8081
druid.extensions.directory=extensions
druid.metadata.storage.type=postgresql
        druid.metadata.storage.connector.connectURI=jdbc:postgresql://your-
host/druid
druid.metadata.storage.connector.user=druid
druid.metadata.storage.connector.password=password
```

36

3. Configuration Specificity: Nodes tailored to specific roles should have configuration files that reflect their functional requirements.

4. Starting Services in Distributed Mode: On each respective node, execute the appropriate startup script according to the roles they serve:

```
bin/start-coordinator-overlay.sh
bin/start-historical.sh
bin/start-middlemanager.sh
```

Integrate configuration management tools such as Ansible or Puppet to automate and maintain consistent configurations across distributed systems.

5. Networking Considerations: Ensure meticulous network setups, with load balancers and firewall configurations as necessitated by security and operational protocols.

Installation Verification

Verify successful installation across services on a standalone or distributed configuration through comprehensive log assessments and interface explorations.

- Accessing the Druid Console: The web console running on default port 8888 provides a comprehensive overview of installed services, audience analytics, and data management tools.

- Log Examinations: Detailed logs for each functional component will be available in the logs directory, prominently featuring metrics, errors, and operational statuses for real-time assessments and retrospective analysis.

By methodically addressing installation and deployment protocols, these directions ensure that Apache Druid operates optimally across varying scales and environments, setting the stage for further configuration and utilization.

2.3 Configuring Druid Components

Effective configuration of Druid components is pivotal for optimizing performance and ensuring reliable data ingestion and query execution. Apache Druid's modular architecture encompasses various components endowed with specific responsibilities, namely the Overlord, Coordinator, Broker, Historical, MiddleManager, and others. This section delves into the configuration intricacies of these components, providing detailed instructions to harness their collective capabilities for enhanced data processing outcomes.

To configure Druid effectively, one must grasp the primary roles and interdependencies of its components:

- **Overlord and Coordinator**:

    - Overlord: Manages task coordination and distribution for data ingestion processes.
    - Coordinator: Oversees data segment distribution and replication across Historical nodes, maintaining data availability and load balancing.

- **Broker**: Acts as a query router to Historical and Real-time nodes, aggregating results for user queries.

- **Historical**: Stores immutable data segments that have been ingested, enabling fast query processing.

- **MiddleManager**: Conducts real-time ingestion and transforms the data into segments for subsequent handoff to Historical nodes.

Each component's configuration must be tailored to its functional demands and the specific infrastructure in use, affecting performance, reliability, and scalability.

Cross-component properties are defined in the common.runtime.properties configuration file. These properties influence basic settings such as logging, directory paths, and service endpoints.

Example Configuration:

38

```
# Common properties for all Druid services
druid.extensions.directory=extensions
druid.extensions.loadList=["druid-hdfs-storage", "druid-kafka-indexing-service"]

# Metadata store
druid.metadata.storage.type=postgresql
druid.metadata.storage.connector.connectURI=jdbc:postgresql://hostname:5432/druid
druid.metadata.storage.connector.user=druid
druid.metadata.storage.connector.password=password

# Deep storage
druid.storage.type=local
druid.storage.storageDirectory=var/druid/segments
```

Further priorities include cloud storage settings if relying on Amazon S3, Google Cloud Storage, or HDFS, with appropriate credentials and access configurations.

Configuring the Overlord and Coordinator involves establishing workload management and segment distribution settings.

- **Overlord Configuration**:

    - Task Management: Adjust properties for task queueing, distribution, and parallelism tuned to system capacity.

    ```
    druid.indexer.runner.type=local
    druid.indexer.queue.startDelay=PT30S
    druid.indexer.runner.javaOpts=-server -Xmx4g -Duser.timezone=UTC
    ```

- **Coordinator Configuration**:

    - Segment Management: Monitor and balance data segments, defining parameters for replication and loading variations to ensure data consistency.

    ```
    druid.coordinator.loadqueuepeon.type=curator
    druid.coordinator.balancer.strategy=cost
    druid.coordinator.period=PT30S
    ```

These configurations are typically stored in the respective runtime.properties for each component.

The Broker is pivotal for routing and aggregating user queries. Its configuration is primarily concerned with query-time operations and resource handling.

```
# Broker-specific configurations
druid.broker.cache.useCache=true
druid.broker.cache.populateCache=true
druid.broker.http.maxIdleTime=PT10M
druid.broker.http.maxQueuedRequests=1024
```

Adjust cache settings based on expected query loads and memory availability. Cache usage dramatically improves repeated query performance by reducing data retrieval times, considering both local and query cache strategies.

Historical nodes serve as the backbone for query execution, holding vast amounts of immutable data. Proper configuration ensures efficient data access and retrieval.

- Example Configuration:

```
druid.segmentCache.locations=[{"path": "/mnt/druid/segment-cache", "maxSize":
    50000000000}]
druid.server.maxSize=100000000000
druid.historical.cache.useCache=true
```

Define data segment cache locations and maximum capacities, tailored by available disk resources. Segment balancer and level settings further optimize query workflows by controlling segment loading distributions.

MiddleManager nodes handle real-time data ingestion, necessitating configurations that accommodate fluctuating data volumes and speed.

- Sample Configuration:

```
druid.worker.capacity=5
druid.indexer.runner.javaOpts=-server -Xmx2g -XX:MaxDirectMemorySize=4g -Duser.
    timezone=UTC
druid.indexer.task.baseTaskDir=var/druid/task
```

Assess task concurrency and memory specifications, ensuring that task slots are appropriately distributed for parallel task execution. It is critical to align the MiddleManager configurations with ingestion backend requirements such as Kafka or Kinesis throughput.

A nuanced understanding of Java Virtual Machine (JVM) optimization can substantially enhance the performance of all nodes:

- **Heap Size and Garbage Collection (GC)**:

```
-server -Xms4g -Xmx4g -XX:+UseG1GC -XX:MaxGCPauseMillis=100
```

- Set Xms and Xmx per node responsibility.
- Employ G1GC or other garbage-collecting processes to reduce delays during execution.

- **Direct Memory Settings**: Specifically for components like Historical and Broker nodes that handle large datasets.

```
-XX:MaxDirectMemorySize=8g
```

Balance memory allocations logically among JVM heap, direct memory, and off-heap (if necessary) to cater to the node's functional prominence.

Reliable data insights are aided by thorough monitoring and well-defined logging configurations:

- **Log Management**:

  - Configure log levels and appenders to capture insights into system operations.
    ```
    log4j.rootLogger=INFO, file, stderr
    log4j.appender.file=org.apache.log4j.RollingFileAppender
    log4j.appender.file.File=${druid.log.path}/druid.log
    ```

- **Metrics Collection**:

  - Utilize Druid's integration with monitoring systems such as Prometheus or Grafana. Implement metric emitter configurations to streamline operational visualization.
    ```
    druid.emitter=prometheus
    druid.emitter.http.flushMillis=1000
    druid.emitter.http.recipientBaseUrl=http://monitoring-service:8080
    ```

Extract actionable intelligence to monitor workload distributions, historical node load lagging, and query performance, providing essential metrics for model auditing and system scaling decisions.

Precision in configuring Druid's components can significantly influence system efficiency, reliability, and scalability. By tailoring each node's parameters to its intended function and workload, robust performance in large-scale and high-demand environments can be achieved. These configurational strategies focus on ensuring data accessibility, maintaining operational scalability, and facilitating quick adjustments to meet evolving data demands, presenting a foundational blueprint for effective Druid deployments.

2.4   Setting Up a Cluster Environment

Setting up an Apache Druid cluster environment entails coordinating multiple nodes across designated roles, enabling the system to handle high availability, fault tolerance, and performance optimization. This process involves strategic deployment planning, intricate network configurations, and diligent resource management. This section provides exhaustive guidance on configuring a multi-node Druid cluster, taking into account considerations such as node role allocation, networking, and performance tuning.

Before proceeding with the physical setup, plan the architecture of your Druid cluster, considering:

- **Role Distribution**: Spread roles across various nodes based on functionality and anticipated load. Standard roles include Master nodes (handling Overlord and Coordinator duties), Query nodes (Brokers), Historical nodes, and Data nodes (MiddleManagers).

  - **Master Nodes** typically demand stable processing capabilities and robust storage for metadata.

  - **Historical Nodes** need fast access storage for efficient querying.

  - **MiddleManagers** require moderate CPU and memory for processing real-time ingestion tasks.

  - **Brokers** benefit from optimized memory and network throughput for query workloads.

- **Capacity Planning**: Assess expected data volumes, query frequency, and complexity. This assessment influences the number of nodes and resources like CPU core count, available RAM, and network infrastructure to match anticipated demands. Model the resource distribution in accordance with business growth predictions.

- **High Availability and Fault Tolerance**: Design the cluster to ensure high availability by replicating key components, employing leader-election mechanisms, and setting up redundant paths for critical workflows.

Networking is crucial for cluster communication and data query performance. Druid requires precise settings to maintain low-latency data exchanges. Network configurations include:

- **Inter-Node Communication**: Ensure each node has clear network access to every other component. This involves configuring proper IP addressing schemes and using DNS for domain resolution across nodes.
  - Implement virtual LANs (VLANs) or subnets for node isolation to reduce packet loss and enhance security.
  - Employ reliable caching DNS solutions.

- **Bandwidth Allocation**: Provide sufficient bandwidth, particularly for Broker - Historical and MiddleManager - Data node communication, which can become bottleneck points owing to the large volume of data transferred during query responses and ingestion.

- **Load Balancing**: Deploy load balancers to manage workloads, distributing queries, and balancing load across Broker nodes. Techniques may involve using reverse proxy solutions with configurations aligned for efficient routing.

```
upstream druid_brokers {
    server broker1:8082;
    server broker2:8082;
}
```

```
location /druid/v2/ {
    proxy_pass http://druid_brokers;
}
```

- **Firewall Rules**: Configurations should allow traffic on relevant ports (e.g., HTTP: 8081, HTTPS: 8082, etc.), establishing ingress and egress rules that sustain secure data and control flows among Druid nodes and external clients while dropping unrelated traffic.

- **Hardware Optimization**:
  - Equip Historical nodes with SSDs to capitalize on read-speed improvements, crucial for responding to high-weight queries.
  - Utilize servers with multi-core processors to parallelize task executions across Overlord, MiddleManagers, and Historical nodes.

- **Operating System Tuning**: Optimize OS settings for handling multiple connections and high I/O demands, involving increased file descriptor limits, swappiness adjustments, and process scaling capabilities.

- **Virtualization and Containerization**: Use lightweight container orchestration, such as Kubernetes or Apache Mesos, for dynamic resource allocation, ease of deployment, and automated scaling. Configure resource requests and limits in deployment manifests for balancing workload distributions.

```
containers:
- name: druid-historical
  image: apache/druid:latest
  resources:
    requests:
      memory: "8Gi"
      cpu: "4"
    limits:
      memory: "16Gi"
      cpu: "8"
```

The next crucial step involves setting up metadata stores and deep storage, providing essential support for Druid's operational pipeline:

- **Metadata Store**: Choose a robust relational database like Post-greSQL as the metadata backend. Configure with high availability in mind using clustering or replication tactics.

  – Example PostgreSQL setup:

```
CREATE DATABASE druid;
CREATE USER druid_user WITH ENCRYPTED PASSWORD 'secure_password';
GRANT ALL PRIVILEGES ON DATABASE druid TO druid_user;
```

- **Deep Storage**: Configure deep storage for segment archiving. Options include cloud services like AWS S3 and Azure Blob Storage or on-premises solutions like HDFS or NFS.

  – Sample S3 configuration in common.runtime.properties:

```
druid.storage.type=s3
druid.s3.accessKey=YOUR_ACCESS_KEY
druid.s3.secretKey=YOUR_SECRET_KEY
druid.storage.bucket=your-bucket-name
druid.storage.baseKey=/druid/segments
```

Apache Druid leverages Zookeeper for critical coordination tasks, such as leader elections and metadata synchronization across nodes.

- **Zookeeper Ensemble Setup**: Configure a cluster of Zookeeper nodes to ensure high availability and fault tolerance.

  – Zookeeper properties example:

```
tickTime=2000
dataDir=/var/zookeeper/data
clientPort=2181
initLimit=5
syncLimit=2
server.1=zookeeper1:2888:3888
server.2=zookeeper2:2888:3888
server.3=zookeeper3:2888:3888
```

- **Zookeeper Configuration in Druid**: Include the coordination configurations in your Druid nodes' runtime.properties files:

```
druid.zk.service.host=zookeeper1:2181,zookeeper2:2181,zookeeper3:2181
druid.zk.paths.base=/druid
```

Performance monitoring and proactive diagnostics are integral to ensuring efficient cluster operations:

- **Metrics Collection**: Utilize Druid's native metric emitters integrated with monitoring systems like Prometheus, Grafana, Datadog, or equivalent. You can configure custom dashboards to visualize cluster health.

- **Log Aggregation**: Centralize Druid logs using ELK Stack or Graylog for detailed troubleshooting, real-time analytics, and alert management, helping track service anomalies or predict potential failures.

- **Deployment Management**: Use CI/CD solutions for deploying and updating clusters, automating the release pipeline to foster consistent and safe environment versioning.

Lastly, prepare for scalability and operational robustness:

- **Auto-scaling Policies**: Codify auto-scaling rules triggered by predefined thresholds of CPU usage, I/O latency, or query volume to dynamically scale MiddleManagers and Brokers.

- **Backup and Recovery**: Schedule periodic backups of metadata, configurations, and segments. Leverage Druid's built-in replication capabilities in association with storage versioning to facilitate rollback scenarios.

- **Maintenance Strategies**: Routine upkeep, including log rotation, metadata pruning, and segment compaction, can contribute to persistently smooth cluster operation.

Establishing efficiencies through strategic planning, network configuration, and careful implementation of Druid's infrastructure provides a robust foundation for enterprise-ready data analytics and processing pipelines. This methodological setup ensures high availability, performance, and reliability, facilitating effective and seamless data operations within the Apache Druid ecosystem.

2.5   Verifying the Installation

Ensuring that Apache Druid is correctly installed involves a series of verification steps that encompass operational, functional, and performance tests. This section provides a detailed guide to validate installation through configuration checks, service verifications, sample data ingestion, and query executions. These processes ascertain the readiness and correctness of Druid's setup, ensuring each component communicates effectively and processes data as anticipated.

Preliminary Configuration Verification

Begin verification by checking pivotal configuration files for syntax and logical correctness. This involves confirming essential properties across Druid's runtime.properties and common configurations with respect to networking, metadata storage, and deep storage:

1. **Syntax Verification**: Confirm there are no syntax errors or misconfigurations by employing configuration file validators or parsers specific to the text format.

2. **Correct Paths and URIs**: - Review file paths and URI configurations in the common.runtime.properties file for accuracy, particularly those related to extensions, storage directories, and metadata:

```
druid.extensions.directory=/opt/druid/extensions
druid.storage.storageDirectory=/var/druid/segments
druid.metadata.storage.connector.connectURI=jdbc:postgresql://my-db-server/druid
```

3. **Database Connectivity**: Test the connectivity to the metadata database using client utilities to confirm credential accuracy and server responses. Execute a basic connect command:

```
psql -h my-db-server -U druid_user -d druid -c "\dt"
```

This command should list tables in the Druid metadata database, indicating successful database connectivity.

47

Service Availability and Process Check

Subsequent steps involve ensuring that each Druid service is running and listening on its expected port:

1. **Process and Port Verification**: - Verify services are actively running by checking system processes. Utilize system utilities such as ps for associated Druid processes:

```
ps aux | grep druid
```

- Confirm services are correctly listening using netstat or ss commands:

```
netstat -tuln | grep -i druid
```

Ensure the expected ports such as 8888 (console), 8081 (Coordinator), 8090 (Overlord), etc., are occupied.

2. **Accessing the Druid Console**: - Access the Druid console typically available via http://{hostname}:8888. Availability of the console signifies the correct startup of central services. Navigating the UI should reveal key operational data points and any underlying issues, reflected as alerts or failures within the console dashboard.

Data Ingestion Testing with Sample Data

Proper data ingestion exemplifies system readiness. Work through data ingestion using sample data sources to confirm connectivity and processing:

1. **Loading Sample Data**: - Utilize Druid-provided datasets, such as the wikipedia example or others. First, ensure that your data source and ingestion tasks are defined within wikipedia-index.json or similar:

```
{
  "type": "index_parallel",
  "dataSchema": {
    "dataSource": "wikipedia",
    "parser": {
      "type": "string",
      "parseSpec": {
        "format": "json",
        "dimensionsSpec": {},
        "timestampSpec": {
          "column": "timestamp",
```

```
          "format": "iso"
        }
      }
    },
    "metricsSpec": [
      {
        "type": "count",
        "name": "count"
      }
    ],
    "granularitySpec": {
      "type": "uniform",
      "segmentGranularity": "day",
      "queryGranularity": "none"
    }
  },
  "ioConfig": {
    "type": "index_parallel",
    "inputSource": {
      "type": "http",
      "uris": ["https://example.com/wikipedia.json"]
    },
    "inputFormat": {
      "type": "json"
    }
  }
}
}
```

Load this task using the Druid Overlord's HTTP endpoint:

```
curl -X 'POST' -H 'Content-Type:application/json' -d @wikipedia-index.json http://
    localhost:8090/druid/indexer/v1/task
```

2. **Monitoring Ingestion Tasks**: - Track ingestion task progress via the Druid Console under Tasks. Successful ingestion indicates healthy task execution and system response, with failed tasks highlighting configuration shortfalls, logged errors, or resource limitations needing remediation.

Query Execution and Functionality Testing

Validate the capability of querying ingested data to confirm system operation and response integrity:

1. **Query Examples**: - Execute typical Druid queries and verify the consistency and correctness of the results:

```
{
  "queryType": "timeseries",
```

49

```
"dataSource": "wikipedia",
"intervals": ["2023-07-01T00:00:00.000/2023-08-01T00:00:00.000"],
"granularity": "day",
"aggregations": [
  {
    "type": "count",
    "name": "edits"
  }
]
}
```

Submit the query to the Broker node and capture its result:

```
curl -X 'POST' -H 'Content-Type:application/json' -d @timeseries-query.json http://
    localhost:8888/druid/v2/sql
```

Expected output should align with ingested data summaries per specified granularity.

2. **Stress Testing with Workloads**: - Implement stress tests using tools like Apache JMeter to simulate concurrent query loads, observing the system's response times, and throughput to verify performance under pressure.

```
jmeter -n -t druid-query-test.jmx -l results.jtl
```

Gauge responsiveness via comprehensive metrics derived from workload patterns, ensuring node and cluster setups can sustain required query operations.

Operational Monitoring and Logs Review

The final validation phase involves assessing the monitoring setup and log integrity:

1. **Log Review**: - Use aggregate log management tools to review Druid logs for errors, warnings, or inconsistencies. Identify patterns indicative of configuration issues or system anomalies:

```
grep -iE "(error|warn)" /var/log/druid/druid.*.log
```

Investigate any entries that reference recurring connectivity issues, segmentation faults, or resource exhaustion warnings.

2. **Monitoring Visualization**: - Verify that monitoring dashboards accurately represent operational metrics such as JVM/System memory use, query latency, and I/O throughput. Tools like Grafana or Prometheus should provide real-time visuals reflecting operational health.

3. **Notifications and Alerts**: - Test the efficacy of alert configurations by simulating fault conditions for proactive monitoring solutions. This ensures that alerting mechanisms are sufficiently tuned to detect and notify in the event of service disruptions or degradations.

Comprehensive Assessment and Adjustments

On completing verification, compile an assessment report detailing configurations, service statuses, and data tests. Address any discrepancies by adjusting configurations, refining resource allocations, or rectifying operational gaps. Fine-tune system components against insights garnered from test results to reinforce system robustness and readiness.

Through structured, extensive verification practices, one can confirm Apache Druid's installation integrity, laying foundational confidence and assurance for production deployments or expansive explorations of data assimilation and processing capabilities.

2.6 Common Installation Issues and Solutions

During the installation and setup of Apache Druid, various issues may arise due to the complex interplay of system components, configurations, and dependencies. This section identifies prevalent installation hurdles and delineates effective solutions to mitigate these challenges. Comprehensive insights will guide through debugging common configuration errors, connectivity pitfalls, resource allocation dilemmas, and address dependency conflicts.

Configuration Errors and Misalignments

One of the frequent causes of installation woes stems from configuration misalignments or syntactical errors within primary property files:

1. **Incorrect Paths and Directory Settings**: - Issue: Druid fails to start due to incorrect data or extension directory paths. - Solution: Validate paths configured in common.runtime.properties. Ensure all specified directories exist and Druid has proper read/write permissions.

```
druid.extensions.directory=/correct/path/to/extensions
druid.storage.storageDirectory=/correct/path/to/data/segments
```

Verify paths using terminal commands:

```
ls -ld /path/to/extensions
ls -ld /path/to/data/segments
```

2. **Metadata Connectivity Problems**: - Issue: Druid services fail to connect to the metadata database or facing frequent disconnections. - Solution: Check configurations for druid.metadata.storage.connector.connectURI, confirming the database server is reachable and credentials are correct.

- Assess connectivity directly:

```
psql -h db-hostname -U db-user -d druid -c "\l"
```

Evaluate database logs for access denials or password mismatches.

Dependency and Library Conflicts

Proper dependency management is crucial for running Druid efficiently:

1. **Java Version Incompatibility**: - Issue: Druid requires a specific Java version or configurations not supported by the installed JDK. - Solution: Ensure Java 8 or later is installed and correctly set as the system's default Java environment. Adjust JAVA_HOME to align with the installed version.

```
export JAVA_HOME=/path/to/correct/java
java -version
```

2. **Extension and Library Conflicts**: - Issue: Conflicts or missing extensions/libraries cause Druid services to fail unexpectedly. - Solution: Confirm all necessary extensions are listed in the druid.extensions.loadList and reside within the specified directory.

```
druid.extensions.loadList=["druid-hdfs-storage", "druid-kafka-indexing-service"]
```

Revisit logs or service console outputs for specific errors relating to unavailable classes or library files.

Network Connectivity and Firewall Settings

Network misconfiguration often leads to poor inter-node communication or sporadic failures:

1. **Node Communication Failures**: - Issue: Druid nodes cannot establish communication, leading to partial service availability. - Solution: Ensure network interfaces are correctly configured and DNS is resolving machine hostnames, with ports open for Druid operations.

Testing typical ports (e.g., 8081 for Coordinator):

```
telnet <node-ip> 8081
```

2. **Firewall Blocking**: - Provision processing mechanisms to verify that firewalls permit necessary bidirectional traffic. Adjust iptables or equivalent firewall settings to allow Druid communication:

```
iptables -A INPUT -p tcp --dport 8081 -j ACCEPT
iptables -A INPUT -p tcp --dport 8082 -j ACCEPT
```

Resource Allocation and Exhaustion

Resource misallocation can cause service inefficiencies or failures experiencing high usage:

1. **Memory and Heap Misconfiguration**: - Issue: Out of memory errors or excessive garbage collection pauses impede functionality. - Solution: Reconfigure JVM heap settings in runtime.properties, ensuring each node has sufficient allocation reflective of its role:

```
-server -Xms8g -Xmx8g -XX:MaxDirectMemorySize=10g -XX:+UseG1GC
```

Use tools like jstat or jmap for analyzing JVM memory usage:

```
jstat -gcutil <pid> 1000
jmap -heap <pid>
```

2. **CPU and I/O Bottlenecks**: - Advocate for realigning task concurrency levels for MiddleManagers or I/O throughput caps for Historical nodes.

Adjust druid.worker.capacity based on parallel task demands:

```
druid.worker.capacity=2
```

Monitor CPU loads employing tools such as iostat or htop.

Zookeeper and Coordination Issues

Druid's reliance on Zookeeper for coordination can be a point of failure if not properly orchestrated:

1. **Zookeeper Connection Loss**: - Issue: Services frequently lose connection to the Zookeeper ensemble. - Solution: Validate Zookeeper connectivity and ensemble health state. Confirm configurations specify accurate Zookeeper server addresses and ports.

Validate using the zkCli.sh utility:

```
/path/to/zk/bin/zkCli.sh -server zookeeper1:2181
```

2. **Configuration Mismatches**: - Casual continuous validation that Druid's paths and node identifiers match those configured within Zookeeper settings.

```
druid.zk.paths.base=/druid
```

Review and remedy Zookeeper logs for leadership election or quorum errors.

Observational Diagnostics and Remediation

Harness systematic diagnostics to uncover hidden discrepancies and iteratively rectify them:

1. **Log Analysis**: Review and collate logs from all Druid nodes and Zookeeper instances, scrutinizing for recurring patterns of errors, exceptions, or warnings.

Integrate tailing tailored to warning/error entries for real-time monitoring:

```
tail -f /var/log/druid/historical.log | grep "error"
```

2. **Job and Task Failures**: - Regularly audit Druid tasks for FAILED states not resolving, tracking inputs and outputs for large discrepancies in ingestion specifications or API responses.

Query failed task details with curl or via the console:

```
curl -X GET http://localhost:8090/druid/indexer/v1/task/<task-id>/status
```

3. **System Monitoring and Load Tracking**: - Develop system monitoring solutions addressing each functional node's health indicators via Prometheus/Grafana dashboards furnishing a holistic visual landscape of system operations.

Upon encountering persistent issues, remediation steps emphasize evaluating cluster sizes, re-tuning existing configurations, or even redistributing workloads among nodes, ensuring service equity.

In summation, recognizing and resolving installation pitfalls within Apache Druid environments necessitate both methodological inspections enveloping configuration, network, resource, and dependency scopes, and the empirical application of small-scale tests pinpointing persistent operational ailments. Through comprehensive exploration and engagement with these solutions, operators can foster robust, resilient Druid installations, aligning with organizational data processing and analytic expectations.

Chapter 3

Understanding Druid Architecture and Key Concepts

This chapter delves into the architectural foundation and key concepts of Apache Druid. It details the modular structure of Druid, explaining the distinct roles and responsibilities of each node type within a cluster. Readers will gain insights into how Druid manages segment storage and employs indexing techniques to facilitate efficient data querying. The text further explores Druid's capability to handle both real-time and batch data processing, emphasizing its design for high-performance analytics. Understanding data sharding, replication, and the querying model are also covered, providing a comprehensive view of how Druid achieves scalability and speed.

3.1 Core Architecture of Apache Druid

Apache Druid is a real-time analytics database designed for delivering rapid queries and concise analysis on large datasets. At the core of Druid's capabilities is its architectural framework, which is built to prioritize high availability, modular scalability, and fault tolerance. Druid achieves these goals through a distributed system architecture comprising several types of nodes, each with specialized roles.

In the architecture of Druid, nodes are the fundamental units that perform various tasks. The Druid cluster operates with a distributed and modular design, allowing different tasks to be executed concurrently with minimal contention. These tasks ensure data storage, querying, ingestion, and coordination are efficiently processed in both real-time and historical data contexts.

Druid modules are designed to handle large-scale data operations independently or in unison. This structured approach facilitates reliability and parallel processing, where each module is responsible for a distinct set of tasks, ensuring that data workloads are managed efficiently. Below is an exploration of the core components and their interplay within Druid's architecture.

- **Broker Nodes:** Broker nodes manage client query requests, deal with query distribution across the cluster, and serve as an intermediary for query results. When a query is received, the broker translates the request into a series of operations, dispatching them to the appropriate nodes in the cluster based on metadata regarding data location and availability. This abstraction layer allows complexity to be handled internally, delivering streamlined query results to clients.

  Broker nodes maintain an awareness of the cluster's state and use that information to route queries intelligently. This information includes the segment metadata of historical and real-time data sources which the broker uses to direct parts of the query to the appropriate processing nodes.

```
SELECT COUNT(*)
FROM website_events
WHERE event_type = 'click'
```

The SQL query shown above, demanding a count of a particular event type, demonstrates the simplicity of client interaction with Druid, while masking the sophisticated interplay between various nodes. The broker node will optimize query efficiency by determining the segments and nodes involved, strategically planning the query's execution path.

- **Historical Nodes:** Historical nodes are dedicated to storing and querying immutable data segments. Serving as the backbone for rendering efficient historical queries, these nodes hold stored data in columnar formats to expedite data retrieval operations. Their primary function is to provide quick access to historical data, selectively scanning only required segments based on the broker's instructions.

  These nodes cache data on local disks, leveraging segment-level storage, which offers advantages in terms of speed and resource management. Locality of reference through caching mechanisms helps in minimizing I/O operations, a crucial factor when dealing with large datasets stored across numerous segments.

- **Coordinator Nodes:** Coordinator nodes play a vital role in Druid's architecture, tasked with the management and reallocation of data segments to ensure balanced resource utilization. Coordinators track segment metadata and decide where and how segments should be distributed among historical nodes. This responsibility ensures that data is evenly distributed, accommodating scaling operations while preventing bottlenecks.

  A major function of the Coordinator node is to execute the segment balancing strategy, ensuring optimal performance when nodes join or leave the cluster.

```
{
  "tier": "hot",
  "types": ["historical"],
  "constraint": {
    "minReplicants": 1,
    "maxLoad": 0.7
  }
}
```

Here, a JSON configuration snippet prescribes a tiered storage layout for segments managed by the coordinator node, imposing constraints on minimum replication and load balancing. The design aims to ensure redundancy and performance smoothness across nodes operating in the same tier.

- **Overlord Nodes:** Overlord nodes are integral to Druid's task management and orchestration. Primarily, they oversee task schedules and manage task lifecycle events such as task allocation, transition, and log collection. Overlords maintain accountability credentials for real-time and batch ingestion tasks while providing oversight to ensure data consistency and availability.

  Their interaction with other Druid nodes typically involves communication with the MiddleManager nodes for task assignments. Overlords are also responsible for ensuring that ingestion tasks are appropriately reattempted if initial processes fail, thereby guaranteeing data integrity and reliability within the Druid system.

- **MiddleManager Nodes:** MiddleManager nodes function as the execution environment for data ingestion tasks. These nodes are responsible for segment creation from raw data. Once prepared, the segments are shuffled to the historical nodes for subsequent query access. MiddleManagers take charge of coordinating various tasks, such as segment merging, and are key components in managing real-time tasks.

  During operation, MiddleManager nodes commonly interact with data streams, converting incoming data into segments, which are then stored locally in an intermediary state before final transmission. This process contributes to Druid's capability to handle real-time analytics with low latency.

- **Data Ingestion Framework:** Druid's data ingestion framework supports both real-time and batch ingestion methodologies. This versatility offers flexibility in handling diverse data inputs.

  - **Real-time ingestion:** Data streamed directly into Druid, immediately available for query operations. Utilizes Middle-

Manager nodes for processing high throughput in minimal time.

- **Batch ingestion:** Traditionally involves ETL processes to ingest data from static sources at scheduled intervals, allowing pre-processing and cleanup before storage.

To illustrate, consider a real-time ingestion scenario involving a Kafka data stream. MiddleManager nodes will pull data from topics, partition the data according to Druid's segmentation policies, and produce new segments very rapidly:

```
{
  "type": "kafka",
  "dataSchema": {
    "dataSource": "example",
    "dimensionsSpec": {
      "dimensions": ["field1", "field2"]
    }
  },
  "tuningConfig": {
    "maxRowsInMemory": 50000
  }
}
```

This configuration showcases settings for a typical real-time ingestion task from a Kafka stream. The 'maxRowsInMemory' parameter indicates the segment size control, influencing how and when segments are committed to historical nodes.

- **Query Execution Model:** The query execution model within Apache Druid is designed to optimize for both speed and resource efficiency. This approach allows for immediate responsiveness, essential in interactive analytics environments. The broker node serves as the query gateway, receiving client queries, parsing them, and dispatching partial queries to historical or real-time nodes as necessary.

The execution process optimizes querying by leveraging Druid's indexing structures. Data is held in a columnar storage format, allowing selective access of required data points by loading only pertinent columns. This columnar format facilitates rapid aggregation and can significantly save system resources compared to row-store formats.

61

In effect, Druid's core architecture not only integrates the functionalities of each node class seamlessly but enhances the performance of analytical tasks executed over distributed data stores. Its design principles emphasize robust modularity and scalability, allowing it to adapt to varying data volumes and use cases in real time efficiently. By applying pathways for rapid data retrieval through optimized segmenting, indexing, and querying practices, Druid stands as a powerful solution for real-time analytics and large-scale data processing.

3.2 Druid Nodes and Their Roles

In the distributed architecture of Apache Druid, nodes serve as the critical backbone, each with specific roles and responsibilities tailored to manage diverse tasks across the system. Understanding these roles is crucial for optimizing Druid's deployment, scalability, and performance. Each node type operates independently or in concert with others, optimizing the handling of vast data volumes and providing a resilient and scalable analytics platform. This section provides a comprehensive examination of the node types within the Druid cluster: Broker, Historical, Coordinator, Overlord, and MiddleManager nodes, delving deeper into their responsibilities, interactions, and importance within the ecosystem.

- **Broker Nodes**

  Broker nodes act as the query routers and processors in a Druid cluster. They receive client queries, break them down into subtasks, and distribute these sub-tasks to the appropriate nodes - Historical or real-time nodes. A broker's primary goal is to ensure that queries are executed efficiently and results are aggregated before sending them back to the client.

  This node maintains a view of what segments are available in the cluster and their locations, using this knowledge to direct parts of a query to the nodes that store the relevant data. Brokers also cache query results to reduce load and improve response times for frequently requested data.

  For example, consider a query request from a client application as follows:

```
SELECT SUM(cost) AS total_cost, city
FROM sales
WHERE time >= '2023-01-01' AND time < '2023-02-01'
GROUP BY city
```

The broker breaks this query into parts, identifying which data segments are pertinent, and dispatches these sub-queries to Historical nodes or MiddleManager nodes if data is still in real-time processing. The Broker then assembles the results, performs any necessary aggregation and grouping, and returns the final result to the client.

Efforts to enhance Broker performance often involve configuring caching strategies or optimizing the query planning algorithms. The goal is to minimize data transfer across the network and maximize node-level processing to reduce latency.

- **Historical Nodes**

  Historical nodes are the storage powerhouses of Apache Druid, designed to handle immutable segment data for historical querying. Their primary function is to process read requests for data stored within segments on local disks, making them integral in handling OLAP (Online Analytical Processing) queries.

  These nodes store data using a columnar format optimized to facilitate fast retrieval and aggregation of large datasets. This design ensures query operations such as filtering, aggregation, and projections can be executed rapidly and efficiently.

  ```
  bin/druid/start -c config/historical.properties
  ```

  Running the above command allows you to configure and start up the Historical nodes, ensuring they are included in the active query ecosystem. Historical nodes communicate with the coordinator nodes regularly to update segment availability, enabling efficient load balancing and fault tolerance.

  Maintaining optimal performance of Historical nodes involves balancing segment storage and considering memory and disk capacity within the cluster to prevent any potential overloading or underutilization of resources.

- **Coordinator Nodes**

  Coordinator nodes are responsible for the management of segment lifecycle and the distribution of these segments across Historical nodes to ensure optimal data availability and redundancy. Their tasks include assigning new segments, rebalancing existing segments, and overseeing segment replication processes.

  Key capabilities of the coordinator include automatic data balancing across historical nodes to prevent bottlenecks, and adjusting replication levels for better fault tolerance and high availability.

  Here is a typical configuration JSON for segment metabolic activities:

  ```
  {
    "indexingPeriod": "PT1H",
    "numReplicants": 2,
    "async": true
  }
  ```

  This settings file allows Coordinators to regulate the size and replication parameters of data segments dynamically, aligning with operational requirements and available resources.

  Strategies for ensuring an efficient Coordinator role involve regular monitoring of data loads and physical disk usage across nodes. By continuously adjusting segment allocations and orchestrating data movement, Coordinators play a pivotal role in maintaining a balanced and efficient data distribution ecosystem.

- **Overlord Nodes**

  Overlord nodes handle task orchestration and manage distributed indexing tasks within a Druid cluster. They are critical to the initiation, monitoring, and life-cycle management of data ingestion tasks, whether batch or real-time workflows.

  Tasks are dispatched by the Overlord nodes to MiddleManager nodes, which perform the resource-intensive ingestion tasks. The Overlord takes responsibility for job scheduling and task routing to ensure that workloads are dynamically distributed. They oversee both stream ingestion for real-time data and batch ingestion from segmented storage systems.

  ```
  {
  ```

```
"type": "index_parallel",
"dataSource": "user_activity",
"tuningConfig": {
  "maxNumConcurrentSubTasks": 4
},
"spec": {
  // ingestion specification
}
}
```

In this scenario, an Overlord node manages ingestion jobs, specifying the maximum number of concurrent tasks to modulate workload. This ensures that MiddleManager nodes utilized for ingestion don't become overloaded and can respond swiftly when a real-time ingestion demand arises.

Efficiency in the Overlord's operation is often enhanced by ensuring that task queues are not overly filled and by optimizing task allocation algorithms to distribute tasks efficiently over available cluster resources, prioritizing real-time task allocation to limit latency.

- **MiddleManager Nodes**

  MiddleManager nodes are the workers tasked with executing ingestion jobs as assigned by the Overlord nodes. They take raw data streams and convert them into indexable Druid segments. These nodes are designed to handle real-time ingestion from streaming data sources typical in scenarios where data must be immediately available for querying.

  Each MiddleManager manages a set of Peon processes. Peons are lightweight Java Virtual Machines (JVMs) responsible for running specific data ingestion jobs, providing isolation and ensuring that tasks can be independently managed and monitored.

```
bin/druid/start-middleManager
```

Executing the start command spins up the MiddleManager service, where it waits for tasks from Overlord nodes. It is crucial to provision MiddleManager nodes adequately, considering the workload and available system resources to optimize ingestion tasks' throughput. Balancing CPU and memory allocation for Peon processes also forms part of effective MiddleManager configuration.

65

- **Node Interactions and Optimization**

  Proper functioning of Druid relies extensively on the coordinated interaction among these node types. Each must communicate effectively to guarantee that data ingestion, storage, querying, and management processes are synchronized for optimal performance.

  Therefore, deployment strategies must consider network configurations that minimize data movement across the nodes and position them to take advantage of locality in data processing. Furthermore, tasks can be finely tuned by modifying configuration files to control aspects like replication factor, caching strategy, memory allocation, and data segmentation tactics.

  Druid relies on the orchestration of these nodes to balance workflows dynamically, intrinsically supporting horizontal scaling. As workload demands fluctuate, clusters can be scaled up by adding more of each node type to meet increased demand, ensuring Druid continues to offer fast, reliable real-time analytic results.

  The node structure within Apache Druid builds a strongly decentralized framework that allows flexibility and robustness within a distributed analytic engine. Each node plays a critical and singular role, contributing to the unified objective of providing prompt, efficient, and scalable analytic processing on significant data sets, whether historical or real-time. Understanding the intricacies of each node's responsibilities prepares you to architect solutions leveraging Druid's full potential.

3.3 Segment Storage and Management

In the architecture of Apache Druid, segments are the fundamental units of data storage and are pivotal to its performance and functionality. A segment in Druid is an immutable chunk of data that represents the output of an ingestion task. These segments are stored across a cluster in a way that enables Druid to efficiently handle queries and maintain available data in conjunction with high ingestion throughput. Understanding segment storage and management is crucial for leveraging Druid's strengths in real-time and batch data analysis.

The lifecycle of a data segment involves several stages, including creation during the ingestion process, storage across distributed nodes in the cluster, management through metadata, and use during query processing. This section examines segment lifecycle management, the architecture supporting it, the impact on system performance, and configuration best practices.

- **Segment Creation and Structure:** Segments are created when raw data is ingested into a Druid cluster. During ingestion, data is partitioned into manageable chunks based on user-defined granularity settings, thereby dictating the size and time span each segment covers.

```
{
  "type": "index_parallel",
  "granularitySpec": {
    "type": "uniform",
    "segmentGranularity": "DAY",
    "queryGranularity": "NONE"
  },
  "tuningConfig": {
    "partitionsSpec": {
      "type": "hashed",
      "targetRowsPerSegment": 5000000
    }
  },
  "inputSource": {
    "type": "local",
    "baseDir": "/data/logs"
  }
}
```

In this configuration file snippet for a parallel indexing task, segments are generated daily ('segmentGranularity' set to '"DAY"') and the partitions are hashed ('partitionsSpec' indicates type 'hashed'). This approach results in segments containing approximately 5 million rows each, aligning the storage granularity with user needs.

Once created, segments are stored in columnar format via an optimized file structure that includes dictionaries, indexes, and metadata, enhancing efficient query processing. This format reduces duplication and improves speed because it allows for quick access to required column data without loading entire rows.

- **Segment Storage Practices:** Segment storage in Druid is facilitated by Historical nodes, which are designed to load and

67

query segments residing on disk. Each segment is self-contained with its data and indexing structures, enabling high parallelization opportunities across the Druid architecture.

Druid supports scalable storage by utilizing deep storage systems to persist segment data files externally. Amazon S3, Hadoop Distributed File System (HDFS), and cloud storage solutions like Azure Blob Storage are commonly employed, allowing segments to be archived and retrieved as needed to meet query demands.

```
{
  "druid": {
    "storage": {
      "type": "s3",
      "bucket": "druid-data-segments",
      "baseKey": "/segments"
    }
  }
}
```

By setting up deep storage through systems such as Amazon S3 (as shown above), organizations can manage cost-effectiveness with regard to maintaining vast volumes of segment data while enabling Druid historical nodes to fetch necessary segment files efficiently during query execution.

When segments are incorporated into Historical nodes for querying, they are typically cached on disk, optimizing the balance between rapid access and minimized disk I/O.

- **Metadata Management and Segment Coordination:** Segment metadata plays a crucial role in the segment management ecosystem. Metadata includes details about each segment such as its identifier, interval, version, size, and partitioning information, stored in the metadata store – often backed by relational database systems like Apache Derby or MySQL.

Druid utilizes Coordinator nodes to orchestrate the segment management process, ensuring that segments are correctly distributed across Historical nodes to provide fault tolerance and load balancing. The Coordinator performs automated tasks such as rebalancing segments among Historical nodes, replicating segments, and handling segment deletion policies per retention rules.

68

For example, the balancing of segments can be influenced through configuration options like:

```
{
  "balancerComputeThreads": 2,
  "balancerStrategy": "cost"
}
```

Here, the 'balancerStrategy' set to '"cost"' indicates that the Coordinator will implement cost-based balancing to minimize resource use during data shuffling and reallocation operations.

Beyond allocation, segment metadata is leveraged to enable the Broker nodes to route query tasks optimally, minimizing time and network resources while affecting data retrieval.

- **Querying and Segment Access Patterns:** Querying in Druid is designed to be highly efficient. The architecture allows specific segments to be identified and targeted for access based on the query parameters, reducing unnecessary scans and computing time.

Druid accesses and processes segments concurrently, providing remarkable speed advantages for analytic operations by limiting data paths. Segmentation is key; by organizing datasets into temporal and hashed partitions, queries can be executed concurrently over a distributed node cluster, allowing for fast, scalable data retrieval.

Aggregating queries happen inline as segments are processed. Druid applies filters before scan operations begin, reducing the volume of data each query operation actions. This is achieved through an indexed data management system, which makes use of bitmap indexes and compressed storage formats to hasten query times, especially in large, multi-terabyte data environments.

```
SELECT AVG(value)
FROM metrics
WHERE category = 'A' AND ___time > '2023-01-01'
```

In executing this query, only relevant segments covering the specified time and category range are loaded into memory. This significantly conserves resource use and accelerates query penetration through smaller, more precise data evaluation.

- **Configuration and Tuning for Segment Management:** Optimal segment management and configuration can significantly enhance a Druid cluster's performance, impacting factors such as storage efficiency, retrieval time, and resource allocation. Recommended tuning practices entail the following:

- **Segmentation Granularity:** Adjust 'segmentGranularity' according to query patterns and data volume. Opt for finer granularity to handle high frequency queries over small timespans or coarser granularity for larger, bigger-picture analytics.

- **Partitioning Strategy:** Choose an appropriate partitioning strategy based on your dataset's characteristics. Use hashed, range, or single-dimension partitioning strategies to complement the natural data distribution and analysis needs.

- **Segment Rebalancing:** Regularly engage segment rebalancing strategies to keep the cluster optimized, preventing any skewed data load that could result in query bottlenecks.

- **Replication Factor:** Set a suitable replication factor for essential data segments to protect against node failures and ensure high availability without excessive storage redundancy.

- **Deep Storage Configuration:** Leverage cost-effective deep storage solutions, ensuring ample throughput for efficient segment archiving and retrieval without risking cloud resource caps.

- **Task Tuning:** Properly set 'maxRowsPerSegment' and 'maxNumSubTasks' to align with hardware and expected throughput. This assists MiddleManager nodes in efficiently handling varying ingestion loads.

By carefully configuring these parameters alongside thorough testing in context with real query loads and data profiles, Druid deployments can be optimized for significant performance.

Integrating Druid's segment storage and management functionality within data architectures provides an adaptable and robust platform that satisfies both immediate and evolving data processing demands —

equipping users with real-time analytic capabilities coupled with historical insights across large-scaled distributed data environments. As organizational data demands continue to grow, organizations will benefit from utilizing Druid's scalable, high-performance analytic engine, wherein effective segment strategy forms the backbone.

3.4 Real-Time and Batch Data Processing

Apache Druid is designed to facilitate high-performance analytics on both real-time and historical data through a unique combination of real-time and batch processing capabilities. This dual functionality enables Druid to address the needs of varied data workloads while ensuring low-latency query performance across massive datasets. This section provides an in-depth exploration of the mechanisms enabling real-time data ingestion, the configuration needed for batch data processing, and the operational details of how Druid achieves seamless integration of both processing types within its architecture.

Real-Time Data Processing

Real-time data ingestion in Druid allows for immediate processing of incoming data streams, facilitating prompt analytical insight with minimal delay. This capability is crucial for applications requiring current data metrics and trends, such as online monitoring systems, ad tech platforms, and business intelligence solutions.

Data enters Druid in real-time through streaming sources such as Apache Kafka, Amazon Kinesis, or other streaming technologies. Middleware nodes like MiddleManager nodes are responsible for managing incoming data, creating segments in near real-time, and storing them temporarily for further processing.

Consider a scenario where data is being streamed from a Kafka topic:

```
{
  "type": "kafka",
  "dataSchema": {
    "dataSource": "real_time_events",
    "parser": {
      "type": "string",
      "parseSpec": {
```

```
      "format": "json",
      "dimensionsSpec": {
        "dimensions": ["userId", "eventType", "timestamp"]
      }
    }
  },
  "granularitySpec": {
    "type": "uniform",
    "segmentGranularity": "minute",
    "queryGranularity": "none"
  }
},
"tuningConfig": {
  "type": "kafka",
  "maxRowsInMemory": 100000,
  "intermediatePersistPeriod": "PT10M"
},
"ioConfig": {
  "consumerProperties": {
    "bootstrap.servers": "localhost:9092",
    "group.id": "druid-consumer"
  },
  "topic": "events_topic",
  "taskCount": 2
}
}
```

In this configuration, the 'ioConfig' section outlines Kafka specifics, directing the MiddleManager node to consume data from the 'events_topic' Kafka topic using a specific group ID. The 'tuningConfig' defines how data is partitioned and persisted, setting in-memory limits and time intervals for intermediate persistency.

Real-time processing is distinguished by the speed at which data is absorbed and made available for querying. Druid achieves this by creating small, transient segments that retain data on the local state until committed into deep storage. This approach enables immediate access to recently ingested data, an essential feature for analytic environments where timeliness is critical.

Further, the capability to partition data based on specific keys ensures that segments are efficiently organized for query scalability and accuracy. After appropriate segments are created and uploaded into deep storage, historical nodes retrieve these segments for long-term storage and query purposes, ensuring a consistent layer between real-time and historical data handling.

Batch Data Processing

Batch processing within Druid caters to the ingestion of bulk data from static or semi-static sources typically through traditional Extract, Transform, and Load (ETL) procedures. Batch processes handle larger volumes of data at scheduled intervals, allowing comprehensive analysis over entire datasets.

Batch ingestion processes can be conducted either using native Druid tasks or by integrating with Hadoop for leveraging its distributed processing capabilities. These tasks are highly configurable, taking advantage of the seamless compatibility with widely-used data stores and systems like Amazon S3, Azure Blob Storage, and Hadoop HDFS.

Below exemplifies a JSON configuration for a batch ingestion task leveraging local files:

```
{
  "type": "index_parallel",
  "dataSource": "historical_sales",
  "intervals": ["2023-01-01/2023-02-01"],
  "inputSource": {
    "type": "local",
    "baseDir": "/path/to/data/files",
    "filter": "*.csv"
  },
  "inputFormat": {
    "type": "csv",
    "findColumnsFromHeader": true
  },
  "tuningConfig": {
    "maxRowsInMemory": 500000,
    "maxNumConcurrentSubTasks": 16
  }
}
```

This setup defines a parallel indexing task using local file input, tuning the task to handle up to half a million rows of data in memory with a provision for 16 simultaneous sub-tasks. By performing ingestion in parallel, Druid can accelerate the process, accommodating high throughput requirements dictated by large datasets.

Batch processing jobs often involve task aggregations and data restructuring for optimization purposes. Unlike real-time tasks, batch ingestion typically constitutes larger segment granularity, which reduces the sheer number of individual segments stored and queried against, improving resource utilization and query performance when analyzing retrospective data.

Integration with Real-Time and Batch Data

The interplay between real-time and batch data processing is what allows Druid to offer a cohesive framework for modern analytics workloads. Data regardless of origin—streaming or static—becomes queryable within the same ecosystem, optimizing the use of Druid's column-oriented storage and fast, scalable query capabilities.

To successfully manage the blend of real-time and batch data:

- **Segment Consolidation:** Over time, Druid has built capabilities to consolidate real-time segments into larger, optimized segments managed by Historical nodes. This reduces the systematic overhead and performance impact associated with maintaining numerous small segments.

- **Schema Management:** Ensuring data consistency across different ingest sources is paramount. Schema definitions should be coordinated, keeping naming, data types, and indexing consistent. Tools within Druid allow dynamic schema adjustments without needing a full re-ingestion, facilitating flexibility in evolving data schemas.

- **Retention Policies:** Implementing robust retention policies enables automatic roll-up and deletion of aged data segments, freeing system resources for the ingest of new data. Such policies maintain storage health and cost efficiency while allowing rapid access to necessary historical data when required.

- **Query Optimization:** By refining the strategies in query execution, including leveraging segment metadata and cache settings, queries can be selectively adjusted based on temporal relevance, preferentially targeting recently ingested real-time data when immediate insights are prioritized or extended periods for comprehensive trend analysis.

- **Resource Allocation:** Adjust MiddleManager and Historical node resource allocation based on active workloads. Real-time processing should avoid resource contention with batch processes, necessitating careful monitoring and possibly distinct hardware deployment when both processes are intensive.

Druid's dynamic blending of real-time and batch processing offers a flexible backend data architecture that conforms to different data use cases and analytical needs. For organizations implementing real-time reporting dashboards or detailed historical reporting systems, this capability highlights Druid's value as a multi-faceted data processing solution.

In summary, Apache Druid's efficient handling of real-time and batch data processing forms a comprehensive and adaptable basis for high-performance analytics. By configuring real-time streams to reflect current trends or applying batch processes for analyzing legacy data, Druid represents an integrated, streamlined approach to processing and querying diverse datasets with efficiency and agility. Whether scaling up to meet large-scale data demands or operating efficiently within resource constraints, Druid stands equipped to tackle varied data challenges head-on, offering reliable and quick insights across temporal dimensions.

3.5 Understanding Druid Indexing

Indexing is a critical aspect of Apache Druid's architecture, allowing the system to provide rapid, scalable query performance across vast datasets. In Druid, indexing refers to the process of structuring data so that it can be quickly retrieved and analyzed. This section explores the unique indexing mechanisms employed by Druid, details the indexing process during data ingestion, and examines the implications on query optimization and system performance.

The indexing strategy in Druid exploits both real-time and batch processing frameworks, designed to transform raw data into a structured segment format that ensures efficient storage and retrieval. The prominence of Druid's indexing abilities lies in its columnar storage design, use of bitmap and dictionary indexes, and the roll-up capability, enabling Druid to optimize both disk usage and query speed.

- **Columnar Storage Format:** Data indexing in Apache Druid begins with how data is stored. Druid uses a columnar data format, which means that data is stored column by column rather than row by row. This storage format is crucial for analytical queries that typically aggregate over a small number of columns in a dataset.

75

```
Column_a | Column_b | Column_c
-------------------------------
  Value1 | Value2 | Value3
  Value4 | Value5 | Value6
  ...
```

In this tabular representation, the columnar storage allows Druid to access only the necessary columns required by a query, eliminating the need to scan entire rows. This reduces I/O overhead and accelerates query processing, especially beneficial when dealing with aggregations over large-scale datasets.

- **Bitmap Indexing:** Bitmap indexing in Druid improves the efficiency with which data can be filtered and aggregated. A bitmap index is a data structure that uses a series of bits to represent the presence or absence of specific values within a column. It is particularly powerful in scenarios where columns have a limited number of distinct values.

```
Value: A | B | C
--------------
Row 1: 1 | 0 | 0
Row 2: 1 | 0 | 0
Row 3: 0 | 1 | 0
...
```

This example illustrates the binary representation of a three-value column using bitmap indexing. For an analytical workload that frequently queries by these column values, bitmaps allow rapid evaluation of conditions by binary operations rather than multiple-value checks, greatly speeding up query execution.

- **Dictionary Encoding:** Druid employs dictionary encoding to compress data columns, an important feature that augments the efficiency of both storage and processing. Dictionary encoding replaces actual column values with numerical surrogates, reducing space requirements and enhancing computational operations.

For instance, consider an encoding map:

```
0: 'New York'
1: 'Los Angeles'
```

```
2: 'San Francisco'
...
```

When a data row references a city, it stores the integer surrogate rather than the full string, optimizing the data footprint. Druid makes good use of this encoding to support its indexing framework, reducing the data's dimensional space and improving access times.

- **Roll-Up Aggregation:** The roll-up is an efficient, lossy compression technique that Druid implements during data ingestion. Roll-up allows Druid to pre-aggregate data based on predefined metrics and dimensions, dramatically reducing data volumes without sacrificing query performance.

Configuring a Druid task for roll-up might look like this:

```
{
  "dataSchema": {
    "granularitySpec": {
      "type": "uniform",
      "segmentGranularity": "HOUR",
      "queryGranularity": "MINUTE",
      "rollup": true
    },
    "metricsSpec": [
      {"type": "count", "name": "count"},
      {"type": "doubleSum", "name": "total_cost", "fieldName": "cost"}
    ]
  }
}
```

Here, roll-up aggregates data to a minute-level granularity, summarizing the cost field as per each distinct combination of dimensions. This technique ensures that repeated queries can be processed over a significantly reduced dataset, boosting speed and responsiveness.

- **Indexing Task Process:** Indexing tasks in Druid are prescribed during the ingestion process, which may vary depending on whether data is streamed in real-time or ingested in batches.

For real-time ingestion, tasks are typically managed by MiddleManager nodes:

```
{
  "type": "kafka",
```

```
"dataSource": "streaming_orders",
"tuningConfig": {
  "type": "kafka",
  "maxRowsInMemory": 100000
}
}
```

During stream processing, data is ingested in micro-batches; indexes are updated dynamically as new entries become available, ensuring that queries can incorporate the freshest data inputs.

In batch ingestion scenarios, indexing tasks are often executed in bulk, using the parallel indexing service:

```
{
  "type": "index_parallel",
  "dataSource": "historical_orders",
  "tuningConfig": {
    "maxRowsPerSegment": 500000,
    "maxNumConcurrentSubTasks": 10
  }
}
```

Parallel tasks calibrate the throughput by defining parameters such as 'maxRowsPerSegment', dictating how data is subdivided and indexed across compute nodes to ensure timely completion.

- **Query Optimizations via Indexing:** The foundational strength of indexing in Druid lies in its ability to accelerate query executions. With the combination of bitmap indexes and pre-aggregated roll-ups, queries perform minimal redundant operations, focusing directly on relevant data subsets.

Consider a query requesting total sales in March:

```
SELECT SUM(sales)
FROM revenue
WHERE __time BETWEEN '2023-03-01' AND '2023-03-31'
```

Here, the use of time partitions enables Druid to skip non-relevant segments immediately. Bitmap indexes filter down further by readily identifying rows corresponding to the specified dates, and any roll-up metrics offer pre-computed totals, as opposed to recalculating from scratch.

Through effective indexing, Druid minimizes the materialization of results, lessens I/O operations, and promotes in-memory computing richness. This design scales extremely well with increasing data volumes and cardinalities.

- **Considerations and Best Practices in Indexing:** To fully leverage Druid's indexing capabilities, practitioners should consider the following best practices:

- Choose Appropriate Granularities: Tailor both query and segment granularities to the most common query use cases. If queries often analyze data minute-by-minute, set segment granularity appropriately to reduce processing overhead.

- Optimize Roll-Up Policies: Determine the dimension columns necessary for roll-up, balancing data redundancy elimination with the granularity needed for typical analytical demands.

- Engage Compression Tools: Implement dictionary encoding thoughtfully, particularly on string-heavy dimensions, where potential savings on storage may outweigh trivial dictionary look-up costs.

- Monitor Cardinalities: Monitor dimension cardinalities, optimizing high-cardinality fields through specialized indexes or structuring data ingestion strategies that accommodate Druid's constraints on direct bitmap indexing capacity.

- Use Complex Metrics Sparingly: While complex metrics extend Druid's analytic possibilities, the computation involved can inflate indexing times. Balance complex metrics' use while respecting component efficiencies.

Apache Druid's architecture for indexing, vibrant in its design and intentionally crafted for speedy analytics, serves as the bedrock for its high-speed query capabilities. By understanding and exploiting these indexing principles, organizations can effectively harness Druid's strengths to gain a competitive edge in high-performance data processing environments, continually operating at the forefront of immediate, in-depth analytical insight.

3.6 Data Sharding and Replication

Data sharding and replication are vital mechanisms within Apache Druid that enable it to handle large datasets with resilience and efficiency. Sharding divides a dataset into smaller, manageable pieces, while replication ensures data availability and fault tolerance by duplicating these shards across nodes. This section will delve into the principles behind sharding and replication in Druid, discuss their execution, analyze their impact on performance, and provide configuration examples and best practices.

Sharding and replication strategies in Druid are fundamental for achieving scalability and reliability across distributed systems. By partitioning data and strategically replicating it, Druid can maintain high availability, distribute the workload evenly, and prevent bottlenecks, providing a robust analytic service in dynamic data environments.

Data Sharding Essentials

In the context of Druid, sharding refers to the process of dividing dataset segments into smaller partitions, known as shards, which can be independently stored and processed across the cluster. Shards are a representation of segment data sliced by a specific partitioning key or dimension, facilitating parallel processing.

The sharding strategy often depends on the dataset characteristics and the query patterns. Druid supports several sharding specifications, including:

- **Hashed Sharding**: Distributes data into partitions based on a hash function applied to one or more dimensions, focusing on even load distribution and areas where the same data occurs across segments.

- **Single Dimension Sharding**: Uses a single column for partitioning, ideal for high cardinality dimensions frequently employed in maximizing parallelism and efficiency.

- **Range Sharding**: Applies for ordered dimensions, dividing data into specified ranges, which is effective for serially configured datasets or those with temporal dimensions.

Below is an example configuration for creating a hashed partition:

```
{
  "tuningConfig": {
    "partitionsSpec": {
      "type": "hashed",
      "targetRowsPerSegment": 1000000,
      "partitionDimensions": ["country", "product_id"]
    }
  }
}
```

In this example, the data is hashed across the '"country"' and '"product_id"' dimensions, creating shards with approximately 1,000,000 records each. This approach allows replication and parallel processing to be effectively optimized.

Exploration of Druid Replication

Replication within Druid ensures data redundancy and fault tolerance, vital for maintaining availability in case of node failures. Each segment can be configured to have multiple copies, distributed across different historical nodes in the cluster. These replicas ensure that even when one node fails, the data remains accessible from its backups.

Replication is configured through:

- **Segment Replication Count**: The number of copies of each shard maintained across the cluster, as defined in the configuration.

- **Tiered Storage Settings**: Allows data to be replicated across storage tiers with different cost-efficiency and performance profiles.

Consider a configuration snippet for setting replication:

```
{
  "druid": {
    "coordinator": {
      "replication": {
        "numReplicants": 2,
        "tieredReplicants": {
          "hot": 1,
          "cold": 1
        }
      }
    }
  }
}
```

```
}
```

Here, 'numReplicants' sets the total number of segment replicas to be maintained, while 'tieredReplicants' assigns replicants across specified storage tiers, balancing between immediacy (hot) and durability (cold) settings.

Balancing Sharding and Replication for Performance

Efficiently balancing sharding and replication can significantly enhance Druid's analytic performance, resource allocation, and fault tolerance capabilities. While sharding promotes data division for parallel processing, replication ensures continuity and reliability.

- **Advantages of Sharding**:

    - Effective Load Balancing: By splitting data, sharding allows workloads to be distributed evenly, preventing any single node from becoming a bottleneck.

    - Enhanced Parallelism: Multiple nodes process shards concurrently, significantly reducing query times.

    - Improved Scalability: Easily adjust the number of partitions to accommodate expanding data loads.

- **Challenges in Sharding**:

    - Complexity in Partitioning Keys: Careful selection of partitioning keys is crucial to avoid hotspots that lead to imbalanced workloads.

    - Increased Metadata Overhead: Each shard produces additional metadata, which can proliferate in environments requiring high segment counts.

- **Benefits of Replication**:

    - High Availability: Replicas provide a safety net against individual node failures.

    - Load Distribution: Queries can be directed to the least-loaded replica, optimizing resource use.

    - Recovery and Fault Tolerance: Rapid recovery from system failures through multiple data sources.

- **Drawbacks of Replication**:

  - Storage Overheads: Multiple replicas consume more storage resources, impacting cost and scalability.

  - Consistency Management: Synchronizing changes across replicas can introduce complexity, especially in real-time ingestion scenarios.

Strategies for Effective Deployment

When balancing these two approaches, consider several strategic implementations that align with business needs and system architecture:

- Select Optimal Dimensions: Choose partition keys that benefit workload distributions, aligning system architecture with data access patterns. In temporal workloads, time-based sharding ensures efficient chronological data retrieval.

- Adjust Replication Factors According to Usage Patterns: Increase replicas for important datasets or when faced with frequent node downtimes to maintain uninterrupted data access.

- Implement Tiered Storage: Where budget allows, employ tiered storage settings to balance performance and expense considerations.

- Monitor System Health: Leverage Druid's monitoring tools to identify bottlenecks or under-replicated segments, adjusting configurations dynamically for optimal performance.

- Test and Iterate: Periodically review the effects of shard and replication strategies, iteratively refining to keep pace with changing workloads or infrastructure.

Configuration and Tuning for Sharding and Replication

Diligently configuring and tuning your Druid cluster for sharding and replication can dramatically improve your organization's capacity to serve rapid analytic demands:

- Segment Tuning: Regular adjustment of the 'targetCompaction-SizeBytes' and 'targetRowsPerSegment' helps Druid manage segment sizes, aligning shard dimensions with query workload for maximum throughput.

- Replication Policies: Establishing responsive replication policies and mechanisms can ensure that backup protocols meet both current operational and growth needs without overwhelmingly increasing storage costs. This is where automated resource allocation strategies via Druid's Coordinator node play a critical role.

- Balancing Costs and Benefits: Determine trade-offs between higher storage demands due to replication and the resilience gains in data availability to create appropriate policies.

By understanding and managing sharding and replication in Apache Druid efficiently, organizations can safeguard against data loss, maximize performance under intensive load, and ensure that analytic systems are both robust and reactive to dynamic demands. Effective sharding and replication alongside strategic provisioning lay an essential groundwork that highlights Apache Druid's strength as a sophisticated, high-performance analytics engine capable of supporting real-time insights across extensive distributed datasets.

3.7 Druid's Querying Model

Apache Druid stands out as an ultra-fast, highly scalable real-time analytics database, capable of complex data workloads through a proficient querying model. Druid's querying model is designed to deliver quick access to data, leveraging distributed query execution and a rich set of query types that support various analytical operations. This section aims to provide an exhaustive exploration of Druid's querying model, elucidating how it operates, the types of queries it supports, performance optimizations, and strategies to leverage its full potential.

The querying model is a cornerstone of Druid's architecture, equipping it for rapid, insightful data exploration across vast data sets. Druid achieves its querying prowess through seamless integration with its segment-oriented storage design, utilizing indexes and parallel processing to resolve queries efficiently.

- **Query Types in Druid**

The types of queries that Druid supports reflect its aim to process large-scale datasets swiftly and effectively. They provide extensive capabilities for data selection, aggregation, filtering, and result set manipulation:

- **Timeseries Queries**: Used for sequential data access, ideal for computing the aggregated value of a measure over a chosen time period. They excel in time-based pattern analysis and trend identification.

  Example of a timeseries query:

  ```
  {
      "queryType": "timeseries",
      "dataSource": "transactions",
      "granularity": "day",
      "aggregations": [
          {"type": "longSum", "name": "total_sales", "fieldName": "sales"}
      ],
      "intervals": ["2023-01-01/2023-12-31"]
  }
  ```

  The above query computes the total sales per day within the specified interval, serving typical use cases like sales trend analysis over time.

- **TopN Queries**: These are designed for efficient retrieval of the top 'N' elements based on a specific metric or dimension. TopN queries optimize for fast computation of most-used items or categories.

  ```
  {
      "queryType": "topN",
      "dataSource": "users",
      "dimension": "country",
      "threshold": 5,
      "metric": "user_count",
      "aggregations": [
          {"type": "count", "name": "user_count"}
      ],
      "intervals": ["2023-01-01/2023-12-31"]
  }
  ```

This TopN query retrieves the top five countries based on user count, a common requirement in demographic studies or marketing analysis.

- **GroupBy Queries**: GroupBy queries perform aggregation across one or more dimensions, enabling complex multi-dimensional analysis akin to SQL GROUP BY operations.

```
{
  "queryType": "groupBy",
  "dataSource": "purchase_data",
  "dimensions": ["country", "product_id"],
  "granularity": "all",
  "aggregations": [
    {"type": "doubleSum", "name": "total_revenue", "fieldName": "revenue"}
  ],
  "intervals": ["2023-01-01/2023-12-31"]
}
```

Here, revenue is aggregated across country and product dimensions, an operation crucial for discovering relations in multidimensional datasets.

- **Scan Queries**: A low-level query type, Scan queries return raw data rows and are not optimized for analytical workloads like Timeseries or GroupBy.

```
{
  "queryType": "scan",
  "dataSource": "event_logs",
  "resultFormat": "list",
  "columns": ["timestamp", "userId", "eventType"],
  "intervals": ["2023-01-01/2023-12-31"]
}
```

This query extracts specific columns from event logs over a time range, effective for data export or exploratory tasks.

- **Select Queries**: These queries provide simple selection capabilities, including drill down details for debugging or data investigation, and are optimized for fast response.

```
{
  "queryType": "select",
  "dataSource": "orders",
  "descending": "true",
  "intervals": ["2023-01-01/2023-01-31"],
  "dimensions": ["orderId", "customerId"],
  "metrics": ["amount"]
```

```
    }
```

Focused on retrieving specific data fields, Select queries deliver detailed insights directly from ingested data.

- **Query Execution and Optimization**

Druid is optimally designed for executing queries in a distributed fashion, engaging multiple nodes in parallel to ensure minimal latency. Broker nodes receive and parse the client query, allocating sub-tasks to Historical or real-time nodes which contain relevant data segments. One of the remarkable aspects of Druid's querying model is its ability to combine the results of each sub-task seamlessly.

Query optimization within Druid involves several strategies that draw on indexing, parallel processing, and segment-oriented operations:

- **Use of Bitmaps and Indexes**: Druid takes advantage of bitmap indexing that enables quick filtering of data segments fitting query conditions, significantly boosting query performance.

- **Segment Pruning**: Segments containing no data relevant to a query are quickly excluded from processing, a method contributing to reducing unnecessary data scans.

- **Time Interval Filtering**: Query localization through time-based partitioning means that only segments containing relevant time data are assessed, leveraging Druid's strong capability in time-sensitive data analysis scenarios.

- **Incremental Aggregation**: Aggregation queries gain efficiency as Druid computes sums, averages, and other metric mixes using strategies that process each segment's data independently yet collaboratively.

Performance optimization in practical terms entails using the right type of query for the task, ensuring the configuration harnesses the full potential of Druid's infrastructure, and continuously monitoring system behavior to refine data partitioning and rulesets.

- **Advanced Query Capabilities**

Alongside standard queries, Apache Druid encompasses more advanced querying capabilities that extend its analytic depth:

- **Expressions**: Druid supports querying with expression-based transformations, allowing complex calculations and condition evaluations within the query context. Example:

```
{
  "queryType": "groupBy",
  "dataSource": "daily_metrics",
  "dimensions": ["region"],
  "granularity": "day",
  "aggregations": [
    {"type": "doubleSum", "name": "total_sales", "fieldName": "sales"}
  ],
  "postAggregations": [
    {
      "type": "expression",
      "name": "sales_tax",
      "expression": "total_sales * 0.1"
    }
  ],
  "intervals": ["2023-01-01/2023-12-31"]
}
```

Here, post-aggregation functions compute additional metrics, such as sales tax, within query logic.

- **Joins**: Druid's native join functionalities enable combining datasets to enrich analytical output, essential for multifaceted insights over dispersed datasets.

- **SQL Interface**: Druid offers SQL-like query handling, translating traditional SQL commands into native Druid queries, easing the transition for users familiar with relational databases.

Performance-enhancing features like data sketches also allow Druid to handle approximate counts and state estimations, beneficial when absolute precision is secondary to understanding trends and patterns.

- **Querying Best Practices**

For best leveraging Druid's querying model, consider the following strategies:

- **Granularity Matching**: Match query granularity with common data access patterns to allow for efficient segment processing and retrieval.

- **Appropriate Query Selection**: Use the query type that best fits the question being asked—Timeseries for chronological aggregations, GroupBy for dimensional analysis, and so on.

- **Prioritize Pre-Aggregations**: Where possible, structure data ingestion to perform aggregations, reducing the burden on query-time computations.

- **Indexing Awareness**: Configure fields for indexing that are frequently filtered or aggregated by queries to expedite processing.

- **Monitor Query Patterns**: Continuously assess query patterns and adjust configuration elements like cache settings, segment retention policies, or node provisioning to address emerging patterns or bottlenecks.

By understanding and leveraging the nuances of Druid's querying model, businesses can fully exploit its rapid data retrieval and analysis capabilities, transforming complex analytic tasks into real-time actionable insights. As data continues to expand and grow in complexity, Druid's querying adaptability and power ensure it remains a pivotal tool in scalable analytic solutions.

Chapter 4

Data Ingestion in Druid

This chapter explores the various methodologies for ingesting data into Apache Druid, which include real-time, batch, and hybrid approaches. It discusses schema design and data modeling as crucial steps for optimizing performance. Readers are guided on configuring data sources and utilizing the Ingestion API to manage data flows effectively. The text also covers the creation of detailed ingestion specifications, highlighting the roles of input sources, parsing formats, and transformations. Real-time and batch ingestion processes are explained with emphasis on effective strategies for handling diverse data streams and large data sets, ensuring efficient data analysis.

4.1 Understanding Ingestion Methods

In Apache Druid, data ingestion is a critical process that determines how information is brought into the system. The mechanism of ingestion can significantly impact the efficiency, speed, and reliability of data querying and analysis. With the rising prevalence of varying data types and sources, understanding the various ingestion methods available in Druid—namely real-time, batch, and hybrid approaches—

becomes imperative. Each of these methods offers unique advantages and challenges, and selecting the appropriate one often depends on the nature of the data and the analytical requirements.

Data ingestion in Druid can be broadly categorized into three types: real-time, batch, and hybrid. Each serves distinct purposes, with real-time ingestion focusing on minimal latency, batch ingestion emphasizing data volume and thorough processing, and hybrid approaches combining elements of both to leverage their strengths.

Real-Time Ingestion is designed for scenarios where data arrives continuously and must be queried promptly. This method is particularly useful in environments that require up-to-the-minute reporting capabilities, such as monitoring industrial processes or financial transactions. Real-time ingestion in Druid is typically facilitated through integration with message queue systems like Apache Kafka or Amazon Kinesis. These systems handle streams of data events that are processed by Druid's indexing services.

The ingestion process involves setting up a stream to deliver data with minimal delay. Here is a conceptual outline of how a real-time ingestion setup might be constructed:

Algorithm 1 Steps for Setting Up Real-Time Ingestion in Druid

---

1: Configure the stream source (e.g., Apache Kafka).
2: Define the data schema, including time parsing and data types.
3: Configure the Druid indexing task to subscribe to the stream.
4: Set up transformations, if necessary, to clean or manipulate incoming data.
5: Monitor data ingestion and adjust configurations for scaling and tuning.

A practical demonstration using Apache Kafka is shown below:

```
Properties props = new Properties();
props.put("bootstrap.servers", "localhost:9092");
props.put("group.id", "druid-ingestion");
props.put("enable.auto.commit", "true");
props.put("auto.commit.interval.ms", "1000");
props.put("key.deserializer", "org.apache.kafka.common.serialization.StringDeserializer
    ");
props.put("value.deserializer", "org.apache.kafka.common.serialization.
    StringDeserializer");
```

```
KafkaConsumer<String, String> consumer = new KafkaConsumer<>(props);
consumer.subscribe(Arrays.asList("druid-stream"));
```

The above configuration sets up a Kafka consumer that consumes from the topic druid-stream. Druid's indexing service can be configured to utilize this consumer to process and ingest data in real time.

The major advantage of real-time ingestion is the immediacy of data availability for analytical queries. This is particularly valuable for dashboards or alerts that operate on threshold alerts.

In contrast to real-time ingestion, **Batch Ingestion** handles data that is accumulated over time. This method is more suitable for periodic processing of significant volumes of data, such as daily logs or transactional databases' exports. Batch processes excel in scenarios that do not require the immediacy of real-time data integration and can be tuned to accommodate larger data sets efficiently.

Batch ingestion in Druid often involves data collected and stored in systems like HDFS, Amazon S3, or local files. Here is a typical batch ingestion setup:

Algorithm 2 Steps for Setting Up Batch Ingestion in Druid

1: Identify data sources (e.g., HDFS, S3).
2: Define the static schema for data, including dimensions and metrics.
3: Create an ingestion specification detailing input formats and parsing configurations.
4: Submit batch ingestion tasks to Druid's ingestion API.
5: Monitor task execution and manage error handling.

An example ingestion specification for batch ingestion, focusing on data from an S3 bucket, is as follows:

```
{
  "type": "index_parallel",
  "spec": {
    "ioConfig": {
      "type": "index_parallel",
      "inputSource": {
        "type": "s3",
        "uris": ["s3://my-bucket/my-data/*.json"]
      },
      "inputFormat": {
        "type": "json"
```

```
    }
  },
  "dataSchema": {
    "dataSource": "my_data",
    "timestampSpec": {
      "column": "event_time",
      "format": "iso"
    },
    "dimensionsSpec": {
      "dimensions": ["user_id", "action"]
    },
    "metricsSpec": [{
      "type": "count",
      "name": "count"
    }]
  }
 }
}
```

Batch ingestion involves defining an ingestion specification, which is a JSON object that includes components such as ioConfig, dataSchema, and other processing details. The ingestion process runs as a separate task, leveraging parallelism to enhance performance.

While both real-time and batch ingestion have their specific use cases, **Hybrid Ingestion Methods** allow for the integration of both approaches. Hybrid methods enable data engineers to process data that demands different latencies. For instance, a system could ingest real-time data for immediate analytics while continuously running batch processes overnight to handle high-volume updates or corrections.

A common strategy in hybrid ingestion is to use real-time ingestion for current data and periodically use batch processing to backfill or correct data as needed.

```
# Process real-time stream
real_time_data = process_stream('kafka', 'realtime-topic')
index_real_time_data(real_time_data)

# Schedule batch processing
schedule_batch_job(process_historical_data)
```

In this pseudocode, real-time data is continuously ingested from a Kafka topic, while historical data is periodically processed via batch jobs. This ensures a balance between immediate data availability and complete coverage over large, historical datasets.

Moreover, the choice of ingestion method in Druid often hinges on several factors, including data latency requirements, volume, and re-

94

source allocation. Real-time ingestion necessitates continuous re-source engagement, whereas batch ingestion can occur during periods of lower system demand.

In practice, the decision matrix for selecting between these ingestion methods should take into account:

- **Latency Requirements**: Determine the acceptable delay for data availability.

- **Data Volume**: Consider not only the current data size but also expected growth.

- **System Resources**: Evaluate the availability and cost implications of compute and storage resources.

- **Complexity of Processing**: Ascertain if the data requires significant transformation or enrichment, impacting the processing choice.

Understanding Druid's ingestion capabilities and tailored application creates a robust data architecture capable of supporting diverse analytical initiatives. Through appropriate method selection, users gain the ability to maintain high-performance querying capabilities while efficiently using infrastructure.

4.2 Schema Design and Data Modeling

Ingesting data into a system like Apache Druid is only the first step in the data management lifecycle. Equally crucial, if not more so, is the design of data schemas and models that optimize querying performance and storage efficiency. Schema design and data modeling are foundational elements that dictate how data is stored, retrieved, and manipulated within Druid, impacting everything from storage costs to query speed and flexibility.

At its core, schema design in Druid involves specifying how data is organized into tabular structures consisting of dimensions, metrics, and timestamp columns. The thoughtful selection and implementation of these components can significantly affect the overall system performance.

Dimensions and Metrics are two fundamental concepts when designing schemas in Druid. Dimensions are attributes of the data that you might filter or group by in queries. Typical examples include categorical data such as user IDs, geographic locations, or product categories. Conversely, metrics represent quantitative measures that one might aggregate in query results. These usually include numerical data like counts, sums, or other mathematical operations applied to data values.

The dataSchema configuration allows you to define the structure of your dataset, as illustrated in the following example:

```
{
  "dataSchema": {
    "dataSource": "ecommerce_events",
    "timestampSpec": {
      "column": "event_time",
      "format": "auto"
    },
    "dimensionsSpec": {
      "dimensions": ["user_id", "product_id", "category", "region"]
    },
    "metricsSpec": [
      {
        "type": "count",
        "name": "event_count"
      },
      {
        "type": "doubleSum",
        "name": "total_sales",
        "fieldName": "sale_amount"
      }
    ]
  }
}
```

In this configuration, event_time is defined as the timestamp column, while user_id, product_id, category, and region are set as dimensions. Metrics include event_count, which counts rows, and total_sales, which sums the sale_amount.

Optimizing schema design necessitates an understanding of the trade-offs between denormalization and database normalization principles. Unlike traditional relational databases that focus heavily on normalization to reduce data redundancy, denormalization in Druid's schema design enhances read performance and simplifies query patterns by

96

storing related data together. This approach can increase storage usage but significantly boost the speed of query execution.

Another aspect to consider is the **Granularity** of data ingested. Granularity settings manage how data is aggregated over time and affect storage size and query performance. Druid supports various granularities like 'all', 'none', 'second', 'minute', 'hour', 'day', 'week', 'month', and 'year'. Lower granularity often results in more fine-grained data with higher storage requirements, while higher granularity can reduce data size at the cost of detail.

```
{
  "granularitySpec": {
    "type": "uniform",
    "segmentGranularity": "day",
    "queryGranularity": "none"
  }
}
```

The segmentGranularity dictates how data is partitioned over time, influencing segment sizes and the performance implications of recomputations. The queryGranularity manages the minimum time granularity for queries, where 'none' retains data at its original granularity.

Another important consideration in schema design and data modeling is the use of **Secondary Indexes** such as bitmap indexes. Bitmap indexing is a powerful feature of Druid that accelerates filtering operations by creating a spatial index over the dimensions. Although these indexes create additional storage overhead, they can expedite query response times considerably. Care should be taken to balance the advantages of indexing with the storage and maintenance overhead.

Roll-up is another powerful feature in Druid, which refers to the pre-aggregation of data during ingestion based on its dimensions and granularity settings. This method can dramatically reduce the data size by aggregating metrics along relevant dimensions, often resulting in significant storage and query efficiency improvements.

```
{
  "tuningConfig": {
    "type": "index",
    "rollup": true
  }
}
```

Above, the rollup option is enabled, which means that Druid will aggregate data across similar dimension tuples during ingestion, reducing the storage footprint.

Deciding whether to apply roll-up involves considerations of both data needs and query patterns. For example, when querying raw data is critical, a non-roll-up approach might be favored. Conversely, where aggregate analysis is sufficient, enabling roll-up can be extremely beneficial.

Transformations and Derived Metrics are another essential component of schema design. Druid allows data transformations and calculations during the ingestion phase, improving query execution performance by preprocessing the data. Custom transformations enable the derivation of new fields or adjustment of existing ones based on specified logic.

```
{
  "transformSpec": {
    "transforms": [
      {
        "type": "expression",
        "name": "adjusted_sales",
        "expression": "sale_amount * tax_rate"
      }
    ]
  }
}
```

Here, a transformation using an expression calculates a new metric adjusted_sales based on existing fields. Such derived metrics can be essential in enhancing analytical insights without requiring complex post-query processing.

Data Types assigned to dimensions and metrics are also pivotal, impacting data precision and storage requirements. Druid supports various data types including strings, longs, floats, and doubles. Correctly choosing data types based on expected values can conserve space and improve processing efficiency.

Partitioning and Clustering strategies should also be considered to optimize data retrieval. Segment partitioning and clustering based on dimensions can optimize query speed and reduce I/O by reducing data that must be scanned. Techniques like sharding data linked to high-cardinality dimensions can greatly benefit from partitioning.

```
{
```

```
"tuningConfig": {
  "type": "index",
  "partitionsSpec": {
    "type": "hashed",
    "numShards": 4
  }
}
}
```

In this example, a partitioning strategy applies hashing to shard data across four partitions, leveraging parallelism to increase ingestion and query performance.

In the context of **Data Modeling for Complex Relationships**, Druid facilitates modeling more intricate datasets by supporting joins and lookups. Although Druid is optimized for OLAP workloads and prefers denormalized, flattened datasets, it can accommodate certain relational patterns via joins and lookups for dynamic reference data integration.

Careful schema modeling in Druid requires balancing the goals of reducing redundancy, optimizing query performance, and ensuring the scalability of data architecture. Practical considerations involve identifying key analytical patterns, understanding the latency and detail requirements of business processes, and anticipating future data growth.

Schema design and data modeling constitute an ever-evolving practice where understanding Druid's strengths and limitations, combined with an iterative approach, can lead to systems that deliver fast, efficient, and scalable query performance, driving insightful analytics for the organization.

4.3 Configuring Data Sources

Configuring data sources in Apache Druid is a critical step that ensures the smooth ingestion and querying of data. This process encompasses defining the pathways through which data is retrieved, specifying the formats and structures expected, and setting parameters that accommodate various source-specific attributes. Thoroughly configuring data sources is crucial for achieving optimal ingestion performance and efficient data flow management within Druid.

The configuration begins with the determination of the **Input Source Type**, which specifies where and how Druid retrieves data. Common input sources include local files, HDFS, Amazon S3, and streaming platforms such as Apache Kafka or Kinesis. Selecting the appropriate input source type is dictated by the nature of the data, the system architecture, and the desired latency.

File-Based Input Sources like HDFS and S3 are typical for batch ingestion, where data is stored in static files, such as JSON, CSV, or AVRO. Configuration involves defining the file paths, parsing formats, and any schema instructions required for accurately reading the data.

Here is a foundational configuration for ingesting data from an S3 bucket:

```
{
  "type": "index_parallel",
  "spec": {
    "ioConfig": {
      "type": "index_parallel",
      "inputSource": {
        "type": "s3",
        "uris": ["s3://my-bucket/data-folder/part-*"]
      },
      "inputFormat": {
        "type": "csv",
        "findColumnsFromHeader": true
      }
    }
  }
}
```

This JSON configuration specifies an S3 input source, pointing to a directory or files using wildcard patterns. The inputFormat field indicates the files' format, with csv reading headers for column names.

Streaming Input Sources cater to real-time ingestion scenarios and involve connecting Druid to message brokering systems like Kafka. Such systems manage continuous data streams and necessitate configurations that subscribe to relevant topics, manage offsets, and potentially enable synchronous record consumption.

Below is an example configuration for a Kafka data source:

```
{
  "type": "kafka",
  "spec": {
    "ioConfig": {
      "consumerProperties": {
```

```
        "bootstrap.servers": "localhost:9092",
        "group.id": "druid-ingestion"
      },
      "topic": "events-topic"
    },
    "taskContext": {
      "useEarliestOffset": true
    }
  }
}
```

In this setup, the Kafka topic events-topic is configured for ingestion. The Druid consumer is part of the group druid-ingestion, using the earliest available offset to manage data from the beginning of the topic.

Aligning the format and structure of the input data is achieved through configuring **Input Formats**. Druid can handle numerous formats such as JSON, CSV, AVRO, PARQUET, and ORC. The correctness of this step is crucial, as misconfigured formats can potentially lead to ingestion failures or data corruption.

An example of an AVRO input format configuration is provided below:

```
{
  "inputFormat": {
    "type": "avro",
    "schema": {
      "type": "record",
      "name": "events",
      "fields": [
        {
          "name": "timestamp",
          "type": "string"
        },
        {
          "name": "user_id",
          "type": "int"
        },
        {
          "name": "purchase_amount",
          "type": "double"
        }
      ]
    }
  }
}
```

The AVRO format not only specifies the field data types but also mandates a precise schema to ensure correctness during deserialization and ingestion operation.

Parsing and Transformation Options are then applied to handle adjustments or enhancements of data as it is read. Parsers manage the breaking down of incoming data; parsing options include choosing delimiters in CSVs or specific expressions for JSON paths.

Below is a configured example of a JSON parser with a transformation:

```
{
  "inputFormat": {
    "type": "json"
  },
  "transformSpec": {
    "transforms": [
      {
        "type": "expression",
        "name": "purchase_with_tax",
        "expression": "purchase_amount * 1.07"
      }
    ]
  }
}
```

This configuration reads JSON data and applies a transformation to compute a tax-adjusted purchase amount involving a simple multiplier expression.

Connection and Security Settings must be accounted for when accessing external systems. This may involve configuring credentials via access keys or certificates, setting up secure connections via SSL, and ensuring compliance with organizational security policies. Ensuring secure data access often involves defining environment-specific settings within Druid's configuration files or services.

A connection configuration could include:

```
{
  "type": "hdfs",
  "paths": ["hdfs://namenode:8020/data/path"],
  "inputFormat": {
    "type": "parquet"
  },
  "credentials": {
    "file": "/path/to/kerberos/krb5.conf"
  }
}
```

The configuration specifies accessing a Hadoop cluster's Parquet files and includes Kerberos configurations for secure connection.

Choosing whether to enable **Hierarchical Data Models** through lookups or joins might also be considered during data source configuration. These models allow additional datasets to be referenced dynamically, facilitating complex operational logic without the need to redesign datasets completely.

Performance Tuning and Scaling considerations play a pivotal role in configuring data sources efficiently. This includes tuning batch sizes, managing buffer allocations, and leveraging parallel processing to maximize throughput and reduce latency. For example:

```
{
  "task": {
    "maxRowsPerSegment": 3000000,
    "maxBytesInMemory": 500000000
  }
}
```

In this scenario, tasks are configured to limit segment size and memory allocation, optimizing for performance while preventing potential overuse of resources.

Configuring metadata storage and managing **State Consistency** is essential for guaranteeing the data's integrity over time, by ensuring that ingestion processes resume correctly after failures and that no duplicate records enter the system.

Finally, understanding and adjusting **Fault Tolerance Features** is integral to robust data source configuration. Implementing retries, ensuring idempotency, and utilizing logging and alert mechanisms support resilience and quick recovery from intermittent issues.

The successful configuration of data sources in Druid involves an intricate balance of setup, performance tuning, format specification, and rigorous security and error-handling practices. By addressing these elements comprehensively, organizations can foster a data infrastructure that is efficient, reliable, and responsive to the evolving needs of data analytics.

4.4 Using the Ingestion API

The Druid Ingestion API is a powerful interface that allows for the submission, management, and monitoring of ingestion tasks. This API is crucial for automating and orchestrating data ingestion workflows within Apache Druid, providing flexibility in handling various data formats and sources. The API offers a set of endpoints that facilitate the ingestion process, allowing users to define tasks, monitor their progress, and handle any errors or exceptions that may arise.

Task Submission is a primary function of the Ingestion API, where JSON task specifications detail how and what data should be ingested. These specifications include configurations for data sources, input formats, parsing strategies, and more. The API is accessed using HTTP POST requests to submit these task specifications to Druid's Overlord service, which is responsible for managing ingestion tasks.

An example task specification for batch ingestion might look like this:

```
{
  "type": "index_parallel",
  "spec": {
    "dataSchema": {
      "dataSource": "clickstream_data",
      "timestampSpec": {
        "column": "event_time",
        "format": "auto"
      },
      "dimensionsSpec": {
        "dimensions": ["session_id", "user_id", "page"]
      },
      "metricsSpec": [
        {
          "type": "count",
          "name": "page_views"
        }
      ]
    },
    "ioConfig": {
      "type": "index_parallel",
      "inputSource": {
        "type": "s3",
        "uris": ["s3://my-bucket/data/2023-01/*.csv"]
      },
      "inputFormat": {
        "type": "csv",
        "findColumnsFromHeader": true
      }
    },
    "tuningConfig": {
      "type": "index_parallel"
    }
  }
}
```

To submit this task specification via the Ingestion API, you would execute an HTTP POST request as follows:

```
curl -X POST 'http://localhost:8081/druid/indexer/v1/task' \
-H 'Content-Type: application/json' \
-d @task-spec.json
```

In this command, task-spec.json is the file containing the task specification, and the Druid Overlord service is accessed at localhost:8081.

Managing Task Lifecycle is another critical aspect of the Ingestion API, providing endpoints to check task statuses, including task creation, completion, and failure states. Important endpoints include:

- /druid/indexer/v1/task/{taskId}/status: Retrieves the status of a specific task. - /druid/indexer/v1/supervisor/{supervisorId}/status: Provides the status of a Kafka indexing service supervisor. - /druid/indexer/v1/tasks: Lists all current and past tasks with their statuses.

Consider the following example for retrieving the status of a specific task:

```
curl -X GET 'http://localhost:8081/druid/indexer/v1/task/{taskId}/status'
```

The API will return a JSON response indicating if the task is running, complete, or failed, along with any messages detailing the task's state:

```
{
  "id": "index_parallel_clickstream_data_2023-01-02T12:00:00Z",
  "status": {
    "id": "index_parallel_clickstream_data_2023-01-02T12:00:00Z",
    "status": "SUCCESS",
    "duration": 12500
  }
}
```

Effective **Error Handling and Retry Logic** is facilitated by the API's feedback mechanisms. For tasks that fail, detailed logs and reports on errors can be retrieved and analyzed to determine the causes and necessary corrective actions. The API provides logs and error messages accessible through specific endpoints, enabling deep troubleshooting and fault isolation for ingestion problems. Automated workflows can incorporate retry logic in response to transient failures or issues resolved by modifying the task's parameters or the data source's availability.

Handling Multiple Data Formats with the API allows for ingesting various file formats and structures in a uniform manner. The API supports native parsing for a diverse set of formats including JSON, CSV, AVRO, and others, specifying parsers in the task specification. Advanced configurations may include custom parsers or extensions if the data does not conform to standard formats, showcasing the flexibility of Druid's ingestion capabilities.

Take for example, a JSON format specification integrated into a task configuration:

```
{
  "inputFormat": {
    "type": "json"
  },
  "jsonParser": {
    "type": "arbitrary_json",
    "flattenSpec": {
      "useFieldDiscovery": true
    }
  }
}
```

This configuration ensures that arbitrary JSON data is parsed according to inferred field structures without pre-defined schemas, leveraging Druid's capacity to dynamically handle semi-structured content.

The API also facilitates **Dynamic Input Source Switching** which can be enabled via script automation or orchestrated workflows. This is particularly beneficial for environments requiring dynamic scaling or realignment of data streams in response to real-time analytics needs, data availability, or query workload shifts.

For example, consider automating ingestion that shifts between Kafka for real-time consumption and S3 for catching up with historical data backlogs:

```
import requests

def submit_task(api_url, task_spec):
    response = requests.post(api_url, json=task_spec)
    return response.json()

def main():
    kafka_task_spec = { /* Kafka Task Specification */ }
    s3_task_spec = { /* S3 Task Specification */ }

    current_hour = datetime.datetime.now().hour

    if current_hour < 12:
        print("Submitting Kafka Ingestion Task")
        submit_task('http://localhost:8081/druid/indexer/v1/task', kafka_task_spec)
```

```
else:
    print("Submitting S3 Ingestion Task")
    submit_task('http://localhost:8081/druid/indexer/v1/task', s3_task_spec)

if ___name___ == "___main___":
    main()
```

In this scenario, the Python script programmatically decides on a task specification based on the time of day, whether to ingest streaming data or batched records.

Overall, the Ingestion API provides comprehensive facilities for customizing, automating, and optimizing data ingestion into Apache Druid. Through its endpoints and capabilities, this API empowers data engineers and operators to effectively manage the data lifecycle, adapt workflows to changing data dynamics, and ensure reliable and efficient data analysis and querying, which is crucial for maintaining a robust data infrastructure.

4.5   Ingestion and Transformation Specs

In Apache Druid, the ingestion process is delineated by detailed specifications that dictate how data is brought into the system and transformed as necessary. Ingestion and Transformation Specifications are critical components, covering the configuration of input sources, parsers, granularity, transformations, and more. They serve as the blueprint for how data is processed from raw formats into a structured, easily queriable form.

An **Ingestion Spec** in Druid is defined in JSON format and encapsulates several key components: dataSchema, ioConfig, and tuningConfig. Each plays a pivotal role in controlling various aspects of the ingestion pipeline.

Data Schema is the first major component, determining how the data is structured once ingested. Key sub-components include:

- timestampSpec: Defines the time column used for indexing. The time column is integral for segment management and ensures temporal organization of data.

107

- dimensionsSpec: Lists the dimensions, which are fields used for filtering or grouping during queries.

- metricsSpec: Describes how to calculate and store metrics, or aggregated values, during ingestion.

Below is an example of a dataSchema configuration:

```
{
  "dataSchema": {
    "dataSource": "user_activity",
    "timestampSpec": {
      "column": "activity_timestamp",
      "format": "iso"
    },
    "dimensionsSpec": {
      "dimensions": ["user_id", "activity_type", "device_type", "location"]
    },
    "metricsSpec": [
      {"type": "count", "name": "event_count"},
      {"type": "longSum", "name": "session_length", "fieldName": "duration"}
    ]
  }
}
```

In this specification, activity_timestamp is the designated timestamp, and several dimensions and metrics are defined, each corresponding to specific analytic needs.

The **IO Configuration** (ioConfig) specifies data source locations and formats. This includes not only batch ingestion sources like file paths (e.g., S3 or HDFS) but also stream ingestion settings for environments using Kafka or other similar services. Input configuration requires declaring input formats and any necessary parsing.

Here is an ioConfig snippet for a Kafka stream:

```
{
  "ioConfig": {
    "type": "kafka",
    "consumerProperties": {
      "bootstrap.servers": "kafka-broker1:9092",
      "group.id": "druid-ingest"
    },
    "topic": "user-activities",
    "autoOffsetReset": "earliest"
  }
}
```

This configuration establishes a Kafka connection, using specified brokers and a consumer group to ingest from the stated topic.

Tuning Configuration (tuningConfig) allows fine-tuning of the ingestion process, addressing performance, memory usage, and resilience. Key parameters include:

- maxRowsInMemory: Control over how many rows are cached in memory before computation.

- numShards: Dictates the number of partitions created for the output.

- resetOffset: In streaming, indicates whether to reset the offset in case of failures.

Consider this example tuningConfig for a parallel ingestion task:

```
{
  "tuningConfig": {
    "type": "index__parallel",
    "maxRowsInMemory": 250000,
    "numShards": 5,
    "partitionsSpec": {
      "type": "hashed",
      "targetPartitionSize": 5000000
    }
  }
}
```

These settings tailor the task's memory footprint and scale, harnessing parallelism for efficiency gains.

A significant facet of Druid ingestion specifications is **Transformation Functions**. Transformations allow modifications of data during its ingestion phase. Transformations often include data cleaning, format conversions, complex field derivations, or augmentations. The transformation spec is defined under the transformSpec section.

An example of adding transformations to an ingestion spec follows:

```
{
  "transformSpec": {
    "transforms": [
      {
        "type": "expression",
        "name": "device__os",
        "expression": "case\__searched(device\__type == 'iOS', 'iOS', device\__type ==
          'Android', 'Android', 'Other')"
      },
```

```
  {
    "type": "expression",
    "name": "geo_hash",
    "expression": "geohash(latitude, longitude, 12)"
  }
  ],
  "filter": {
    "type": "selector",
    "dimension": "activity\_type",
    "value": "login"
  }
 }
}
```

Two transformations are applied here: determining the operating system as derived from device_type and computing a geo_hash. Additionally, a filter selectively processes only login activities.

Druid's versatile handling of **Complex Data Types**, including nested or denormalized structures, is often managed with bespoke transformations and parsing scripts, usually via extension points. This flexibility is key when integrating heterogeneously structured datasets that don't align directly with out-of-the-box capabilities.

One of Druid's distinguishing strengths lies in its choice of **Granularity Specifications**, playing a paramount role in balancing data completeness with query efficiency. Granularity is set for both segment and query levels:

- segmentGranularity: Controls how data is physically stored per segment.

- queryGranularity: Determines how data is aggregated or summarized during ingestion.

The ingestion tool must craft these granularity parameters mindfully, seeking balance between performance demands and the detail needed for downstream analytics.

```
{
  "granularitySpec": {
    "type": "uniform",
    "segmentGranularity": "hour",
    "queryGranularity": "minute",
    "rollup": true
  }
}
```

Here, segments are created on an hourly basis, while rolled-up data can be queried at a minute's granularity, optimizing for performance efficiency while maintaining sufficient detail.

Moreover, Druid's **Guards Against Data Anomalies** or inaccuracies within the ingestion spec reduce potential errors during processing. These are handled through metrics validation, schema checks, and setting precision standards for numerical types, which prevent propagation of corrupted data through validation steps.

A good practice in complex ingestion scenarios is integrating **Automated Testing Procedures**. These procedures ensure ingestion configurations perform correctly under varied data structures and evolving schemas, preserving the system's integrity.

A combined view of these specifications can be seen in a comprehensive task configuration, designed to align every aspect of ingesting data with broader operational and analytical strategy. The ingestion spec orchestrates a sophisticated dance of thorough data preparation from source ingest to endpoint availability, underlining every insight extracted and every decision made.

Conclusion

Incorporating a well-crafted ingestion and transformation specification is essential for adapting Apache Druid to complex, high-demand environments. This customization harnesses the full power of Druid, allowing for a tailored experience that matches business needs with technological prowess. By thoroughly defining each component within an ingestion specification, businesses ensure that their Druid clusters provide efficient, scalable, and accurate analytics necessary for modern data-driven decision processes.

4.6 Real-Time Data Ingestion

The capability for real-time data ingestion in Apache Druid underpins its reputation as a powerful database for analytical workloads. Real-time ingestion allows for the immediate availability of data as soon as it is generated, facilitating instant analytical querying. This section delves into the setup, mechanisms, and optimizations involved in configuring Druid for real-time ingestion, particularly leveraging Apache Kafka and other streaming platforms.

Understanding Real-Time Ingestion Mechanics is fundamental. Real-time ingestion in Druid is typically achieved through the use of indexing services that subscribe to data streams, continuously ingesting and processing this data as it arrives. The pivotal components in this infrastructure are the indexing services and the middle managers.

- *Indexing Services* are responsible for retrieving data from streaming platforms such as Kafka. They create real-time Druid segments which are stored continuously in memory and periodically (or upon completion) finalized and persisted to deep storage.

- *Middle Managers* handle the task dispatch, ensuring scalability and parallel processing. They manage task execution, perform necessary compute operations, and handle intermediate data before transferring it to permanent storage.

The typical flow for setting up real-time ingestion starts with configuring a Kafka indexing task. To do this, specific properties and settings need to be accurately specified in the ingestion task specification:

```
{
  "type": "kafka",
  "dataSchema": {
    "dataSource": "real_time_events",
    "timestampSpec": {
      "column": "event_time",
      "format": "auto"
    },
    "dimensionsSpec": {
      "dimensions": ["user_id", "event_type", "platform"]
    },
    "metricsSpec": [
      {"type": "count", "name": "event_count"}
    ]
  },
  "ioConfig": {
    "consumerProperties": {
      "bootstrap.servers": "localhost:9092",
      "group.id": "druid-consumer-group"
    },
    "topic": "real-time-topic",
    "inputFormat": {
      "type": "json"
```

```
    }
  },
  "tuningConfig": {
    "type": "kafka",
    "maxRowsInMemory": 100000,
    "intermediatePersistPeriod": "PT10M",
    "maxTotalRows": 5000000
  }
}
```

This specification indicates that Druid will listen to the 'real-time-topic' on a Kafka server configured at 'localhost:9092'. Settings such as 'maxRowsInMemory' and 'intermediatePersistPeriod' ensure the system efficiently handles in-memory operations and manages data persistence.

Leveraging Streaming Architectures optimizes real-time data ingestion by aligning it with the streaming paradigms. Platforms like Kafka provide high-throughput and fault-tolerant features, making them suitable for capturing and disseminating large volumes of live data. Integrating such architectures with Druid requires careful planning:

- *Partition Strategy*: Data can be partitioned across various Kafka topics to reduce bottlenecks and enhance processing speed.

- *Consumer Configuration*: Adjusting consumer group settings ensures balanced data consumption across multiple indexing tasks and prevents overloading any single node.

- *Fault Tolerance and Resilience*: Utilizing built-in resilience features such as auto-offset resets or consumer group balancing ensures recovery from transient errors without manual intervention.

Real-time data typically originates in various formats and structures, necessitating flexible **Parsing and Transformation** capabilities within the ingestion pipeline. This involves defining parsers and using transformations to ensure correct field types and derived metrics necessary for analytical insights. For example:

```
{
  "transformSpec": {
    "transforms": [
```

113

```
{
  "type": "expression",
  "name": "is_mobile",
  "expression": "platform == 'iOS' || platform == 'Android'"
}
],
"filter": {
  "type": "selector",
  "dimension": "event_type",
  "value": "click"
}
}
}
```

In this case, a transformation calculates whether an event came from a mobile platform, while filtering exclusively for 'click' events to streamline the dataset and reduce noise.

Optimizing for Low-Latency is crucial in real-time environments where the timing of data availability translates to a competitive advantage. Ensuring low latency involves:

- *Minimizing Ingestion Delays*: Configuring small batch sizes for intermediate persistence reduces waiting time for data to be available for querying.

- *Efficient Query Execution Plans*: Designing queries that leverage indices and reduced resource footprints ensures that insights are gained swiftly.

- *System Resource Management*: Allocating sufficient memory and compute resources to manage real-time tasks reduces bottlenecks.

Introducing **Error Handling and Monitoring** mechanisms is essential for maintaining seamless real-time ingestion processes. This includes enabling detailed logging, setting up alerts for task failures, and automatic recovery actions allowing the system to self-heal from interruptions.

A multi-tier **Scalability Strategy** must be implemented to accommodate growing data volumes and variety. Scalability involves not only increasing resources but also leveraging parallelism and task distribution across multiple nodes. This approach ensures Druid remains responsive even as demand escalates.

114

Security and Compliance Considerations for real-time ingestion involve securing data in transit and ensuring only authorized nodes and users can interact with the data pipeline. Setting up SSL/TLS encryption for communication channels and employing authentication mechanisms such as Kerberos are standard practices to maintain secure operations.

Finally, **Testing and Validation** of real-time ingestion configurations ensure the system handles live data as expected. Testing simulates load, validates data integrity upon ingestion, and measures end-to-end latency, informing iterative optimizations for further enhancements.

With the correct configurations and infrastructure, Druid's real-time ingestion empowers organizations to achieve unprecedented insight using the freshest data, closing the gap between data generation and decision-making. This enables a new spectrum of opportunities in analytics, transforming reactive models into proactive, data-driven strategies.

4.7 Batch Ingestion Processes

Batch ingestion in Apache Druid is a crucial operation that allows for the efficient processing of large volumes of data accumulated over time. Unlike real-time ingestion, batch tasks ingest data in chunks, offering the possibility to process historical records, perform backfills, or handle data corrections. This process is vital for scenarios with high data volume, where performance and accuracy are prioritized over immediacy.

Batch ingestion can be configured to source data from various storage systems such as local files, HDFS, Amazon S3, or even directly from databases. This flexibility enables organizations to structure their data pipelines according to their infrastructure and strategic needs.

Batch Ingestion Mechanisms involve several stages, starting from data retrieval, pre-processing, segment creation, to finally persisting these segments into deep storage. Each stage is customizable through configuration to optimize the balance between processing speed, resource use, and data fidelity.

A common batch ingestion approach is through the use of the index_-parallel task, which allows data to be ingested in parallel, efficiently utilizing available resources. Here is an example of an ingestion specification for processing data from an S3 bucket:

```
{
  "type": "index_parallel",
  "spec": {
    "ioConfig": {
      "type": "index_parallel",
      "inputSource": {
        "type": "s3",
        "uris": ["s3://my-druid-data/2023-logs/*.json"]
      },
      "inputFormat": {
        "type": "json",
        "flattenSpec": {
          "useFieldDiscovery": true
        }
      }
    },
    "dataSchema": {
      "dataSource": "web_logs",
      "timestampSpec": {
        "column": "timestamp",
        "format": "iso"
      },
      "dimensionsSpec": {
        "dimensions": ["ip_address", "url", "session_id", "user_agent"]
      },
      "metricsSpec": [
        {"type": "count", "name": "request_count"}
      ]
    },
    "tuningConfig": {
      "type": "index_parallel",
      "maxNumWorkers": 10,
      "maxRowsInMemory": 500000,
      "maxTotalRows": 10000000
    }
  }
}
```

This setup describes an ingestion task targeting JSON files within an S3 bucket, specifying dimensions and metrics relevant to log analytics. The tuning configuration optimizes task execution using multiple workers and memory-efficient processing.

Defining Robust IO Configurations is essential in batch ingestion. This involves setting input sources correctly and optimizing handling for various data formats. Formats such as CSV, ORC, and AVRO are widely used, each with its own configuration nuances:

116

```
{
  "inputFormat": {
    "type": "csv",
    "listDelimiter": "|",
    "columns": ["timestamp", "ip_address", "url", "session_id", "user_agent"]
  }
}
```

A csv input format with a specified delimiter enables parsing configurations tailored to the source file's structure, ensuring accurate ingestion.

In batch processes, **Scheduling and Coordination** of tasks are pivotal to avoid conflicts and optimize system resource usage. Tasks can be orchestrated via workflow management tools like Apache Airflow or via simple cron jobs, ensuring they run during off-peak hours or after data availability windows.

Batch ingestion also often involves a **Pre-Processing Stage**, where data transformations are applied to structure or clean the data before final ingestion. This may involve filtering records, applying computed columns, or mapping and reducing operations to match the schema requirements:

```
{
  "transformSpec": {
    "transforms": [
      {
        "type": "expression",
        "name": "full_url",
        "expression": "concat(url, '?session=', session_id)"
      }
    ],
    "filter": {
      "type": "and",
      "fields": [
        {"type": "selector", "dimension": "user_agent", "value": "Mozilla"},
        {"type": "bound", "dimension": "timestamp", "lower": "2023-01-01T00:00:00"}
      ]
    }
  }
}
```

This transformation concatenates the URL with session identifiers and filters incoming data to include only requests from Mozilla browsers after a specific date.

Granularity and Partitioning Strategies play a key role in optimizing batch ingestion by determining how data is chunked and indexed over time. Segment granularity impacts how data is organized in storage, influencing query performance and partition management.

```
{
  "granularitySpec": {
    "type": "uniform",
    "segmentGranularity": "day",
    "queryGranularity": "minute",
    "rollup": true
  }
}
```

By setting segmentGranularity to 'day', data is segmented on a daily basis, while the queryGranularity defines the finest resolution to which data should be aggregated.

When processing high volumes, efficient **Memory and Resource Management** within the tuningConfig is vital to preventing bottlenecks. Configuring worker threads, memory buffers, and persistence thresholds ensures the tasks operate smoothly without exceeding available resources.

Error Handling and Fault Tolerance should incorporate retry mechanisms and logging to capture task failures and facilitate correction. Implementations ensure that data integrity is maintained and processing can resume automatically from points of failure. Leveraging Druid's retry configurations or orchestrating with robust schedulers ensures resiliency.

With batch ingestion, **Cost Efficiency** is also an important consideration, particularly when using cloud storage and compute resources. Optimizing segment sizes, data schemas, and query patterns can significantly reduce overheads and enhance overall cost-effectiveness.

Finally, thorough **Testing and Validation** is essential to confirm that ingestion specifications process data correctly and scalably. Simulation of ingestion on sample datasets can help identify bottleneck issues or schema errors early, facilitating a seamless production rollout.

By effectively employing batch processing capabilities within Druid, organizations can leverage high-efficiency data pipelines that support broad analytical contexts, rendering them prepared for insights derived from both historical trends and contemporary patterns. This strategic integration enables businesses to maximize value from their data assets through well-informed decision-making.

Chapter 5

Druid Querying Basics

This chapter introduces the foundational aspects of querying within Apache Druid, covering different query types such as timeseries, topN, groupBy, and select. It explains the distinctions between Druid's SQL interface and native query formats, guiding readers in choosing the appropriate method for their needs. The chapter elaborates on the query execution process, basic syntax, and core query structures, providing examples for clarity. Techniques for filtering, aggregating, and grouping data are detailed, alongside constructing time-based queries using Druid's granularity features. Additionally, the use of JSON structures for crafting native queries is discussed to enhance query handling capabilities.

5.1 Query Types and Use Cases

Apache Druid, a high-performance real-time analytics database, supports a range of query types, each designed for specific use cases and performance optimization on multidimensional datasets. Understanding these query types and their respective use cases is crucial for effectively leveraging Druid's capabilities. This section covers the primary query types in Druid: timeseries, topN, groupBy, and select queries,

119

providing details on their structure, execution, and applicable scenarios.

The query types in Druid are tailored to facilitate various analytical operations. Their fundamental aim is to extract, refine, and present data in forms that cater to organizational needs for business intelligence and operational insights.

The **timeseries** query type is quintessential for chronological data analysis. Druid excels in handling time-series data due to its inherent time-based partitioning architecture. Timeseries queries aggregate data over specified time intervals, generally returning one data point per interval, formed by aggregating the values of all records within that interval. This makes them particularly useful for generating time-series charts and dashboards where tracking changes over time is essential. For such queries, analyzing metrics like daily website visits, weekly revenue, or monthly temperature averages becomes seamless.

Consider a basic timeseries query, structured as follows:

```
{
  "queryType": "timeseries",
  "dataSource": "website_traffic",
  "granularity": "day",
  "aggregations": [
    {
      "type": "longSum",
      "name": "total_visits",
      "fieldName": "page_views"
    }
  ],
  "intervals": ["2023-01-01T00:00:00.000Z/2023-01-31T00:00:00.000Z"]
}
```

This query retrieves daily total page views for the month of January 2023. The granularity is set to 'day', meaning the result is aggregated over daily intervals. The aggregation function 'longSum' sums the page views to compute the total for each day. By modifying the 'granularity' field, these timeseries queries can be adjusted to different time resolutions such as minute, hour, month, or year, as well as custom granularities.

The **topN** query type is crafted for analytics focusing on top-ranking results, such as identifying leading categories, sites, or products, generally where cardinality is reasonably low. TopN queries return the top N elements based on certain criteria like most visited pages, highest selling products, or most active users. They are computationally efficient, which allows them to quickly return ranked results with reduced memory consumption.

A topN query example is depicted below:

```
{
  "queryType": "topN",
  "dataSource": "ecommerce_sales",
  "dimension": "product_id",
  "threshold": 5,
  "metric": "revenue",
  "aggregations": [
    {
      "type": "doubleSum",
      "name": "revenue",
      "fieldName": "order_value"
    }
  ],
  "granularity": "all",
  "intervals": ["2023-01-01T00:00:00.000Z/2023-01-31T00:00:00.000Z"]
}
```

This query identifies the top 5 products by revenue sold in January 2023. The 'threshold' defines the number of top entries to return, and the metric 'revenue' on which the ranking is based is computed using a 'doubleSum' aggregation on the 'order_value' field. The 'dimension' defines the categorical field used for ranking, here being 'product_id'.

The **groupBy** query type is among the most versatile in Druid, suitable for multi-dimensional data analysis involving slicing and dicing data along various attributes. These queries are designed to group data by specified dimensions and perform aggregates on measures, akin to SQL GROUP BY operations. GroupBy queries are typically more computationally expensive than topN queries but provide more comprehensive insights.

An example groupBy query could be:

```
{
  "queryType": "groupBy",
  "dataSource": "ecommerce_sales",
  "dimensions": ["product_id", "country"],
  "granularity": "all",
  "aggregations": [
    {
      "type": "doubleSum",
      "name": "total_revenue",
      "fieldName": "order_value"
    },
    {
```

```
    "type": "count",
    "name": "transaction_count"
  }
],
"intervals": ["2023-01-01T00:00:00.000Z/2023-01-31T00:00:00.000Z"]
}
```

Here, the sales data is grouped by both 'product_id' and 'country', providing a revenue breakdown by product and location for the given interval. The double aggregation strategy ('doubleSum' and 'count') illustrates the flexibility of groupBy queries to perform diverse calculations in a single execution.

The **select** query functions as a way to retrieve raw data records from the Druid storage, specified by certain filters and intervals. Although select queries are not typically used for analytics due to their lack of aggregation, they are crucial for drilling into detailed or non-aggregated views of the dataset, acting much like a traditional database SELECT statement. This is critical for exploratory data analysis or data verification tasks.

Here's a typical select query example:

```
{
  "queryType": "select",
  "dataSource": "ecommerce_sales",
  "dimensions": ["order_id", "customer_id"],
  "metrics": ["order_value", "discount"],
  "granularity": "all",
  "pagingSpec": {"pagingIdentifiers": {}, "threshold": 100},
  "intervals": ["2023-01-01T00:00:00.000Z/2023-01-31T00:00:00.000Z"]
}
```

In this query, the 'dimensions' and 'metrics' parameters guide which fields to retrieve. The 'pagingSpec' specifies how many records to return (the 'threshold'), which is useful for navigating large result sets through pagination.

Intrinsically, the choice of query type in Druid depends on several factors such as the desired level of aggregation, data velocity, complexity of required results, and performance considerations. Each query type involves different trade-offs. Timeseries and topN prioritize speed by operating primarily in-memory, whereas groupBy offers depth at the cost of added complexity in both compute and result size. Select queries provide raw, granular insights that can form the base for more refined datasets.

Given Druid's architectural design optimized for time-indexed data, timeseries queries align well with real-time dashboarding and interval-based analytics. Conversely, topN and groupBy serve scenarios necessitating operational intelligence, where pinpoint thresholds or categorical summaries are emphasized for rapid decision-making.

Real-world applications often require combining different query types to meet multifaceted business analytics needs. For instance, a comprehensive sales dashboard may pull data using timeseries for trending, topN for key performers, and groupBy to examine cross-sectional patterns amongst various demographics. This cooperative utilization effectively maximizes the insightful potential embedded within Apache Druid's querying capabilities.

In practical deployments, it is also common to refine queries by employing filters, aggregation functions, and custom reducers to precisely tailor the analytic outcome to business requisites. Understanding how to dissect and construct these queries enables data architects and analysts to fully harness Apache Druid's capacity for high-throughput, sophisticated data interrogation.

By providing structured and pointed analyses, query types in Druid alleviate the complex demands of processing large-scale datasets, delivering analytical efficiency and actionable intelligence to elevate strategic data utilization.

5.2   Druid SQL and Native Queries

Apache Druid offers dual mechanisms for querying: Druid SQL and native JSON queries. These paradigms serve different purposes and target distinct user skills, streamlining the extraction of insights from complex data sets. This section delves into the differences between these query types, highlighting scenarios where each offers advantages, thereby providing a guide for choosing the appropriate method.

Druid SQL effectively abstracts Druid's infrastructure with an SQL-like language familiar to numerous practitioners. It expands the comprehensibility of query formulation and introduces a wide audience of SQL-proficient users into the realm of Druid analytics. Built on Apache Calcite, Druid's SQL interface supports analytic SQL capabilities such as complex filtering, aggregations, groups, and more nuanced window functions, making it a robust tool for complex analytical tasks.

Conversely, Druid's native querying format employs JSON structures optimally designed for high performance and flexibility, affording more direct interaction with Druid's capabilities. The JSON query structure caters to use cases necessitating precise control over query execution and takes advantage of Druid's unique functions like custom aggregations and extensions. This characteristic makes native queries the preferred choice for real-time data processing and integration scenarios.

Consider a use case requiring the calculation of daily active users from a dataset of user logins, exploring both Druid SQL and native JSON query approaches.

A Druid SQL query solving this task might appear like:

```
SELECT
  FLOOR(__time TO DAY) AS day,
  COUNT(DISTINCT user_id) AS daily_active_users
FROM
  login_events
WHERE
  __time >= TIMESTAMP '2023-01-01 00:00:00'
  AND __time < TIMESTAMP '2023-02-01 00:00:00'
GROUP BY
  FLOOR(__time TO DAY)
ORDER BY
  day
```

In this SQL query, it utilizes standard SQL SELECT, WHERE, GROUP BY, and ORDER BY clauses making it accessible to users familiar with relational databases. The capability to format timestamps and group data by day is simplified by SQL syntax, providing a clear path from requirement to execution.

Contrastingly, accomplishing similar results with the native JSON query structure would involve:

```
{
  "queryType": "groupBy",
  "dataSource": "login_events",
  "granularity": "day",
  "dimensions": [],
  "aggregations": [
    {
      "type": "cardinality",
      "name": "daily_active_users",
```

```
    "fieldNames": ["user_id"]
  }
],
"intervals": ["2023-01-01T00:00:00.000Z/2023-02-01T00:00:00.000Z"],
"limitSpec": {
  "type": "default",
  "limit": 1000,
  "columns": [
    { "dimension": "___time", "direction": "ascending" }
  ]
}
}
```

Here, the query operates directly with Druid's ability to aggregate using cardinality on user identifiers, inherently recognizing the unique count through distinct analysis. Explicit configuration of intervals and dimensions provides flexibility over exactly how data aggregation transpires, offering a fine control unencumbered by SQL's abstraction layers.

The decision to deploy either SQL or native queries principally revolves around the context and user requirements. SQL's strength lies in its familiarity and ease of use, well suited for straightforward reporting tasks. It encapsulates operations with minimal boilerplate, facilitating not only rapid prototyping but also collaborative environments where SQL is the lingua franca.

On the other hand, JSON queries leverage Druid's core capabilities, offering performance-tuned executions and access to its advanced features. JSON's direct correlation to Druid's optimal execution path implies diminished translation overhead and enhanced capacity to customize processing components — from aggregation specifics to execution strategies.

In enterprise applications where agility and scalability are crucial, hybrid utilization of SQL for standard analysis, alongside JSON for intensive data engineering pipelines, can harmonize productivity with performance. This delineation ensures that analysts can iterate quickly on SQL, whereas engineers can harness the power Druid's engine offers through precise JSON configurations.

Consider an advanced scenario moving beyond simple counts to analyze complex metrics such as conversion rates on an e-commerce platform. This might involve aggregating user sessions, contrasting visit data with transaction confirmations, perhaps prioritizing opportunities for cross-sale recommendations:

```
SELECT
  product_category,
  COUNT(order_id) / NULLIF(COUNT(DISTINCT session_id), 0) AS
      conversion_rate
FROM
  web_traffic
JOIN
  transactions ON web_traffic.session_id = transactions.session_id
WHERE
  web_traffic.__time BETWEEN TIMESTAMP '2023-01-01 00:00:00' AND
      TIMESTAMP '2023-02-01 00:00:00'
GROUP BY
  product_category
```

This SQL adeptly joins and aggregates high cardinality data using familiar constructs; integrating analytics across multiple dimensions reflects the SQL interface's high-level ergonomic strength.

The equivalent JSON representation would necessitate leveraging Druid's multi-stage pipeline configuration, illustrating the advantage of its intricate command over partitioning and sorting intricacies. For monumental datasets requiring custom distributed aggregation strategies, native queries exhibit inherent proficiencies.

For example:

```
{
  "queryType": "groupBy",
  "dataSource": "web_traffic",
  "granularity": "all",
  "dimensions": ["product_category"],
  "aggregations": [
    {
      "type": "filtered",
      "filter": {
        "type": "selector",
        "dimension": "transaction_complete",
        "value": "true"
      },
      "aggregator": {
        "type": "count",
        "name": "purchase_count"
      }
    },
    {
      "type": "cardinality",
      "name": "session_count",
      "fieldNames": ["session_id"]
    }
  ],
  "postAggregations": [
    {
```

```
"type": "arithmetic",
"name": "conversion_rate",
"fn": "/",
"fields": [
  { "type": "fieldAccess", "fieldName": "purchase_count" },
  { "type": "fieldAccess", "fieldName": "session_count" }
]
    }
],
"intervals": ["2023-01-01T00:00:00.000Z/2023-02-01T00:00:00.000Z"]
}
```

This query amplifies precision analytics within Druid, deploying conditional filtering and post-aggregation calculations that showcase customizable logic flows, making the most of Druid's distributed and real-time processing characteristics.

What becomes evident is that while Druid SQL enhances accessibility and democratizes data analytics with its declarative syntax, native queries provide an unmatched level of finesse in handling high throughput scenarios, becoming indispensable for operations at scale or where raw analytical power is paramount.

Technical decisions hinge on a qualitative understanding of the application domain: specialization asserts that within data-intensive environments, an effective combination of SQL simplicity for analysis and JSON specificity for integration empowers a full-spectrum analytical strategy.

Both Druid SQL and native queries embody facets of the Apache Druid's prowess — one through human-centric language articulation and the other through machine-centric precision execution — allowing organizations to harness the analytical gifts of Druid to their strategic advantage.

5.3 Query Execution Process

Understanding the query execution process in Apache Druid is central to grasping how this powerful analytics engine processes vast amounts of data in real-time with impressive speed and efficiency. Druid's architecture uniquely supports distributed query execution, which is critical for achieving scalability and maintaining performance. This section explores in detail how queries are propagated, managed, and executed within the Druid ecosystem, focusing on the roles of broker and historical nodes, along with various components that facilitate the query processing pipeline.

The query execution process in Druid involves several key steps that transform user queries into actionable results, leveraging Druid's distributed and columnar storage design. Upon receiving a query, Druid progresses through parsing, planning, distribution, execution, and finally, result aggregation.

When a query is submitted, it is first received by the Druid Broker node. The Broker's initial task is to parse the query, then determine its type and structure whether it be timeseries, topN, groupBy, or any other supported query type. This identification is crucial as it informs the subsequent planning and routing decisions.

At the heart of Druid's processing efficiency is the broker's role in query planning and task assignment. The broker dispatches subqueries to various segments depending on data availability and the need for computational efficiency. These segments are abstract units of partitioned data that reside across Druid's Historical and Real-time Nodes.

$$\text{Broker Node} \xrightarrow{\text{Distributes Queries}} \{\text{Historical Nodes, Real-time Nodes}\}$$

A fundamental responsibility of the Broker is to consult Druid's metadata store, typically backed by a relational database, which maintains segment metadata. This metadata enables the Broker to map queries to the precise segments that contain the required data subsets over the specified time intervals. Accurate metadata management ensures that Druid does not scan unnecessary data segments, thus optimizing query latency.

Historical nodes, key to Druid's storage and durability, serve as the primary executors of read-only queries against stored data. These nodes are optimized for handling batch-indexed data, providing rapid access to historical records. The process from allocation to execution on historical nodes involves:

- Segment Retrieval: Historical nodes fetch the relevant segments indicated by the broker's query plan.

128

- Aggregating and Filtering: These nodes apply necessary aggregation functions and filters to minimize the data footprint throughout the execution.

- Intermediate Results Alignment: Results of subquery execution are streamlined, often involving data chunking for more efficient inter-node communication.

Real-time nodes, on the other hand, ingest and query data simultaneously, performing incremental indexing to integrate new data entries on-the-fly. Queries targeting real-time data undergo a dynamic process as they incorporate latest streaming records, maintaining the data system's contemporaneity.

Real-time Nodes: Ingestion ‖ Query Execution

A typical Druid query transpires over a distributed real-time data architecture. For instance, consider a straightforward timeseries query recapitulated in both its JSON structure and SQL expression:

JSON Query:

```
{
  "queryType": "timeseries",
  "dataSource": "user_actions",
  "granularity": "hour",
  "aggregations": [
    {
      "type": "count",
      "name": "action_count",
      "fieldName": "user_events"
    }
  ],
  "intervals": ["2023-09-01T00:00:00.000Z/2023-09-02T00:00:00.000Z"]
}
```

SQL Equivalent:

```
SELECT
  FLOOR(__time TO HOUR) AS hour,
  COUNT(user_events) AS action_count
FROM
  user_actions
WHERE
  __time BETWEEN TIMESTAMP '2023-09-01 00:00:00' AND TIMESTAMP
    '2023-09-02 00:00:00'
GROUP BY
  FLOOR(__time TO HOUR)
```

During execution, the Historic and Real-time nodes undertake fragment-specific computations, each contributing to constructing the progressive result set specified by the global query plan. This distributed computation is central to achieving high throughput and low latency.

Merging Results: Upon receiving subquery results, the Broker node proceeds to merge these intermediate results. Druid employs several strategies to efficiently combine partial results, benefiting from columnar storage to manage large datasets effectively. Operations like shuffling and merging leverage partial aggregation, which diminishes the computational load across all involved nodes.

For instance, using a groupBy query that might involve multiple dimensions and metrics aggregation, the strategy orchestrates data shuffle between cluster nodes based on partitioning keys. This framework substantially reduces the sharding complexity and merges distributed aggregates into a unified result set.

The final aggregation and processing of data are predominantly performed by the Broker node. It is the Broker node that constructs the complete response object to the client, carrying out final sorting, additional filtering, and pagination if required. As results accumulate, the Broker node exercises Druid's internal compression and serialization capabilities to reduce the response footprint, heightening the delivery speed to end-users' applications.

Underlying this intricate orchestration are several optimizations, including:

- Bitmap Indexing: Efficiently narrows down the data range with bitmap indices, easing filtering operations.

- Query Caching: Across different levels, both result-level and segment-level caches improve data retrieval times significantly.

- Parallel Query Execution: Harnesses multi-threading to expedite various stages of the distributed query process, maximizing CPU utilization across nodes.

Automation and optimization strategies such as segment auto-compaction and balancing of segment distribution further enhance the overall performance. These components together ensure that Druid can handle petabyte-scale workloads with agility and consistency.

When deploying Druid in production, comprehending the query execution process allows data engineers and administrators to diagnose performance bottlenecks, fine-tune query pathways, and strategically balance workloads. By exercising best practices in configurational adjustments and resource allocation, Druid's system reaches its ideal throughput capabilities, even as data volume and complexity intensify.

The query execution process in Apache Druid is a testament to the system's design principle of balancing real-time performance with batch query effectiveness, illustrating a sophisticated tapestry of coordination across distributed nodes — promoting a fluid, powerful analytical experience.

5.4 Basic Query Syntax and Structure

The ability to effectively formulate queries in Apache Druid is vital to unlocking its full analytical capabilities. At the core of interacting with Druid lies the understanding of its basic query syntax and structure, integral for both SQL users and those writing native JSON queries. This section provides an overview of these fundamental elements, offering insights into their constructs and illustrating their application through examples.

Apache Druid supports two primary query languages: the SQL-like interface and the native JSON format. Each possesses its distinct advantages, allowing users to select the appropriate tool based on familiarity, complexity, and task requirements.

Druid SQL Query Syntax:

Druid's adoption of SQL offers simplicity for users acquainted with traditional relational databases. It adheres to SQL-92 and extends with functionalities suited to multidimensional analytics. A typical SQL query example in Druid might involve querying a dataset to retrieve aggregated metrics:

```
SELECT
```

```
  product_category,
  SUM(order_amount) AS total_sales
FROM
  sales_data
WHERE
  ___time BETWEEN TIMESTAMP '2023-01-01 00:00:00' AND TIMESTAMP
    '2023-01-31 23:59:59'
GROUP BY
  product_category
ORDER BY
  total_sales DESC
```

This query exemplifies standard SQL features used in Druid: SELECT for choosing columns, SUM for aggregating the total sales amount, WHERE for filtering based on a time range, GROUP BY for categorization, and ORDER BY for sorting results.

Druid leverages time column ___time as its inherent temporal dimension, crucial for queries that look to harness its time-series capabilities. Adjustments in your WHERE clause are pivotal as they define the time window for Druid's efficient segment retrieval process.

Advanced SQL users can utilize SQL functions and extensions such as window functions for complex temporal analytics, bringing forth sophisticated features like cumulative sums and analytics across sliding windows.

Consider this example demonstrating a more complex SQL operation using window functions:

```
SELECT
  region,
  order_date,
  order_value,
  SUM(order_value) OVER (PARTITION BY region ORDER BY order_date) AS
    cumulative_sales
FROM
  regional_sales
WHERE
  order_date BETWEEN TIMESTAMP '2023-01-01' AND TIMESTAMP '2023-01-31'
```

This query calculates a cumulative total of sales over time within each region, illustrating the power of SQL when analyzing data patterns across partitions and ordering data for cumulative calculations.

Native JSON Query Syntax:

For those requiring more fine-tuned control or seeking to exploit Druid's advanced functionalities like custom aggregation or filtering behaviors, native JSON queries offer this capability. Despite a steeper learning curve, JSON's descriptive structure communicates directly with Druid's processing framework, making it highly potent for optimal performance tuning and complex query specifications.

The basic format of a native JSON query may resemble the following structure:

```
{
  "queryType": "timeseries",
  "dataSource": "sales_data",
  "granularity": "day",
  "filter": {
    "type": "and",
    "fields": [
      {"type": "selector", "dimension": "product_category", "value": "electronics"},
      {"type": "time", "dimension": "__time", "intervals": ["2023-01-01T00:00:00.000Z
          /2023-01-31T23:59:59.999Z"]}
    ]
  },
  "aggregations": [
    {"type": "doubleSum", "name": "total_sales", "fieldName": "order_amount"}
  ],
  "intervals": ["2023-01-01T00:00:00.000Z/2023-01-31T23:59:59.999Z"]
}
```

In this JSON query, the granularity is set to daily, making it ideal for day-over-day analysis. The filter utilizes logical conditions to refine data selection. The aggregations specify how measures are calculated—in this instance, using doubleSum to total order amounts.

JSON syntax allows for more detailed expressions, particularly beneficial when engaging complex nested aggregations, dimensions with specific filtering requirements, or when integrating with custom extensions developed to enhance Druid's capability.

Structuring Queries for Performance:

A significant aspect of constructing effective Druid queries resides in their structure. The configuration of queries influences the speed and efficiency of data processing, impacting both latency and resource utilization. Queries should be structured to exploit Druid's column-oriented storage, segment partitioning, and parallel processing capabilities.

- **Granularity Optimization:** Setting the granularity in queries dictates the resolution of the aggregation. Finer granularity results in more detailed data but may increase processing overhead, whereas coarser granularity enhances performance by reducing the number of data points processed.

- **Filter Strategies:** Employing filters early in the query design improves efficiency by reducing the volume of data. Leveraging bitmap indices through conditions such as selector, bound, and regex can help in sharply narrowing down data segments prior to computation.

- **Aggregation Functions:** Choosing the appropriate aggregation function optimizes performance based on the nature of the dataset and analytical intent. Functions such as longSum, double-Sum, hyperUnique, and cardinality assist in constructing tailored analytics with precision.

- **Query Caching and Indexing:** Utilizing Druid's built-in caching mechanisms can significantly boost query speeds by reusing previously computed segment results. Indexing schedules should correspond to querying patterns to minimize redundant disk I/O.

Comprehensive Example:

Developing a complex query structure might involve integrating these elements to deliver in-depth analytics, such as monitoring user engagement across multiple dimensions:

```
{
  "queryType": "groupBy",
  "dataSource": "user_engagement",
  "granularity": "week",
  "dimensions": ["product_category", "user_location"],
  "filter": {
    "type": "and",
    "fields": [
      {"type": "selector", "dimension": "user_status", "value": "active"},
      {"type": "expression", "expression": "__time >= 1672531200000 AND __time <
          1675209600000"}
    ]
  },
  "aggregations": [
    {"type": "longSum", "name": "page_views", "fieldName": "view_count"},
    {"type": "cardinality", "name": "unique_users", "fieldNames": ["user_id"]}
  ],
  "intervals": ["2023-01-01T00:00:00.000Z/2023-01-31T00:00:00.000Z"],
  "limitSpec": {
    "type": "default",
```

```
"columns": [
   {"dimension": "product_category", "direction": "ascending"},
   {"dimension": "unique_users", "direction": "descending"}
  ]
 }
}
```

This query provides weekly insights into user activities, categorized by product and location, for active users over a specified time frame. By employing both longSum for counting page views and cardinality to distinctively evaluate user diversity, the JSON structure is used to convey intricate reporting needs directly.

Both SQL and JSON, through their syntax and structure, equip users to phenomenally query and analyze data with Druid. Selection between these interfaces depends on the user's requirement for simplicity or control; regardless of the pathway chosen, mastering their basic syntax and structure enables unlocking Apache Druid's analytics potential across multifarious data landscapes.

5.5 Filtering, Aggregating, and Grouping Data

The ability to selectively filter, aggregate, and group data is foundational to deriving meaningful insights from complex datasets in Apache Druid. These operations enable analysts and data scientists to focus on relevant data slices, summarize large volumes of data, and categorize results in ways that reveal underlying patterns. This section provides a comprehensive guide to these core operations within Druid's querying capabilities, explaining their principles, applications, and providing illustrative examples.

Filtering Data:

Filters in Druid act as constraints that determine which data points are included in query results. By applying filters appropriately, users can exclude unnecessary data, reducing the volume of data processed and improving query performance. Druid offers a wide array of filtering options that can be used in combination to refine datasets efficiently.

Basic filters include:

- Selector Filter: This is probably the most straightforward filter, used to select rows where a dimension matches a specific value.

```
"filter": {
  "type": "selector",
  "dimension": "product_category",
  "value": "electronics"
}
```

- Bound Filter: Suitable for selecting numeric or time ranges.

```
"filter": {
  "type": "bound",
  "dimension": "order_amount",
  "lower": "100",
  "upper": "500",
  "lowerStrict": false,
  "upperStrict": true
}
```

- Regex Filter: Utilized for matching dimensions against regular expressions.

```
"filter": {
  "type": "regex",
  "dimension": "user_agent",
  "pattern": "^Mozilla.*Firefox.*$"
}
```

- In Filter and Not Filter: Define composite logic for inclusions or exclusions.

```
"filter": {
  "type": "in",
  "dimension": "country",
  "values": ["USA", "Canada", "UK"]
}
```

Complex filter configurations can be embedded using logical operators and, or, and not, enabling multi-condition filtering strategies.

```
"filter": {
  "type": "and",
  "fields": [
    {
      "type": "selector",
      "dimension": "activity",
      "value": "purchase"
    },
    {
```

```
  "type": "not",
  "field": {
    "type": "selector",
    "dimension": "payment_status",
    "value": "cancelled"
  }
 }
]
}
```

In practice, well-architected filters leverage Druid's indexing capabilities to ensure efficient data parsing, especially with bitmap indices that expediently resolve matches or mismatches per dimension.

Aggregating Data:

Aggregation in Druid, akin to database summarization, involves the transformation of multiple data points into singular statistical representations. It's an essential tool for reducing data complexity and extracting high-level insights.

Druid supports several aggregation functions, some of which include:

- LongSum and DoubleSum: Additive aggregators for integer and floating-point numbers, respectively, often used for summing sales or visit counts.

```
"aggregations": [
  {
    "type": "longSum",
    "fieldName": "page_views",
    "name": "total_page_views"
  }
]
```

- Min and Max: Return the smallest or largest value in a column, useful for determining minimum or maximum sales prices.

```
"aggregations": [
  {
    "type": "max",
    "fieldName": "temperature",
    "name": "max_temp"
  }
]
```

- Count: Simple row counter, typically used for tallying record numbers.

```
"aggregations": [
  {
    "type": "count",
    "name": "total_transactions"
  }
]
```

- Cardinality: **Determines the number of distinct values within a dimension and is instrumental in analyzing unique visitors or distinct product views.**

```
"aggregations": [
  {
    "type": "cardinality",
    "name": "distinct_users",
    "fieldNames": ["user_id"]
  }
]
```

Aggregation functions encapsulate the efficiency of columnar processing by reducing data movement — a prominent benefit when handling big data volumes across distributed nodes.

Grouping Data:

Grouping involves organizing data into sets based on specified dimensions, forming the basis for summarized reporting and cross-sectional analysis. Druid's ability to group data extends beyond simple categorization by supporting multi-dimensional groupBy operations, analogously complex as SQL's GROUP BY feature.

Grouping example in JSON:

```
{
  "queryType": "groupBy",
  "dataSource": "web_logs",
  "granularity": "day",
  "dimensions": ["device_type", "country"],
  "aggregations": [
    {
      "type": "count",
      "name": "view_count"
    }
  ],
  "intervals": ["2023-01-01T00:00:00.000Z/2023-01-31T00:00:00.000Z"]
}
```

The query above groups web logs by device_type and country, providing daily counts of records, categorically organized by each combination of group dimensions over a given time frame.

Effective grouping strategies improve data accessibility, particularly in business intelligence (BI) applications where comparisons between different segments, such as demographic groups, products, or regions, can provide actionable insights.

Combined Usage and Optimization:

The potency of Druid's filtering, aggregating, and grouping lies in combining these operations to distill raw data into comprehensive insights. Optimization emerges when these operations are orchestrated to exploit Druid's intrinsic capabilities:

- **Minimize Data Movement**: Well-defined filters early in a query significantly limit unnecessary segment scans, reducing data movement during aggregation.

- **Leverage Indexing**: Filtering based on indexed dimensions ensures rapid row selection, crucial for performance in large datasets.

- **Scale with Granularity**: Choosing appropriate granularity maximizes processing efficiency to suit analytical objectives, whether daily usage trends or annual growth metrics.

- **Utilize Post-Aggregation Operations**: Extend aggregative capacity using calculated fields to apply arithmetic and logical operations on pre-aggregated data.

Consider this comprehensive example demonstrating an optimized query configuration:

```
{
  "queryType": "groupBy",
  "dataSource": "sales_transactions",
  "granularity": "week",
  "dimensions": ["store_location", "product_type"],
  "filter": {
    "type": "and",
    "fields": [
      {
        "type": "bound",
        "dimension": "transaction_amount",
        "lower": "10",
        "upper": "100"
```

```
    },
    {
      "type": "selector",
      "dimension": "promotion_applied",
      "value": true
    }
  ]
},
"aggregations": [
  {
    "type": "doubleSum",
    "fieldName": "transaction_amount",
    "name": "total_revenue"
  },
  {
    "type": "cardinality",
    "fieldNames": ["transaction_id"],
    "name": "transaction_count"
  }
],
"postAggregations": [
  {
    "type": "arithmetic",
    "name": "average_transaction_value",
    "fn": "/",
    "fields": [
      { "type": "fieldAccess", "fieldName": "total_revenue" },
      { "type": "fieldAccess", "fieldName": "transaction_count" }
    ]
  }
],
"intervals": ["2023-01-01T00:00:00.000Z/2023-02-28T00:00:00.000Z"],
"limitSpec": {
  "type": "default",
  "limit": 200,
  "columns": [
    {"dimension": "total_revenue", "direction": "descending"}
  ]
}
}
```

This query exemplifies a real-world application scenario: determining weekly total revenue and average transaction value for promotions, grouped by store location and product type. Such queries aid businesses in strategic planning, optimizing inventory, and targeting promotions based on granular data insights.

Integrating filtering, aggregation, and grouping in Apache Druid not only enhances decision-making capabilities by illuminating contrasts and trends hidden in large datasets but also harnesses the full potential of Druid's platform, transforming raw data into a strategic asset with timely, relevant analytics.

5.6 Time-Based Queries and Granularity

At the heart of Apache Druid's analytical prowess is its robust handling of time-based queries, leveraging its time-indexed design to optimize data processing. Time-based queries are essential in applications requiring the analysis of trends, seasonal effects, or changes over time spans, such as in financial markets, IoT analytics, or operational monitoring. This section explores the mechanics of time-based querying in Druid and the crucial role that granularity plays in shaping these queries for performance and insight.

Understanding Time-Based Queries:

Time-based queries allow users to explore datasets dynamically segmented by time intervals. These are not limited to mere filtering by dates but involve complex analytics such as computing aggregates by time slice, spotting anomalies in time series, or identifying long-term patterns.

Druid capitalizes on its segment structure to efficiently handle time-based queries by partitioning data segments over time. This organization minimizes the amount of unnecessary data scanned during a query, largely enhancing speed and efficiency.

An illustrative JSON example of a time-based query could be:

```
{
  "queryType": "timeseries",
  "dataSource": "user_activity",
  "granularity": "minute",
  "aggregations": [
    {
      "type": "count",
      "name": "activity_count"
    }
  ],
  "intervals": ["2023-01-01T00:00:00.000Z/2023-01-02T00:00:00.000Z"]
}
```

This query retrieves minute-level counts of user activities for a single-day period, leveraging Druid's inherent time management to assess high-resolution user interactions.

One of the key benefits of Druid's time-based capabilities is its ability to manage both real-time and historical data seamlessly, empowering applications that depend on timely and retrospective insights.

Granularity in Time-Based Queries:

Granularity refers to the precision at which data is aggregated or analyzed over time. Druid supports various levels of granularity:

- All: The entire dataset is treated as a single chunk.

- None: Records data at its raw level.

- Granular intervals such as second, minute, hour, day, week, month, and year.

Each granularity level in Druid affects how the data is aggregated temporally, impacting both the resolution of insights and the speed of query execution.

For example, a fine granularity like 'minute' can reveal sudden spikes or dips in a dataset, useful in detecting anomalies like server downtimes or stock surges, whereas coarser granularity such as 'month' emphasizes long-term trends and cyclical patterns.

Consider the necessity of determining daily active users over a quarterly period:

```
{
  "queryType": "timeseries",
  "dataSource": "website_logs",
  "granularity": "day",
  "aggregations": [
    {
      "type": "hyperUnique",
      "name": "unique_visitors",
      "fieldName": "visitor_id"
    }
  ],
  "intervals": ["2023-01-01T00:00:00.000Z/2023-03-31T23:59:59.999Z"]
}
```

This query, by setting 'day' as the granularity, calculates unique visitors daily over a three-month period—a granularity suited for observing broad user engagement patterns and plotting retention graphs.

Granularity Effects on Storage and Query Performance:

Granularity is a critical decision point when designing Druid queries, linked closely to both storage efficiency and query performance:

- **Storage Implications**: Finer granularities result in higher data resolution but can rapidly increase data volume, potentially elevating storage costs or impacting the system's processing capacity over extensive date ranges.

- **Performance Impact**: Coarse granularity diminishes data aggregation levels, speeding up queries by reducing the computational effort needed to process numerous data points together. Fine granularity, however, extends detailed insights at the cost of increased computation time and resource usage.

Balancing granularity requires insight into the trade-offs between the need for detailed data and the efficiency of query execution, which is crucial for maintaining responsive analytics without overwhelming the Druid environment.

Constructing and Analyzing Time-Based Queries:

When designing time-based queries, it's essential to define not only the granularity but also the specific intervals you wish to analyze. Intervals in Druid specify the period over which to execute the query, forming a bounding box around the potential data to be included in calculations.

For example, an analyst looking to review social media interactions during a holiday season may write:

```
{
  "queryType": "timeseries",
  "dataSource": "social_media_engagement",
  "granularity": "hour",
  "filter": {
    "type": "and",
    "fields": [
      {"type": "selector", "dimension": "post_type", "value": "holiday_greetings"},
      {"type": "time", "dimension": "__time", "intervals": ["2023-12-20T00:00:00.000Z
        /2023-12-27T23:59:59.999Z"]}
    ]
  },
  "aggregations": [
    {
      "type": "longSum",
      "name": "total_interactions",
      "fieldName": "interactions"
    },
    {
      "type": "hyperUnique",
      "name": "unique_posters",
      "fieldName": "user_id"
    }
```

```
    ]
}
```

In this query, hourly granularity matches the high engagement period during a limited timeframe, extracting detailed post interaction metrics and evaluating user uniqueness in seasonal content.

Advanced Time-Based Query Techniques:

Beyond basic time-interval selection, advanced users may implement mixed granularity strategies or custom roll-ups for additional analytic complexity—a powerful feature within Druid that combines data into summary views to expedite query responses in certain contexts.

Custom granularities can also be specified by the user, such as 5-minute intervals:

```
"granularities": {
  "type": "duration",
  "duration": 300000
}
```

This setup defines five-minute buckets, adaptable in real-time data analytics where minute-by-minute details lend value to operational decision-making.

Real-World Applications:

- **Financial Analytics**: Intraday stock trend analyses require minute or even second-level granularity to capture market shifts and trading volumes.

- **E-commerce Sales Monitoring**: Day-level granularity aids in understanding daily revenue cycles, optimization of product placement, and recognizing shopping trends.

- **IoT Sensor Data**: Sensor data may require granularity adjustments based on condition monitoring needs, such as hourly readings for environmental changes or finer calibrations for detecting anomalies in machinery operation.

Granularity Roll-Ups and Efficiency:

In Druid, leveraging roll-ups allows data compaction by pre-aggregating metrics, effectively reducing storage demands and

144

accelerating query times. This pre-aggregation process, while introducing some degree of data resolution loss, significantly boosts system efficiency, creating an important trade-off matrix for system architects to navigate.

By properly utilizing these time-based query and granularity strategies, users can achieve an unparalleled balance of insight resolution and system performance, crafting a responsive and insightful analytical environment via Apache Druid that meets diverse and demanding business needs.

5.7 Introduction to JSON Query Language

The JSON query language in Apache Druid stands out for its exceptional flexibility and power, enabling fine-grained control over the data querying process. As a cornerstone of interaction within Druid, JSON queries allow users to leverage the full potential of Druid's real-time analytics and high scalability. This section introduces the structure, usage, and practical applications of the JSON query language, elucidating its role in crafting efficient data queries.

Foundation of JSON Queries:

At its core, Druid's JSON query system is designed for precision, permitting users to access a detailed level of control over how queries are processed and results are aggregated. Unlike SQL that provides a familiar, high-level interface, JSON queries interact more directly with Druid's capabilities, offering specific tuning possibilities for performance and specialized data retrieval requirements.

JSON serves as the transport language to express the structure and intent of requests, delivering a highly succinct yet expressive means to define complex constructs necessary for robust analytics tasks. Druid exploits JSON to structure queries that involve distinct parameters such as query type, data source, filters, aggregations, intervals, and more.

Basic Structure of JSON Queries:

A JSON query in Druid comprises a series of fields defining the key components of a query. The typical fields include:

- queryType: Specifies the type of query (e.g., "timeseries", "topN", "groupBy").

- dataSource: Indicates the dataset or source against which the query is executed.

- granularity: Determines the time resolution for data grouping.

- filter: Implements conditions to exclude or include specific data.

- aggregations and postAggregations: Defines the selection of measures and subsequent operations on these measures.

- intervals: Specifies the timeframe for which the data is queried.

Basic Example:

Consider a simple timeseries query to count daily sales:

```
{
  "queryType": "timeseries",
  "dataSource": "sales_data",
  "granularity": "day",
  "intervals": ["2023-01-01T00:00:00.000Z/2023-01-31T00:00:00.000Z"],
  "aggregations": [
    {
      "type": "longSum",
      "name": "total_sales",
      "fieldName": "sales_amount"
    }
  ]
}
```

This JSON structure specifies that the query will retrieve data aggregated daily for the month of January 2023, summing all entries under the sales amount.

Advanced Filters and Logic:

One of JSON's strengths is its ability to implement nuanced filters. Through a combination of logical operators and filters, complex criteria can be met.

Composite Filter Example:

```
"filter": {
  "type": "and",
  "fields": [
    {
      "type": "selector",
      "dimension": "region",
      "value": "North"
    },
    {
      "type": "not",
      "field": {
        "type": "selector",
        "dimension": "customer_segment",
        "value": "unsubscribed"
      }
    },
    {
      "type": "bound",
      "dimension": "order_amount",
      "lower": "50",
      "upper": "250",
      "upperStrict": true
    }
  ]
}
```

Such filters allow evaluation of datasets based on a multi-criteria set, here isolating regions and specific customer segments with transactional bounds, a typical necessity when performing segmentation analysis.

Aggregation and Post-Aggregation:

JSON queries comprehensively set the stage for aggregation operations, offering the flexibility to manipulate statistical properties of datasets. Standard aggregations include totals, counts, averages, etc. Post-aggregations provide calculated fields on already aggregated results, enhancing the depth of analysis.

Example JSON with Post-Aggregation:

```
{
  "queryType": "groupBy",
  "dataSource": "store_transactions",
  "granularity": "week",
  "dimensions": ["store_id"],
  "aggregations": [
    {
      "type": "doubleSum",
      "name": "total_revenue",
      "fieldName": "revenue"
    },
```

```
{
    "type": "count",
    "name": "transaction_count"
  }
],
"postAggregations": [
  {
    "type": "arithmetic",
    "name": "average_revenue_per_transaction",
    "fn": "/",
    "fields": [
      { "type": "fieldAccess", "fieldName": "total_revenue" },
      { "type": "fieldAccess", "fieldName": "transaction_count" }
    ]
  }
],
"intervals": ["2023-01-01T00:00:00.000Z/2023-03-31T00:00:00.000Z"]
}
```

This example calculates total and average revenue per transaction weekly, illustrating JSON's ability to derive meaningful insights beyond basic aggregates.

Integrating Real-Time and Historical Data:

A compelling feature of JSON queries in Druid is their capacity to handle both real-time and historical data. JSON queries are inherently designed to manage streaming data seamlessly while also querying established historical records without modification of the query parameters, providing a unified view of all data.

Integrating data from event streams and log archives concurrently enables businesses to act on real-time insights while maintaining contextual awareness over historical trends, all orchestrated through precise JSON configurations.

Performance Optimizations:

Performance considerations are pivotal when crafting JSON queries. To truly leverage Druid's power, awareness of query optimization features is crucial:

- **Segment Resolution**: Queries should be scoped by clear intervals to minimize scan volume, crucially affecting performance.

- **Efficient Use of Filters**: Applying filters that exploit Druid's bitmap indexing can drastically reduce the footprint of data processed.

148

- **Appropriate Granularity**: Choosing suitable granularity reflects not only on the expected resolution of result insights but also on the computation strain — finer granularities can inflate workload, whereas coarser ones expedite it.

- **Cache Utilization**: Make use of Druid's caching at various system levels to speed up data retrieval without compromising freshness.

In practice, balancing these elements means translating operational analytics requirements into precise JSON syntax for optimal execution in Druid's environment.

Real-World Scenarios and Applications:

JSON queries are instrumental across multiple deployments:

- **Predictive Analytics**: Healthcare or retail industries extensively use JSON queries to forecast demand and identify opportunities via time series forecasting and historical pattern analysis.

- **Monitoring Systems**: Engineering and DevOps leverage JSON queries to keep tabs on server health metrics, error rates, and threshold breaches for systems intervention.

- **Personalization Engines**: Through dynamic user profile assessments, businesses use JSON to deploy tailored experiences by querying customer behavior and preference datasets.

These examples underscore the range and responsiveness afforded by JSON queries, enabling rapid iteration and expansive data interaction.

By mastering JSON queries, users endow their Druid-based applications with unparalleled customization and control, precisely tailoring data interrogation to match intricate analytical requirements while also ensuring that they are responsive to the ever-evolving landscapes of modern data-driven environments. JSON empowers users to craft elaborate, highly tuned queries undeterred by typical SQL limitations, achieving fine-tuned, high-velocity analytics tailored to specific massive-scale workloads that characterize current and future business paradigms.

Chapter 6

Advanced Query Techniques

This chapter explores advanced querying capabilities in Apache Druid, focusing on complex aggregations and post-aggregation calculations. It covers the execution of join operations and the use of lookups to manage complex data relationships. Techniques for deploying subqueries and approximate algorithms for query optimization are discussed to enhance performance and efficiency. Advanced filtering methods and strategies for analyzing time series data are outlined, ensuring sophisticated data analysis. Additionally, the chapter provides guidance on optimizing query performance, including caching and configuration settings to address large-scale data challenges effectively.

6.1 Complex Aggregations and Post-Aggregations

Apache Druid's aggregations form the backbone of its analytical capabilities, providing robust tools to synthesize and distill vast datasets into comprehensible insights. Complex aggregations extend basic functionalities, allowing users to handle intricate data scenarios. By pairing these with post-aggregation operations, the flexibility and depth of analysis in Druid are significantly enhanced.

Aggregations in Druid are fundamental operations that compute a single value from a set of input rows. Common aggregators include sum, count, min, and max, among others. Each of these functions is optimized to run efficiently across distributed storage nodes. A pivotal feature of Druid is its ability to carry out these operations in a low-latency manner, ensuring interactive querying even against large datasets.

To initiate a comprehension of complex aggregations, consider the following structure:

```
{
  "queryType": "groupBy",
  "dataSource": "your_data_source",
  "granularity": "day",
  "dimensions": ["dimension1"],
  "aggregations": [
    {
      "type": "longSum",
      "name": "total_value",
      "fieldName": "value_field"
    },
    {
      "type": "hyperUnique",
      "name": "unique_users",
      "fieldName": "user_id"
    }
  ],
  "postAggregations": [
    {
      "type": "arithmetic",
      "name": "average_value_per_user",
      "fn": "/",
      "fields": [
        {
          "type": "fieldAccess",
          "fieldName": "total_value"
        },
        {
          "type": "fieldAccess",
          "fieldName": "unique_users"
        }
      ]
    }
  ],
  "intervals": ["2023-01-01/2023-01-31"]
}
```

This query aggregates data on a daily basis, summing values and determining the number of unique users via the hyperUnique aggregator. It then applies a post-aggregation to compute the average value per user. The arithmetic post-aggregator performs basic mathematical operations (addition, subtraction, multiplication, division) using fields or other post-aggregations within the query.

Complex aggregations may involve multi-step calculations that necessitate breaking down the query into smaller, interlinked components. Here, post-aggregations are vital; they perform secondary computations on the results of initial aggregations. They are written in a specialized format that can include an array of different operations including arithmetic, field access, and more complex mathematical functions.

To illustrate a scenario involving computed post-aggregations, consider a situation where you need the growth rate of a particular metric over successive days. You can calculate this growth rate directly in Druid, facilitating time-sensitive analytics directly at query time:

```
{
  "queryType": "timeseries",
  "dataSource": "sales_data",
  "granularity": "day",
  "aggregations": [
    {
      "type": "doubleSum",
      "name": "daily_sales",
      "fieldName": "sales"
    }
  ],
  "postAggregations": [
    {
      "type": "arithmetic",
      "name": "growth_rate",
      "fn": "-",
      "fields": [
        {
          "type": "fieldAccess",
          "fieldName": "daily_sales"
        },
        {
          "type": "fieldAccess",
          "previous":{
            "type": "fieldAccess",
            "fieldName": "daily_sales"
          }
        }
      ]
    }
  ],
  "intervals": ["2023-02-01/2023-02-07"]
```

```
}
```

The above query tracks sales data and calculates the day-over-day growth rate. Notice the approximation of previous value; though Druid does not natively support lag functions, similar operations can be performed externally prior to ingestion, or with advanced ingestion specs involving lookups or transformations.

For more sophisticated scenarios, consider leveraging sketch-based algorithms that provide approximate but highly performant solutions for statistics over large data sizes. The theta-sketch aggregation, for instance, provides distinct count approximations, crucial for large cardinality datasets where exact counts are computationally expensive.

Theta sketch aggregators are used as follows:

```
{
  "type": "thetaSketch",
  "name": "approx_unique_sessions",
  "fieldName": "session_id"
}
```

This sketch offers an efficient way to calculate unique counts with a configurable accuracy-precision trade-off. By controlling the sketch size parameter, users can balance memory usage and computation precision to suit their needs. Post-aggregation operations also extend to merging two sketches or computing their union or intersection through advanced operations.

Furthermore, complex aggregations benefit from layers of pre-computation and intermediate row calculations potentially through Druid extensions or custom code. This affords preconfigured metrics and KPIs that are computed during the ingestion process, reducing on-the-fly computation load and expediting result delivery when querying.

To address growing analytical needs, Druid's abilities can be further enhanced with extensions or customized scripts. This implies that while Druid's native aggregations and post-aggregations capabilities are extensive, developers should always select aggregation strategies best aligned with their data's unique characteristics and their enterprise's performance constraints.

The application's operational mode should also dictate aggregation parameters; for example, real-time analytics may prioritize speed and update frequency over the absolute accuracy that might be essential for scheduled batch analytics.

Join capabilities often complement aggregations excellently. By synthesizing datasets from multiple sources into joined tables, more advanced complexities and data interrelations are managed effectively, bringing forth a suite of transformative capabilities, suitable for dynamic aggregation strategies.

Ultimately, the complexity of the aggregation and post-aggregation operations in Druid can help transform raw data into meaningful intelligence, guiding strategic initiatives, enhancing operational efficiencies, and driving data-centric decision-making.

6.2 Join Operations and Lookups

Apache Druid offers capabilities for join operations and lookups, which are critical for integrating multiple data sources and enriching data with additional dimensions. These functionalities provide a framework for executing complex, multi-relational queries that are pivotal in analytics contexts requiring detailed and layered data insights.

Join operations in Druid enable the melding of data from different datasources, providing a fused view that encompasses relevant attributes from each component table. This is particularly useful when datasets are normalized into structural formats like star or snowflake schemas. The typical join operation in Druid allows for combining a primary dataset, often your main storage of time-series data, with secondary facets or classifications held within other datasources or external systems.

Consider the JSON structure of a simplified query format involving join operations in Druid:

```
{
  "queryType": "join",
  "left": {
    "type": "query",
    "query": {
      "queryType": "scan",
      "dataSource": "orders",
      "columns": ["order_id", "customer_id", "order_total"],
```

```
      "intervals": ["2023-01-01/2023-01-31"]
    }
  },
  "right": {
    "type": "lookup",
    "query": {
      "queryType": "scan",
      "dataSource": "customer_lookup",
      "columns": ["customer_id", "customer_name"]
    }
  },
  "on": {
    "equals": ["left.customer_id", "right.customer_id"]
  },
  "outputColumns": ["order_id", "customer_name", "order_total"]
}
```

This basic join operation defines a relationship between two Druid datasources: 'orders' and 'customer_lookup'. The 'on' clause specifies the join condition as the equivalence of 'customer_id' between the two tables. The resulting set fields specified in 'outputColumns' provide a concise result containing 'order_id', 'customer_name', and 'order_total'.

Druid supports several strategies for performing joins, including:

- **Broadcast Joins**: Effective for joining a large datasource with a smaller dimension table. The smaller table is broadcasted to the individual processing nodes, which enables parallel join execution across distributed fragments of the larger dataset.

- **Hash Joins**: Utilized when comparable datasets are involved, allowing Druid to hash the join keys and perform the join efficiently in a distributed fashion. This may necessitate ample memory on each processing node.

- **Nested Loop Joins**: Generally employed as a fallback method when other more efficient join methods are inapplicable, mainly due to resource constraints or data distribution incompatibilities.

Beyond traditional join operations, Druid offers a practical feature known as lookups, which are particularly advantageous for rapidly translating IDs or codes into comprehensible strings or metrics. This

156

translation is akin to a key-value mapping where certain fields in a data-source are replaced or enhanced through external data that resides in lookup tables.

Lookups are defined in Druid as services that map keys within event fields to values from external datasets. They can originate from a variety of external sources including relational databases, files, or through direct configuration in Druid clusters. A straightforward configuration could look like this:

```
{
  "lookup": "country_lookup",
  "version": "v1",
  "map": {
    "1": "United States",
    "2": "Canada",
    "3": "Mexico"
  }
}
```

Given this lookup configuration, any aggregation query targeting a 'country_code' column could reference 'country_lookup' to replace numeric identifiers with their respective country names. This process significantly enhances query legibility and comprehension without materially increasing query latency.

Here is how lookups may be integrated directly within query specifications:

```
{
  "queryType": "groupBy",
  "dataSource": "sales_transactions",
  "granularity": "all",
  "dimensions": [
    {
      "type": "lookup",
      "dimension": "country_code",
      "outputName": "country_name",
      "lookup": "country_lookup"
    }
  ],
  "aggregations": [
    {
      "type": "doubleSum",
      "name": "total_sales",
      "fieldName": "sales_amount"
    }
  ],
  "intervals": ["2023-01-01/2023-01-31"]
}
```

In the above example, the 'groupBy' query aggregates 'sales_amount' by 'country_name', which is dynamically resolved using a lookup table. This dynamic resolution capability simplifies query-writing, facilitating scalable aggregation operations based on human-readable dimensions.

Implementing joins and lookups involves thoughtful consideration of numerous factors:

- **Performance**: Join operations, particularly those involving large datasets, can be resource-intensive. Selections of appropriate join strategies and adequate indexing on join keys can mitigate performance challenges. Understanding Druid's segment architecture and underlying storage layout also aids in optimizing data access paths.

- **Consistency and Maintenance**: It is crucial to manage lookup tables efficiently for consistency, especially when these are dynamically updated. Regular refresh operations and version control can prevent discrepancies between lookup states and data queries.

- **Schema Evolution**: Data schema alterations impacting primary keys, foreign keys, or lookup mappings need attentive management. Ensuring that schema changes do not introduce breaking changes to existing joins or lookup configurations warrants careful versioning and regression testing.

Expanding Druid's native support for dynamic joins and lookups is possible through customization and the use of extensions. The integration of user-defined functions (UDFs) or external libraries enables specialized operations that reflect unique business logic or data processing requirements beyond conventional implementations.

Ultimately, join operations and lookups must be viewed as integral components of Druid's querying engine, facilitating meaningful integration and exploration of diverse datasets. By implementing careful strategies for their deployment, operational complexity can be managed while maximizing analytical value derived from interconnected data ecosystems.

6.3 Using Subqueries Effectively

Subqueries in Apache Druid provide a mechanism for constructing layered and more complex queries by embedding one query within another. This nesting allows the execution of a series of operations in a single request, streamlining complex analysis workflows and improving the expressiveness of query capabilities. Properly constructed subqueries can enhance data processing, reduce computational overhead, and achieve advanced data manipulations that would otherwise require additional query logic or preprocessing steps.

Subqueries in Druid usually take the form of a query within the dataSource field of another outer query, allowing for inner query results to be directly used as input for further computations. The outer query can then apply additional transformations, aggregations, or filters building atop the subquery's output.

To illustrate the application of subqueries, consider the scenario of needing to compute daily averages but then analyze weekly trends based on these daily figures. Using subqueries, this can be approached efficiently as follows:

```
{
  "queryType": "groupBy",
  "dataSource": {
    "type": "query",
    "query": {
      "queryType": "timeseries",
      "dataSource": "hourly_traffic",
      "granularity": "day",
      "aggregations": [
        {
          "type": "doubleSum",
          "name": "daily_hits",
          "fieldName": "hits"
        }
      ],
      "intervals": ["2023-01-01/2023-01-31"]
    }
  },
  "granularity": "week",
  "dimensions": [],
  "aggregations": [
    {
      "type": "doubleMean",
      "name": "average_daily_hits",
      "fieldName": "daily_hits"
    }
  ],
```

```
   "intervals": ["2023-01-01/2023-01-31"]
}
```

In this example, the subquery computes daily aggregates of hits from an hourly_traffic datasource. The outer query then calculates weekly averages of these daily figures. Such usage effectively enables multi-granularity analysis by computing intermediate results before proceeding with further operations.

Subqueries are particularly useful in scenarios that require filtering or transformations on a specific subset of a dataset before applying broader operations. This reduces the volume of data the outer query must process and can lead to performance efficiencies, particularly in large-scale data environments.

Consider a use case where you need to isolate high-value transactions, and subsequently, perform additional filtering or aggregation:

```
{
  "queryType": "groupBy",
  "dataSource": {
    "type": "query",
    "query": {
      "queryType": "scan",
      "dataSource": "transactions",
      "filter": {
        "type": "bound",
        "dimension": "transaction_value",
        "lower": "10000",
        "lowerStrict": false
      },
      "columns": ["transaction_id", "transaction_value", "transaction_date"],
      "intervals": ["2023-01-01/2023-01-31"]
    }
  },
  "granularity": "all",
  "dimensions": ["transaction_date"],
  "aggregations": [
    {
      "type": "doubleSum",
      "name": "total_high_value_transactions",
      "fieldName": "transaction_value"
    }
  ]
}
```

This query uses a subquery to filter out transactions where transaction_value is greater than or equal to 10,000 units. The outer groupBy query then performs an aggregation over these filtered results. This pattern of query design enables focused analysis and helps eliminate irrelevant data from computations early in the query lifecycle.

Druid's ability to handle subqueries efficiently hinges on several aspects:

- **Endpoint Exclusion**: By leveraging pruning and early materialization, Druid can sometimes avoid processing for specific partitions that don't contribute to the final results.

- **Parallel Execution**: Subqueries in Druid benefit from distributed computing architecture, allowing subquery components to run concurrently across nodes, distributing the workload and enhancing processing speed.

- **Resource Management**: Effective caching mechanisms store intermediate subquery results, which can dramatically speed up repeated queries by reducing redundant computations.

Despite their versatility, subqueries in Druid should be approached with an awareness of potential pitfalls:

- **Complexity**: Over-reliance on subqueries can result in intricate query structures that are harder to debug and maintain. A balance must be struck between query conciseness and clarity.

- **Performance**: Although subqueries reduce individual query burden, complex nested operations can sometimes lead to increased overall query times due to layered computation dependencies.

- **Scalability**: Subqueries that demand large sets of intermediate data storage may risk straining available resources, particularly in memory-constrained environments.

A strategic approach to designing effective subqueries involves:

- Pre-processing data as much as possible to limit the scale of subquery operations.

- Using indices and sorted columns to facilitate faster access and reduce the need for extensive filtering in subqueries.

- Partitioning your data appropriately to ensure that subqueries utilize Druid's segment architecture optimally.

By embracing the power of subqueries in Druid, one can harness complex data interactions and layered analytical paradigms directly within Druid's querying infrastructure, enabling powerful insights from even the most demanding datasets.

6.4 Approximate Algorithms for Query Optimization

In the context of big data analytics, achieving precise query results at scale often entails prohibitive computational cost and latency. Apache Druid addresses this challenge by incorporating approximate algorithms that provide rapid, near-exact answers with significantly reduced resource requirements. These approximation techniques leverage statistical constructs to process large volumes of data efficiently while still delivering insights of acceptable accuracy.

Approximate algorithms are particularly advantageous when working with Druid for query optimization, as they balance precision and performance through smart trade-offs. This section explores Druid's primary approximate algorithms, including hyperUnique, theta sketches, and others, illustrating their application and the strategic benefits they provide.

- **HyperUnique Algorithm**

The hyperUnique aggregator in Druid is an implementation based on HyperLogLog, a cardinality estimation algorithm that provides effective distinct counting techniques. HyperUnique is employed to estimate the number of unique elements in a dataset without requiring explicit storage of each element.

Here's an illustrative example of a query that employs the hyperUnique aggregation:

```
{
  "queryType": "groupBy",
```

```
"dataSource": "web_events",
"granularity": "day",
"dimensions": ["event_type"],
"aggregations": [
    {
      "type": "hyperUnique",
      "name": "unique_users",
      "fieldName": "user_id_hll"
    }
],
"intervals": ["2023-01-01/2023-01-31"]
}
```

The query estimates the number of unique users interacting with different event types on a daily basis. Compared to exact counting methods, hyperUnique substantiates significant performance improvements especially when dealing with datasets characterized by high cardinality, such as user identifiers, session IDs, or transaction references.

Key benefits encompass:

- **Memory Efficiency**: HyperUnique uses a constant amount of memory irrespective of dataset size, which is invaluable in maintaining scalability across distributed nodes in Druid clusters.

- **Execution Speed**: With low overhead, hyperUnique computes faster as it obviates the need for large-scale data shuffling and sorting.

While hyperUnique provides impressive speed and efficiency, it inherently trades exactitude for speed via statistical approximation models. The accuracy level, generally configurable within tolerable bounds, is suitable for a myriad of use cases such as user behavior analytics, fraud detection, and system monitoring.

- **Theta Sketches**

Theta sketches extend the capabilities of HyperLogLog, offering more flexibility and rich operations for set expressions such as unions, intersections, and differences. This proves invaluable when querying segmented sets or conducting set-based operations across multiple dimensions.

Example of theta sketch usage in a Druid query:

163

```
{
  "queryType": "timeseries",
  "dataSource": "purchase_data",
  "granularity": "week",
  "aggregations": [
    {
      "type": "thetaSketch",
      "name": "unique_buyers",
      "fieldName": "buyer_id_sketch"
    }
  ],
  "postAggregations": [
    {
      "type": "thetaSketchEstimate",
      "name": "estimated_unique_buyers",
      "fieldName": "unique_buyers"
    }
  ],
  "intervals": ["2023-01-01/2023-03-31"]
}
```

In the above query, theta sketch aggregation determines the cardinality of buyers per week. Theta sketches' advanced coverage includes:

- **Set Operations**: Compute combinations of sets (e.g., finding overlap between different buyer segments or sales campaigns).

- **Precision Tuning**: Offers configurable parameters for balancing speed, precision, and memory use via the sketch size parameter ('nominalEntries').

Compared to HyperLogLog, theta sketches maintain higher precision consistency across different operational contexts and exhibit greater versatility in compositing results across hierarchical data structures.

- **Top-N Queries with Approximation**

For queries focused on the top elements in a dataset based on particular metrics, top-N queries excel by retrieving only the most relevant records. These queries inherently apply approximation to prioritize speed over scanning entire datasets, making them ideal in user interface components such as dashboards.

An example of a Top-N query in Druid:

```
{
```

```
"queryType": "topN",
"dataSource": "video_views",
"dimension": "video_title",
"threshold": 5,
"metric": "views_count",
"aggregations": [
    {
      "type": "longSum",
      "name": "views_count",
      "fieldName": "view_count"
    }
],
"intervals": ["2023-01-01/2023-02-01"],
"granularity": "all"
}
```

This query targets the top 5 viewed videos in a month. By reducing the result set to only what's necessary, it minimizes processing time and resource allocation, particularly relevant in scenarios requiring real-time display updates.

- *Considerations for Using Approximate Algorithms*

Adopting approximate algorithms demands a critical understanding of the application's tolerance for estimation errors. Key considerations include:

- **Use Case Suitability**: Determine whether the query scenario permits approximation. While approximate algorithms are excellent for trend analysis and volume estimation, they are less appropriate where legal or compliance mandates necessitate definitive accuracy.

- **Parameter Configuration**: Take care to adjust algorithm parameters to match performance goals. For example, theta sketches' 'nominalEntries' affect memory allocation and precision, necessitating careful tuning.

- **Result Interpretation**: Users should be aware of the potential variance ranges in results and the statistical significance of findings derived from approximations. Documentation and training can enhance understanding and proper application.

Approximate algorithms in Druid thus provide a foundational tool for handling large-scale analysis efficiently. By empowering rapid exploration and operational transaction processing, these mechanisms significantly alleviate computational loads, contributing to robust analytics and prompt data-driven decision-making flexibility.

6.5 Advanced Filtering Techniques

In data analytics, filtering is crucial for refining datasets by extracting the most relevant information that adheres to specific criteria. Apache Druid, with its robust capabilities, offers a spectrum of advanced filtering techniques that empower users to drill down into expansive datasets, isolating critical insights efficiently. This section explores the structure and application of filters in Druid, outlining their role in query optimization and data analysis.

Filters in Druid are integral to querying operations, providing mechanisms for excluding irrelevant data, thus reducing the dataset scale to enhance processing speed and query accuracy. They can be applied across various dimensions, supporting complex scenarios through logical operations, range selection, regular expressions, and spatial filtering.

- **Logical Filters**

  Logical filters allow the combination of multiple simple filters within a query through logical operators such as 'AND', 'OR', and 'NOT'. These operators enable the representation of intricate conditions essential for narrowing down datasets to highly specific sub-populations.

  A basic example of logical filtering is illustrated below:

  ```
  {
    "queryType": "scan",
    "dataSource": "user_purchases",
    "filter": {
      "type": "and",
      "fields": [
        {
          "type": "selector",
          "dimension": "country",
          "value": "USA"
        },
        {
          "type": "bound",
  ```

```
        "dimension": "purchase_amount",
        "lower": "100",
        "lowerStrict": true
      }
    ]
  },
  "columns": ["user_id", "purchase_amount", "purchase_date"],
  "intervals": ["2023-01-01/2023-01-31"]
}
```

In this query, an 'AND' filter limits results to users in the USA with purchase amounts greater than 100 units during the specified time interval. Logical filters like this enable the construction of complex conditions by layering simple filters.

- **Range and Bound Filters**

  Range filters serve to limit data to a specified interval, crucial in performance optimization as they allow exclusion of irrelevant data points early in the processing pipeline. The 'bound' filter type lets users define open and closed range limits with strictness.

  A typical use case is filtering for a range of metrics:

```
{
  "queryType": "groupBy",
  "dataSource": "temperature_readings",
  "granularity": "day",
  "filter": {
    "type": "bound",
    "dimension": "temperature",
    "lower": "20",
    "upper": "30",
    "lowerStrict": false,
    "upperStrict": true
  },
  "dimensions": ["sensor_id"],
  "aggregations": [
    {
      "type": "count",
      "name": "reading_count"
    }
  ],
  "intervals": ["2023-01-01/2023-02-01"]
}
```

This query aggregates temperature readings by sensor ID exclusively for temperatures ranging from 20 degrees, inclusive, up to but not including 30 degrees.

- **Regular Expression Filters**

167

Regular expression (regex) filters offer pattern-based filtering to match complex string criteria within fields. They enable highly specific character sequence matching, making them ideal in cases such as anomaly detection, log file processing, or data quality checks where patterns do not conform to simple determinate forms.

Example of a regex filter:

```
{
  "queryType": "scan",
  "dataSource": "text_logs",
  "filter": {
    "type": "regex",
    "dimension": "log_message",
    "pattern": "\\berror\\b.*\\bcritical\\b"
  },
  "columns": ["log_id", "log_message", "timestamp"],
  "intervals": ["2023-01-01/2023-01-02"]
}
```

This query finds log messages containing the word "error" followed by "critical", capturing log entries that qualify as urgent attention cases.

• **Spatial Filters**

Spatial filters allow refining queries based on geographic data. These filters assess location-based fields within data points, enabling queries that interact with spatial attributes such as coordinates. They are particularly useful in location-based services, logistics, geospatial analysis, and mapping applications.

Illustrative spatial filter usage:

```
{
  "queryType": "scan",
  "dataSource": "geo_events",
  "filter": {
    "type": "spatial",
    "dimension": "location",
    "bound": {
      "type": "rectangular",
      "minCoords": [-122.0, 37.0],
      "maxCoords": [-121.0, 38.0]
    }
  },
  "columns": ["event_id", "event_name", "location"],
  "intervals": ["2023-01-01/2023-01-31"]
}
```

The query isolates events whose locations lie within the latitude and longitude bounds specified, thereby focusing only on data falling within a particular geographic area.

- **Nested Filters**

  Nestable filters permit strategic composition of various filter types, enabling flexible filtering architectures where multiple filtering layers are applied sequentially or simultaneously based on the specific data exploration needed.

  Strategically nesting filters can enhance performance by ensuring only relevant data passes through each stage, minimizing the workload of subsequent filters.

```
{
  "queryType": "groupBy",
  "dataSource": "sales_data",
  "granularity": "month",
  "filter": {
    "type": "and",
    "fields": [
      {
        "type": "or",
        "fields": [
          {
            "type": "selector",
            "dimension": "product_category",
            "value": "Electronics"
          },
          {
            "type": "selector",
            "dimension": "product_category",
            "value": "Toys"
          }
        ]
      },
      {
        "type": "bound",
        "dimension": "sales_amount",
        "lower": "1000",
        "lowerStrict": false
      }
    ]
  },
  "dimensions": ["store_id"],
  "aggregations": [
    {
      "type": "doubleSum",
      "name": "monthly_sales",
      "fieldName": "sales_amount"
    }
  ],
  "intervals": ["2023-01-01/2023-12-31"]
```

169

```
     }
```

This query combines an 'OR' filter for product categories with an 'AND' filter for sales amounts to yield a refined result set that contributes to highly targeted sales analytics.

Effective Use of Advanced Filtering

Implementing filters effectively requires a foundational understanding of both dataset structure and query performance characteristics:

- **Performance Impact**: Proper use of filters can greatly reduce unnecessary data processing, but poorly placed filters may result in additional computational costs. Understanding the order of filter application and its interaction with Druid's segment-based architecture is crucial for optimizing query speed.

- **Index Utilization**: Leverage Druid's indexing capabilities where feasible to expedite filter operations on high-cardinality dimensions. Bitmap indexes, in particular, are highly effective for speeding up range and selector filters.

- **Filter Complexity**: Consider the balance between filter complexity and performance. Simpler filters that execute early can rule out large swathes of data, whereas complex or nested filters should apply only after initial pruning to minimize overhead.

- **Caching Strategies**: Utilize cache settings smartly to persist frequently used filter conditions and their results, reducing overhead for repeated queries with consistent filtering logic.

Advanced filtering techniques in Druid are crucial for extracting relevant data subsets from large datasets efficiently. By understanding and leveraging these techniques, users can achieve optimal performance and gain valuable insights tailored to specific analytical needs, enhancing the overall efficacy of their data-driven initiatives.

6.6 Time Series Analysis and Trends

Time series analysis is a critical component of data analytics, focused on tracking changes over time to predict future trends and assess temporal patterns. Apache Druid, designed as a real-time data store, is particularly well-suited for processing and analyzing time series data. This section delves into methods and strategies for effectively harnessing Druid's capabilities to conduct time series analysis and extract meaningful insights from temporal datasets.

Druid handles time series data natively, leveraging its columnar storage format optimized for time-based queries. Each row of data in Druid is inherently associated with a timestamp, making temporal queries efficient and natural. Furthermore, Druid's ability to ingest real-time data streams allows for near-instantaneous analysis of rapidly changing datasets.

- **Time Granularity and Aggregation**

In time series analysis, selecting the appropriate time granularity is crucial. Granularity signifies the level of detail captured in the time axis of a dataset. Druid supports various granularities ranging from milliseconds to years, enabling queries to summarize data at the desired timeframe. Aggregations over time dimensions provide a condensed view, facilitating analysis such as seasonal trends, growth rates, and overall patterns.

Consider a time series query with hourly granularity:

```
{
  "queryType": "timeseries",
  "dataSource": "energy_consumption",
  "granularity": "hour",
  "aggregations": [
    {
      "type": "doubleSum",
      "name": "total_energy",
      "fieldName": "energy_usage"
    }
  ],
  "intervals": ["2023-01-01/2023-01-07"]
}
```

This query provides hourly summaries of energy consumption over the first week of January 2023. Summarizing data over specific time intervals makes it easier to observe patterns and deviations.

Conversely, daily or weekly granularity might illustrate longer-term trends, such as seasonal energy usage patterns or the impact of external factors like weather changes.

- **Trend Analysis Techniques**

Trend analysis aims at identifying patterns or movements in the data over time. Druid facilitates several approaches for trend analysis, including moving averages, seasonal decomposition, and anomaly detection.

- **Moving Averages**

A moving average smooths fluctuations and highlights longer-term trends or cycles in time series data. It is calculated by averaging a subset of data points surrounding those whose average is sought. Druid can compute moving averages efficiently thanks to its aggregation framework.

Example using a simple moving average in Druid:

```
{
  "queryType": "timeseries",
  "dataSource": "stock_prices",
  "granularity": "day",
  "aggregations": [
    {
      "type": "doubleSum",
      "name": "daily_close",
      "fieldName": "close_price"
    }
  ],
  "postAggregations": [
    {
      "type": "arithmetic",
      "name": "5_day_average",
      "fn": "avg",
      "fields": [
        {
          "type": "window",
          "fieldName": "daily_close",
          "window": 5
        }
      ]
    }
  ]
}
```

```
  ],
  "intervals": ["2023-01-01/2023-01-31"]
}
```

The query calculates the 5-day simple moving average for daily stock closing prices. Moving averages reduce noise from random variation, allowing stakeholders to track genuine trends.

• Seasonal Decomposition

Seasonal decomposition separates a time series into seasonal components and trends. This provides insights on cyclical patterns and inherent seasonality, often crucial in domains like retail, where consumer behavior exhibits fluctuations based on seasons.

While Druid does not natively support full-fledged time series decomposition, preparation of input data using ETL processes or employing extensions can facilitate such analysis. Users can then utilize decomposed components in Druid queries for visualization and decision-making.

• Anomaly Detection

Identifying anomalies involves recognizing unusual patterns or deviations that do not conform to expected behavior. Anomalies can indicate significant occurrences warranting investigation, such as equipment failure or fraudulent activity.

Druid's flexible querying capabilities, including complex filters and post-aggregation calculations, aid in anomaly detection, albeit often supplying input for further machine learning models implemented externally for advanced anomaly discovery.

```
{
  "queryType": "timeseries",
  "dataSource": "network_traffic",
  "granularity": "hour",
  "aggregations": [
    {
      "type": "doubleSum",
      "name": "data_transfer",
      "fieldName": "bytes_transferred"
    }
  ],
```

```
"postAggregations": [
  {
    "type": "arithmetic",
    "name": "traffic_variance",
    "fn": "-",
    "fields": [
      {
        "type": "fieldAccess",
        "fieldName": "data_transfer"
      },
      {
        "type": "doubleMean",
        "fieldName": "data_transfer",
        "filter": {"type": "time", "period": "7" }
      }
    ]
  }
],
"intervals": ["2023-01-01/2023-01-31"]
}
```

The query detects variance or dips and spikes in hourly network traffic against a weekly mean baseline, serving as initial anomaly detection.

- **Temporal Forecasting**

Temporal forecasting involves using historical data to predict future events. While Apache Druid excels at current and historical data analysis through fast aggregations and slicing, forecasting typically requires statistical models available in specialized tools integrated with Druid outputs.

For example, exporting time series aggregate outputs to a platform like Apache Spark or R can enable predictive modeling, employing algorithms such as ARIMA, STL, or Prophet beyond Druid's built-in analytical routines.

Post-analysis, integrating forecasted trends back into Druid via ingestions or batch load processes allows visualization and monitoring alongside real-time data.

- **Time Series Visualization**

Visualization plays a vital role in interpreting time series data. Druid's ability to quickly supply data to visualization tools like Apache Superset, Grafana, or Tableau reinforces the utility of temporal data. Charts such as line plots, heat maps, and area graphs effectively represent trends, anomalies, and seasonal patterns.

Additionally, visualizations of time series data often incorporate interactive features allowing users to zoom, slice, and compare different intervals, aiding insight extraction and communication.

- *Challenges and Best Practices*

Time series analysis in Druid, while highly effective, presents certain challenges:

- Data Granularity Selection: Choosing the right granularity is essential; too fine a granularity may slow down query performance with excessive detail, while too coarse a granularity might obscure valuable insights.

- Segment Granularity: Aligning the segment granularity with expected query patterns can notably improve efficiency, as Druid retrieves contiguous data segments.

- Data Enrichment: Integrating supplementary data through joins or lookups enhances context but may increase the complexity of time series queries.

Best practices encourage leveraging Druid's flexibility for various time-based analyses while supplementing with external systems for advanced modeling, ensuring a balanced approach for real-time and historical evaluations.

Druid's robust abilities in handling time series data empower analysts to derive extensive insights from streaming data. By utilizing advanced query techniques and integrating with forecasting tools, organizations can unlock predictive capabilities, complement operational strategies, and maintain a competitive edge through timely data-driven decisions.

6.7   Optimizing Query Performance

Efficient query performance is a cornerstone of effective data analytics, ensuring that insights are derived promptly and with minimal resource expenditure. Apache Druid, as a high-performance real-time analytics database, provides numerous mechanisms for optimizing query performance. This section examines several strategies and considerations for optimizing the performance of queries within Druid environments, covering aspects from data ingestion to query execution and resource management.

Druid's architectural design underpins its ability to deliver fast query responses. The combination of distributed processing, columnar storage, and sophisticated indexing strategies forms the foundation upon which query optimization strategies are built. To harness these capabilities fully, it is vital to understand and apply practical optimizations that cater to the specific needs of your operational environment.

Optimal Data Ingestion

Performance optimization begins at data ingestion. The ingestion process is fundamental as it determines how well data is structured, indexed, and stored, impacting query efficiency.

Segment Granularity

Choosing an appropriate segment granularity is critical. Druid organizes data into segments, which are the fundamental units of storage and querying. The granularity at which data is partitioned into segments can drastically affect query performance, particularly for time-based queries.

For example, if your queries predominantly access daily data, setting the segment granularity to 'day' can enhance performance due to reduced I/O operations and faster retrieval:

```
{
  "type": "index",
  "spec": {
    "dataSchema": {
      "granularitySpec": {
        "type": "uniform",
        "segmentGranularity": "day",
        "queryGranularity": "none"
      }
```

```
    }
  }
}
```

Additionally, aligning segment granularity with frequent query time-frames ensures that queries touch only necessary segments, thereby minimizing unnecessary data reads.

Data Partitioning

Effective partitioning and sorting of data can further enhance query performance. Druid supports various partitioning strategies that can significantly impact the speed and efficiency of queries:

- Time-based Partitioning: By partitioning data based on time intervals, you can improve the performance of time-bound queries and reduce the impact of time-based filtering operations.

- Hash-based Partitioning: Useful for large datasets where queries often involve specific keys or dimensions. Hash partitioning distributes the data evenly across nodes, balancing workloads and reducing hot spots.

- Range Partitioning: Effective for dimensions with continuous values, supporting range-based filtering optimally.

Compaction and Optimization Tasks

Periodic compaction tasks consolidate smaller segments into larger ones, aiding query performance by reducing overhead from handling numerous tiny segments. Compact, well-organized data can lead to more efficient query planning and execution.

```
{
  "type": "compact",
  "dataSource": "user_activities",
  "segmentGranularity": "month"
}
```

Compaction tasks can also integrate optimizations such as rollups, where data is pre-aggregated, lowering storage needs and query times for aggregative queries.

Indexing Strategies

177

Druid's indexing capabilities are paramount in optimizing query performance. The strategic use of indices results in faster data retrieval and filtering:

- Bitmap Indexes: Efficient for filtering on high-cardinality dimensions. Bitmap indexes accelerate query filtering by minimizing data scans.

- Inverted Indexes: Enable fast lookups and are particularly beneficial when combined with low-cardinality dimensions.

- Global Dictionaries: Provide quick access to dimension values, reducing the overhead involved in comparisons.

Efficient indexing hinges on understanding the nature of queries. Focus indexing efforts on dimensions that appear frequently in filters or group-by conditions.

Query Execution Optimization

Query execution in Druid takes advantage of parallel processing and intelligent data access strategies. Optimizing execution entails:

Query Granularity

Selecting the right query granularity can balance detail and performance:

- Coarser granularities can improve performance by summarizing data, reducing the volume processed at query time.

- Fine granularity is better for precise calculations and detailed analytical tasks.

Predicate Pushdown

Employing filters effectively using predicate pushdown can reduce data load. Predicate pushdown allows filtering operations to occur as close to the data source as possible, minimizing unnecessary data transfer and processing.

Using logical conditions and combining filters strategically aids in this process. For example:

```
{
  "queryType": "groupBy",
  "dataSource": "sales",
  "granularity": "all",
  "dimensions": ["region"],
  "filter": {
    "type": "and",
    "fields": [
      {"type": "selector", "dimension": "product_line", "value": "Electronics"},
      {"type": "bound", "dimension": "sales_amount", "lower": "1000"}
    ]
  },
  "aggregations": [{"type": "doubleSum", "name": "total_sales", "fieldName": "
      sales_amount"}],
  "intervals": ["2023-01-01/2023-03-31"]
}
```

Resource Allocation

Allocating resources effectively ensures balanced workloads and minimizes bottlenecks. Druid utilizes computational resources across broker nodes and real-time or historical nodes, distributing query execution tasks for parallel processing.

Adjusting task allocation, configuring peon settings, and efficient data sharding contribute to enhanced processing speeds.

Caching and Result Reuse

Caching mechanisms significantly influence query response times, especially in environments with recurring query patterns. Druid's multilayer caching supports both local and distributed caches, storing segments and result sets for immediate retrieval in repeat queries.

- Query Result Caching: Stores the output of previous queries for fast access if identical queries are executed.

- Segment Cache: Caches segments locally on historical nodes, reducing data retrieval latency.

Advanced Techniques

Advanced optimization techniques involve:

- Lookups and Joins Optimization: Streamline queries involving lookups and joins by minimizing data through early filtering and

179

using broadcast strategies to handle dimension table joins efficiently.

- Schema Evolution Management: Proactively manage schema changes to prevent adverse impacts on query performance. Maintain backward compatibility where possible and test comprehensively before deploying schema updates.

- Hybrid Workloads: For environments dealing with both analytical and transactional data, configure separate tiers in Druid or utilize other database systems for transaction processing, reducing interference with analytics queries.

Monitoring and Diagnostics

Regularly monitoring query performance and employing diagnostic tools helps identify performance bottlenecks. Druid provides insights through query metrics, system logs, and support for plug-ins and extensions that facilitate performance tracking and troubleshooting.

Identifying slow queries and analyzing their query plan can provide clues to issues such as inefficient filtering, suboptimal resource allocation, or data distribution challenges. Regular audits of configuration settings, review of query patterns, and engagement with community forums or support channels offer opportunities for continuous optimization.

In summary, optimizing query performance in Druid involves leveraging appropriate strategies throughout the data lifecycle, from ingestion through indexing and execution. By strategically adjusting settings and tools to specific workload demands, organizations can achieve remarkable improvements in speed, accuracy, and resource efficiency, empowering proactive and agile data-driven decision-making.

Chapter 7

Scaling and Performance Optimization

This chapter addresses the strategies for effectively scaling Apache Druid to manage increased data loads and query demands. It explores configurations for optimizing node performance, focusing on memory, disk, and CPU resource management. Techniques for tuning Druid segments to enhance performance through proper sizing, replication, and compaction are detailed. The use of caching to improve query speed and load distribution is discussed alongside methods for balancing loads and managing resources. Readers will gain insight into optimizing both ingestion and query processes and learn to identify and resolve performance bottlenecks to ensure efficient system operation.

7.1   Understanding Druid's Scaling Capabilities

Apache Druid is a real-time analytics database designed to handle large-scale data and deliver sub-second query performance. Its architecture, which incorporates distributed data storage and compute engines, allows it to scale both horizontally and vertically to accommodate increased data volumes and query loads efficiently. The system's ability to scale seamlessly is essential for enterprises that process massive datasets and require rapid insights. This section delves into the architectural components and configurations that facilitate Druid's powerful scaling capabilities.

Druid achieves scaling through a combination of several key design principles: the separation of data storage and query processing, the use of flexible data partitioning mechanisms, and distributed job execution. Each of these principles enables Druid to efficiently manage resources and balance load across multiple nodes, enhancing its capability to scale linearly with data volume and user demand.

Data Storage and Query Processing

In Druid, data storage and query processing are separated physically and logically. This separation enables the independent scaling of these two components as the load increases, offering significant performance improvements.

The data storage layer is responsible for data ingestion, partitioning, and persistence. It primarily involves the "Data Server" nodes, which comprise of "Historical", "MiddleManager", and "Deep Storage" nodes. Historical nodes serve as the backbone of data storage, dealing with immutable data segments that are persisted in deep storage and loaded into the cluster. MiddleManager nodes handle real-time data ingestion and preliminary processing, thus supporting both batch and real-time workflows. Deep Storage acts as the long-term storage solution for Apache Druid and is typically backed by distributed file systems like HDFS or cloud-based storage services like Amazon S3.

Conversely, the query processing layer, composed of "Broker" and "Coordinator" nodes, focuses on handling incoming queries and distributing workloads effectively across the cluster. Broker nodes receive queries from clients and then fan-out those queries to relevant Historical and MiddleManager nodes, collating the results before returning them to clients. Coordinator nodes are responsible for overseeing the distribution of segments across the Druid cluster, ensuring data is effectively balanced for high availability and redundancy.

Flexible Data Partitioning

Partitioning is a crucial aspect of Druid's scalability, allowing large datasets to be divided into smaller, manageable segments. Druid's partitioning mechanism operates on row-level granularity, leveraging time-based partitioning as the foundation. This approach enables the efficient filtering and retrieval of data, particularly for time-series datasets.

By implementing time-based shards and hash-based partitioning, Druid can distribute data evenly across multiple Historical nodes, preventing any single node from becoming a bottleneck. More specifically, Druid can either partition data using uniform-sized segments (time partitioning) or based on specific dimensions for finer control over segment allocation (hash partitioning). This flexible approach allows organizations to choose a partitioning strategy that best aligns with their data requirements and query patterns.

Consider the following example of a partitioning strategy:

```
{
  "type": "index_parallel",
  "spec": {
    "dataSchema": {
      "dataSource": "example_data",
      "granularitySpec": {
        "type": "uniform",
        "segmentGranularity": "DAY",
        "queryGranularity": "HOUR"
      },
      "partitionSpec": {
        "type": "hashed",
        "targetPartitionSize": 5000000
      }
    }
  }
}
```

In the example above, data is partitioned based on a daily segment granularity while maintaining hourly granularity for query execution. A hashed partition spec assigns records into partitions of approximately 5 million rows each. Such configurations ensure optimal query performance, reducing latency and distributing workload evenly.

Distributed Job Execution

Druid's architecture is designed to execute ingestion and query jobs in a distributed manner across multiple nodes. This parallelization ensures that increases in data volume or user queries do not critically affect the system's response time or throughput.

The ingestion process typically involves dividing data into chunks that are processed concurrently across MiddleManager nodes. Druid uses task-based processing frameworks such as Kafka or native batch ingestion to support this distributed ingestion pipeline. Parallel tasks ingest data segments and submit them to Historical nodes, where they are indexed, compressed, and persisted.

```
{
  "type": "realtime",
  "spec": {
    "ioConfig": {
      "type": "realtime",
      "kafka": {
        "consumerProperties": {
          "bootstrap.servers": "localhost:9092",
          "topic": "topics",
          "group.id": "group"
        }
      }
    }
  }
}
```

In this example, the 'Realtime' ingestion task consumes data from Kafka, distributing it across available MiddleManager threads for concurrent processing.

Queries are similarly distributed, with Druid's Broker nodes orchestrating query execution. Brokers recursively construct query plans, then issue subqueries to relevant Historical nodes based on data partition information. Results are merged and reduced before being returned to the requesting user. This distributed execution model leverages network bandwidth, CPU, and memory resources effectively, enhancing scalability.

Load Balancing and Replication

Load balancing in Druid is orchestrated by Coordinator nodes that ensure optimal data distribution and replication. Coordinator nodes monitor the data segments hosted on each Historical node, using rules-based policies to enforce segment placement, reallocation, and replication. Segment replication provides fault tolerance and ensures that queries have multiple execution paths to avoid single points of failure.

Consider a replication strategy example:

```
{
  "rules": [
    {
      "type": "loadByInterval",
      "interval": "2016-01-01/2022-01-01",
      "targetCompactionSizeBytes": 20000000,
      "tieredReplicants": {
        "_default_tier": 2
      }
    }
  ]
}
```

In this configuration, data within the specified interval is replicated twice across "_default_tier" nodes, thus ensuring redundancy and reliability.

Additionally, Druid utilizes consistent hashing for hit-and-dispatch queries, facilitating load distribution across Broker nodes and maximizing throughput. This method allows for the effective management of request load, irrespective of the number of concurrent users accessing the system.

Scaling Druid offers a remarkable opportunity to manage immense amounts of data with low latency and high availability. By understanding and leveraging the architectural elements and configurations outlined here, users can lay a foundational pathway towards an efficient and scalable Druid deployment. Thereby, enterprises can harness the power of real-time data analytics to drive valuable insights and informed decision-making processes.

7.2 Node Configuration for Optimal Performance

Optimizing node configuration is crucial in achieving peak performance in an Apache Druid deployment. Each Druid node type has specific roles and resource requirements, and fine-tuning these settings can lead to significant improvements in data ingestion rates, query processing times, and overall system reliability. This section discusses the optimal configuration of Druid nodes, emphasizing memory allocation, disk usage, and CPU considerations, to ensure the effective utilization of cluster resources.

- **Memory Allocation**

Memory management is one of the most critical aspects of node configuration since inadequate memory settings can lead to performance degradation, excessive garbage collection, and ultimately service outages. Each Druid node type requires particular memory settings, guided by its functional role in the architecture.

For Historical Nodes, which manage storage and data retrieval, the majority of system memory should be allocated to JVM heap space. This is because Historical Nodes often deal with large data sets that are actively queried. For these nodes, the size of the off-heap memory is also significant, particularly for column storage and bitmap index caches.

```
druid.processing.buffer.sizeBytes=1GB
druid.processing.numMergeBuffers=2
```

This configuration allocates a 1GB buffer for query processing, allowing up to two simultaneous merge operations. Adjusting these numbers based on available system memory and workload patterns ensures efficient query execution without causing out-of-memory errors.

MiddleManager Nodes, responsible for real-time data ingestion and processing, also require careful memory configuration. These nodes benefit from a balanced distribution between heap and direct memory settings, as both types of memory are crucial for ingestion tasks.

```
druid.indexer.fork.property.druid.processing.buffer.sizeBytes=512MB
druid.indexer.fork.property.druid.processing.numThreads=4
```

The fork properties determine the allocation of memory and processing threads for indexing tasks within the MiddleManager node. In this scenario, 512MB is reserved for processing buffers, with four processing threads enabled for ingestion tasks.

Broker Nodes maintain query cursors and need adequate heap memory allocation for effective query planning and result merging. Coordinating between Historical Nodes necessitates notable memory allocation tuned based on query size and complexity.

Coordinators primarily manage cluster metadata, such as segment assignments and load balancers; therefore, their memory usage is less demanding compared to other nodes. Generally, ensuring sufficient memory for cache and coordination tasks is crucial.

Segment caches on all nodes benefit from allocated off-heap memory, particularly for frequently accessed data. Configuring maximum cache sizes relative to available memory ensures balanced performance and prevents excessive garbage collection.

- **Disk Usage**

Disk performance and storage configurations significantly impact a Druid cluster's responsiveness and processing capabilities. Adequate disk provisioning, with both capacity and speed in mind, is essential to support ingestion, storage, and real-time analytics tasks.

Historical Nodes should be provisioned with high-throughput, fault-tolerant disk configurations since they handle a significant portion of the stored data. Secondary storage mechanisms, such as RAID configurations on local disks, or distributed storage solutions like HDFS or Amazon S3, offer redundancy and data accessibility.

When ingesting data, replication and compaction tasks lead to data storage spikes. A well-provisioned storage system, with appropriate disk capacity, is necessary to avoid interruptions or delays during these tasks.

SSD storage provides significant improvements over HDDs for read-heavy workloads by decreasing data-fetch latency during query operations. For Historical nodes, where latency is an issue, having SSDs can improve data access times, a major consideration if processing time-sensitive datasets.

187

```
mount | grep /mnt/druid
Filesystem Type  Size Used Avail Use% Mounted
/dev/sdb1 ext4 932G 453G 431G 52% /mnt/druid
```

Here, '/mnt/druid' is mounted on a high-performance SSD, ensuring ample space and optimal read/write speeds for our Druid data directories.

MiddleManager Nodes utilize disk resources during real-time data processing and should have redundant storage setups to accommodate the high I/O load. Ensuring that storage devices minimize latency is particularly salient when processing streaming data sources.

- **CPU Considerations**

CPU resources are pivotal in determining Druid's data processing and querying speeds. Each node type should be provisioned with sufficient CPU cores, balanced relative to its workload and expected resource demand.

Historical Nodes benefit from multiple processing threads for data retrieval and query execution. The value of 'druid.processing.numThreads' determines the parallel execution ability and should be set according to the number of CPU cores available:

```
druid.processing.numThreads=7
```

In this example, seven threads are available for parallel query processing, balancing CPU utilization while preventing system contention.

MiddleManager Nodes require CPU resources sufficient for real-time data ingestion and task execution. Correctly scaling 'druid.worker.capacity', which sets the number of concurrent tasks, helps maintain efficiency:

```
druid.worker.capacity=6
```

This configuration assigns the MiddleManager node six task slots, ensuring that multiple ingestion tasks can be handled concurrently.

Broker Nodes require an allocation of CPU resources that aligns with the query load and complexity. Configuring 'numProcessingThreads' accordingly ensures that query handling threads do not exceed CPU constraints, avoiding bottlenecks:

```
druid.broker.http.numProcessingThreads=9
```

This setting allows the Broker node to handle nine processing threads for incoming queries, facilitating effective query distribution.

Coordinators manage administrative tasks and require less intensive CPU resources than data-intensive nodes. However, providing adequate resources remains important for facilitating prompt metadata operations and minimizing latency in segment propagation.

Through careful configuration of memory, disk, and CPU resources, Druid nodes can achieve exemplary performance, tapping into the maximum potential of underlying hardware infrastructure. This optimization not only enhances data ingestion and query response times but also ensures that resource use is both balanced and efficient. For organizations looking to scale their Druid implementation successfully, tailoring each node type's configuration to its designated role is a critical step in building a robust deployment capable of handling complex data processes securely and swiftly.

7.3   Tuning Druid Segments

Apache Druid's capability to efficiently manage large datasets is significantly influenced by its segment tuning strategies. Segments are the fundamental units of storage in Druid, containing data indexed for fast retrieval. Proper tuning of these segments leads to optimization in storage space, query performance, and resource utilization. This section thoroughly examines methods for adjusting segment sizes, replication levels, and compaction tactics, thereby enhancing the overall performance and reliability of a Druid deployment.

Segment Size Configuration

One of the primary considerations when tuning Druid segments is determining their optimal size. Segment size impacts both the speed of data retrieval during query execution and the efficiency of storage resources.

For Druid to strike a balance between performance and resource utilization, segments should ideally range between 300MB to 700MB in size. Segments that are too small may lead to excessive metadata load and increased query overhead, whereas overly large segments can delay query response times and reduce cache efficiency.

Consider the following segment configuration example:

```
{
  "type": "index_parallel",
  "spec": {
    "dataSchema": {
      "granularitySpec": {
        "segmentGranularity": "HOUR"
      },
      "partitionSpec": {
        "type": "dynamic",
        "targetSegmentRows": 5000000
      }
    }
  }
}
```

Here, an hourly segment granularity is combined with dynamic partitioning based on target rows, aiming for a segment size suitable for efficient querying and processing.

Careful attention should be paid to 'segmentGranularity', which determines the time granularity for segment roll-up. Selecting a granularity that aligns with your data's temporal structure allows for optimized segment creation and resource utilization.

Replication Strategy

Segment replication in Druid enhances data availability, reliability, and ensures consistent performance under failure scenarios. Properly configured replication settings ensure that queries have multiple execution paths, reducing potential points of failure.

The replication factor defines the number of copies of each segment maintained across the Druid cluster. A higher replication factor increases data availability but demands more storage and network resources.

An example of configuring replication for increased fault tolerance is as follows:

```
{
```

```
"rules": [
  {
    "type": "loadByInterval",
    "interval": "2023-01-01/2023-12-31",
    "tieredReplicants": {
      "\_default\_tier": 3
    }
  }
]
}
```

In the above configuration, segments within the specified time interval have a replication factor of three across nodes in the '_default_tier'. This ensures that any node failures do not affect data availability.

For organizations that prioritize high uptime and reliability, advising multiple replication layers enables additional data redundancy, catering to both high priority and workload distribution.

Compaction Strategies

Compaction is an integral aspect of segment tuning that reduces fragmentation, combines small segments, and enhances query performance. Druid's compaction processes consolidate data, leading to storage savings and optimized caching.

Compaction tasks can be configured to execute on demand or scheduled regularly based on data update patterns. The following configurations establish compaction task parameters:

```
{
  "type": "compact",
  "dataSource": "example_data",
  "inputSegmentSizeBytes": 500000000,
  "targetCompactionSizeBytes": 750000000,
  "tuningConfig": {
    "maxRowsPerSegment": 10000000
  }
}
```

This example demonstrates a compact task for 'example_data'. The task triggers only if input segments exceed 500MB, targeting a segment set of 750MB, with segment rows capped at 10 million.

Compaction strategies must account for system load, ensuring that when compaction tasks are executed, they do not interfere with ongoing ingestion or compromise query performance.

Column Configuration and Data Rollup

191

Another aspect of segment tuning is the strategic configuration of data columns and roll-up settings. In Druid, data roll-up is an aggregation mechanism where input rows are consolidated, leading to the efficient storage of repetitive data. Proper implementation requires configuring dimension and metric specifications.

Rolling-up data offers savings in both storage and improved query times, particularly for highly granular datasets frequently queried at summary levels:

```
{
  "type": "index_parallel",
  "spec": {
    "dataSchema": {
      "dimensionsSpec": {
        "dimensions": [
          "dimension1",
          "dimension2",
          {
            "type": "float",
            "name": "metric1"
          }
        ]
      }
    }
  }
}
```

Here, 'dimensionsSpec' specifies the dimensions to aggregate by, while metrics (such as 'metric1') are calculated per incoming segment row. Effectively tuning column configurations ensures the role of each column is conducive to roll-up processes.

Roll-up strategies often require balancing. It is critical to ensure that aggregation levels maintain analytical value while minimizing the impact on data granularity.

Analyzing and Monitoring Segment Performance

Understanding segment performance through continuous monitoring is essential for sustained tuning efforts. The Druid Console provides insights into segment size distribution, load status, and query performance, allowing for prompt management action when necessary:

```
curl -X GET http://<coordinator-host>:8081/druid/coordinator/v1/metadata/
  segments/<datasource>
```

Using the above REST endpoint, users can gather segment metadata, offering visibility into segment distribution, load status, and size details.

Additionally, consider leveraging performance metrics related to query latencies, hit/miss cache ratios, and the distribution of query execution times to guide further segment adjustments. Such metrics provide valuable feedback on the configuration strategies and their direct consequence on system efficiency.

Segment tuning is an iterative process that requires careful planning, insight into data usage patterns, and judicious resource management. By optimally configuring segment size, replication, and compaction tactics, a robust Druid deployment capitalizes on enhanced performance metrics reflected through improved query times and lowered operational costs. The commands, configurations, and rational approaches to segment tuning discussed herein facilitate continued excellence in high-performance analytics with Apache Druid. The ability to adaptively fine-tune these parameters showcases Druid's flexible architecture designed to cater to evolving data and query demands for enterprises.

7.4 Leveraging Druid Caching

Caching is a pivotal component in enhancing the performance of data query systems, particularly in reducing latency and load across computing resources. Apache Druid implements efficient caching mechanisms that help optimize query response times and improve throughput. By understanding and leveraging these caching strategies, practitioners can ensure that Druid handles large volumes of data queries more efficiently. This section explores the types of caching available in Druid, their configurations, and the practical considerations necessary for achieving optimal performance.

- **Types of Caches in Druid**

Druid employs two primary types of caches: query result caching and segment-level caching. Each of these caches serves to decrease redundancy in data processing and network transmission, therefore enhancing the system's overall performance and response times.

Query Result Caching

Query result caching stores the results of executed queries, preventing the need for re-execution of identical queries within specified time frames or conditions. This caching occurs at the Broker node level and is beneficial in environments with recurring query patterns or dashboards.

The following configuration enables and controls query result caching:

```
druid.broker.cache.useCache=true
druid.broker.cache.populateCache=true
druid.cache.type="caffeine"
druid.cache.sizeInBytes=100000000
```

Here, Druid utilizes the Caffeine cache, a high-performance caching library, with a 100MB allocation dedicated to storing query results at the Broker level. The configuration flags enable cache utilization and population.

Segment-Level Caching

Segment-level caching stores individual segments or data blocks in the Historical and MiddleManager nodes, thus reducing retrieval times during query processes.

```
druid.server.cache.useCache=true
druid.server.cache.populateCache=true
druid.cache.type="caffeine"
druid.cache.sizeInBytes=500000000
```

With a segment cache of 500MB, this configuration assures that segments frequently accessed during query execution remain readily available, providing quick access and response.

- **Configuring Caching Parameters**

Configuring caching correctly is crucial for optimizing resource usage and ensuring that caching strategies align with operational requirements. Each parameter within Druid's caching configuration plays a role in controlling the cache's life cycle, its size limits, and data retention policies.

Expiration and Eviction Policies

Caching configurations must consider expiration and eviction policies for maintaining space efficiency and relevance of cached data. By configuring time-to-live (TTL) parameters, users can control the lifespan of cached data:

```
druid.cache.expirationTime=PT10M
```

The example above sets the cache expiration to 10 minutes, thereby ensuring that data remains fresh and accurate. Eviction policies, such as Least Recently Used (LRU), further manage how space is freed in circumstances where the cache is full:

```
druid.cache.evictionPolicy=LRU
```

Cache Peers

For query result caching, utilizing cache peers allows for clustering multiple Broker caches, enabling them to share cache entries. This configuration yields a distributed caching layer effectively spreading the caching load:

```
druid.cache.peers=["broker1:8080", "broker2:8080"]
```

Monitoring and Metrics

Monitoring cache performance using metrics provides insights into cache effectiveness and areas for improvement. Druid's cache hit/miss ratio is a critical performance metric:

```
curl -X GET http://<broker-host>:8081/druid/v2/datasources/<datasource>/metrics
```

This API call returns comprehensive metrics on cache performance, guiding administrators to adjust configurations according to workload patterns and system behavior. Analyzing these metrics helps in determining the appropriate cache size and policies.

• Operational Considerations in Cache Management

While caching offers substantial performance benefits, it introduces additional complexities in operational maintenance. Careful management helps avoid common pitfalls associated with stale and inconsistent data.

Data Staleness and Consistency

One of the primary challenges with caching is managing the freshness of data. The TTL settings should match the update frequency and data sensitivity. In real-time analytics scenarios, ensuring that incoming data propagates quickly requires tuning cache parameters that do not overly prioritize stale data retention.

Resource Overhead

Caching, particularly in-memory, draws on system RAM which could otherwise serve querying or ingestion processes. As such, balancing cache size with other resource needs requires constant vigilance and periodic recalibrations based on system load.

- **Performance and Scalability Benefits**

The practical impact of leveraging efficient caching mechanisms in Druid manifests in enhanced performance and greater scalability. By offloading repetitive query processing tasks, caching contributes to reduced CPU and network load, extending the cluster's effective capacity for concurrent users:

```
Cache Hit Ratio:
Cache Hits: 87, Cache Misses: 13 (out of 100 queries)
```

A cache hit ratio as shown above indicates that the majority of queries are served directly from cache, thus saving on expensive computation and data retrieval costs. Such performance metrics validate the value derived from strategic caching.

- **Dynamic Caching Adjustments**

To keep pace with evolving query workloads and data growth, cache configurations must be regularly evaluated and adjusted. Dynamic tuning ensures continued alignment with the overall system throughput and speed objectives.

Adaptive Cache Policies

Built on queueing theory, adaptive policies adjust parameters like TTL and eviction strategies in response to real-time metrics:

```
druid.cache.dynamic.adjustment=true
```

This setting enables dynamic adjustments in cache parameters, allowing Druid to autonomously adapt to changes in workloads or usage patterns.

Tailoring caching strategies to the uniqueness of each data model, query pattern, and business requirement is crucial in maximizing the potential of Druid's powerful caching capabilities. Whether it's past query responses or frequently accessed data segments, caching operates to streamline and accelerate access, facilitating the swift and efficient delivery of insights. Through diligent configuration and tuning methods outlined in this text, leveraging Druid's caching can transform data systems into responsive, high-performance analytic platforms, capable of meeting the demands of modern enterprises.

7.5 Load Balancing and Resource Management

Effective load balancing and resource management are essential in ensuring that an Apache Druid cluster operates efficiently under a variety of workloads. As Druid deployments scale, balancing the distribution of data and computation tasks across nodes becomes crucial for maintaining low-latency query responses, optimal resource utilization, and high availability. This section explores the techniques and strategies for implementing load balancing and resource management in a Druid deployment, focusing on the configuration and practical considerations that lead to a well-tuned, high-performance system.

Understanding load balancing in Druid involves distributing data segments, queries, and computation tasks across multiple nodes to prevent any single node from becoming a performance bottleneck. The primary goal is to achieve an even distribution of workload, optimizing resource utilization while retaining fault tolerance.

Druid employs several mechanisms to achieve load balancing:

- **Segment Distribution**

  The Coordinator node manages segment distribution by periodically checking the load status of Historical nodes. It determines

197

the ideal assignment of segments based on rules defined by the cluster administrator. Through dynamic load balancing, data is shuffled across nodes to ensure balanced resource utilization.

The key configuration for segment balancing involves specifying load and drop rules:

```
{
    "rules": [
        {
            "type": "loadByInterval",
            "interval": "2019-01-01/2024-01-01",
            "tieredReplicants": {
                "hotTier": 2
            }
        }
    ]
}
```

In the above configuration, segments within the specified interval are replicated twice in the "hotTier," ensuring that data access remains prompt and evenly distributed.

- **Query Distribution**

  Broker nodes handle the distribution of query requests, fanning them out to the appropriate Historical and MiddleManager nodes based on data availability and workload distributions. They ensure that query execution is spread across the cluster so that no single node handles an excessive number of request loads.

- **Resource Awareness**

  Druid's resource awareness involves understanding the capacity and load characteristics of each node, factoring in CPU, memory, and I/O essentials when distributing workloads. This awareness facilitates strategic task assignments that mitigate overloading any part of the infrastructure.

Resource management encapsulates strategies to allocate, monitor, and optimize the use of computing resources in a Druid cluster, ensuring that hardware and software assets are effectively harnessed for performance and scalability.

- **Auto-scaling**

Druid supports integration with container orchestration and cloud management tools to automatically scale nodes up and down depending on current workload demands. Such elasticity ensures optimal resource management, dynamically adjusting available capacity and maintaining cost-effectiveness.

For instance, setting up auto-scaling in a cloud environment might involve:

```
{
    "autoScaling": {
    "type": "ec2",
    "minInstances": 4,
    "maxInstances": 10,
    "launchConfig": {
       "name": "druid-cluster",
          ...
       }
    }
}
```

In this EC2 example, the cluster scales between four and ten instances based on resource usage metrics. Such configurations prevent resource wastage, adapting resources to fluctuating demand.

- **Resource Isolation**

  Using resource isolation ensures that different workloads and processes do not interfere with one another, maintaining predictable performance. This can be achieved by configuring resource limits for Druid nodes, partitioning CPU and memory resources:

```
druid.processing.numThreads=8
druid.processing.buffer.sizeBytes=1GB
```

  Using dedicated threads and memory buffers ensures that background tasks like segment loading do not compete with query execution, stabilizing performance.

- **Priority and Queue Management**

  Administering task priorities and queues allows critical workloads to be executed promptly. Druid includes support for assigning priorities to various tasks:

```
{
```

199

```
"taskPriority": 75,
"taskQueue": "high-priority-tasks"
}
```

The above configuration assigns a high priority to specific tasks, ensuring they precede less critical operations in execution sequences.

Druid's extensive monitoring capabilities provide insights into key performance metrics that can guide effective resource management practices. Understanding load distribution, node performance, and task execution provides clues for optimizing configurations and scaling approaches.

- **Utilizing Metrics for Load Balancing**

  Metrics such as segment count, CPU and memory utilization, and query processing times are fundamental indicators of load and can inform proactive adjustments to configurations:

  ```
  Node Metrics:
  CPU Utilization: 70%
  Memory Utilization: 60%
  Segment Load: 250 segments
  ```

  High resource utilization metrics may necessitate scaling node resources or redistributing tasks. Keeping abreast of these data points facilitates maintaining a balanced and optimal environment.

Several considerations must be addressed when implementing effective load balancing and resource management in a Druid deployment.

- **High Availability**

  Ensuring high availability requires data redundancy through segment replication and fault tolerance mechanisms that guarantee continuity of service even in case of node failures. Cross-region replication is an advanced technique allowing clusters to sustain operations despite regional outages.

200

- **Performance Tuning**

  Routine performance tuning based on monitoring insights and operational data involves adjusting segment sizes, buffer configurations, and query distribution mechanisms to sustain peak performance.

  ```
  druid.indexer.task.fork.property.druid.processing.buffer.sizeBytes=512MB
  ```

  Tuning buffer sizes in the task ingestion pipeline enhances system responsiveness, preventing under-utilization or saturation of resources.

- **System Scalability**

  Long-term scalability aligns with future data growth and usage trends. Planning resource additions or enhancements is essential for ensuring sustainable system operations under expanding data volumes and query complexities.

Load balancing and resource management within Apache Druid are paramount for achieving a responsive, reliable, and efficient analytics platform. With intelligent configurations and proactive management strategies, Druid can seamlessly deliver high-performance analytic capabilities, irrespective of scale or workload dynamics. Organizations thus position themselves to harness real-time insights and derive value from vast datasets, driving innovation and decision-making efficiencies with precision.

7.6 Optimizing Ingestion and Query Processes

In an Apache Druid deployment, optimizing both data ingestion and query processes is essential for ensuring high throughput and minimizing latency. Efficient ingestion strategies streamline data flow from diverse sources into Druid, while optimized query processes ensure rapid and reliable data retrieval. This section delves into the configurations, techniques, and considerations that underpin optimized ingestion and query performance, providing insights into building a robust and responsive Druid system.

Data Ingestion Optimization

The ingestion phase is crucial in transforming raw data from source systems into indexed Druid segments. The efficiency of this process affects not only the speed at which data becomes queryable but also the accuracy and reliability of downstream analytic operations.

Ingestion Pathways

Druid supports multiple ingestion methods, including real-time ingestion using Kafka or Kinesis and batch ingestion via Hadoop or native methods. Choosing the appropriate pathway based on data volume, velocity, and variability is pivotal.

```
{
  "type": "kafka",
  "kafkaConfig": {
    "bootstrapServers": "kafka-broker:9092",
    "topic": "druid-events",
    "consumerProperties": {
      "group.id": "druid-ingestion"
    }
  }
}
```

Using Kafka, as shown in the example above, supports real-time feeding of high-velocity data streams into Druid, enabling immediate data availability for analysis. For larger, more static datasets, batch processing may offer a more resource-efficient approach.

Schema Design

Effective schema design can greatly influence ingestion speed and storage efficiency. Define schemas that capture essential data dimensions and metrics that align closely with anticipated query patterns.

```
{
  "dataSchema": {
    "dataSource": "events",
    "granularitySpec": {
      "segmentGranularity": "DAY",
      "queryGranularity": "NONE"
    },
    "parser": {
      "parseSpec": {
        "format": "json",
        "dimensionsSpec": {
          "dimensions": ["userId", "eventType", "country"]
        }
      }
    }
```

```
    }
}
```

Setting 'segmentGranularity' and 'dimensions' appropriately ensures the resulting segments align with both storage efficiency and retrieval speed, minimizing unnecessary overhead.

Parallelization and Task Tuning

Leveraging Druid's parallel ingestion capabilities can dramatically increase throughput. Assign multiple tasks to ingestion processes by configuring the following properties:

```
{
  "tuningConfig": {
    "maxNumTasks": 10,
    "numThreads": 3
  }
}
```

In this case, up to 10 ingestion tasks run concurrently, each making use of three threads, thereby enhancing data throughput and reducing time-to-ingest.

Query Process Optimization

Once data is ingested into Druid, efficient query processing mechanisms ensure quick retrieval and analytics execution. Several strategies contribute to optimized query performance.

Indexing and Aggregation

Indexing strategies play a crucial role in how quickly a query can access data. Each dimension field in Druid can be dictionary-encoded, bitmap-indexed, or forward-indexed based on analytical requirements.

```
"dimensionsSpec": {
  "dimensions": [
    "userId",
    {
      "type": "string",
      "name": "eventType",
      "multiValueHandling": "SORTED_SET"
    }
  ]
}
```

The configuration of 'multiValueHandling' can enable specific opti-

203

mizations for queries involving multi-valued dimensions, reducing complexity and enhancing speed.

Query Granularity and Roll-up

For use cases involving summary analysis over time, configuring granularity and roll-up properties can consolidate data and hasten query response times:

```
{
  "queryGranularity": "HOUR",
  "rollup": true,
  "appendAggregations": [
    {
      "type": "count",
      "name": "count"
    }
  ]
}
```

Enabling roll-up aggregates data on ingest, allowing for compact storage and swift retrieval, particularly suitable for lightweight aggregations and dashboarding applications.

Caching Strategies

Effective caching strategies lower repeated query loads and enhance response times. The caching mechanisms at various Druid nodes can be tested and optimized for specific workloads.

```
druid.broker.cache.useResultLevelCache=true
druid.broker.cache.populateResultLevelCache=false
```

This configuration utilizes result-level caching at the Broker level, enabling queries to bypass redundant processing for identical requests.

Query Prioritization

Correlating the priority of queries with their relative importance ensures critical operations receive adequate resources. Assist with this by setting query priorities system-wide or per request:

```
druid.query.priority.default=50
```

Each query receives a priority level, scheduling execution and resource allocation depending on operational requirements.

Monitoring and Optimization Metrics

Utilizing Druid's extensive monitoring capabilities helps continually manage and tune ingestion and query processes. Key metrics provide insight into performance and can direct future optimizations.

Performance Metrics

Monitoring query latencies, segment distribution, and resource utilizations offers data-driven insights driving optimizations.

```
Query Performance:
Query Latency: 200ms
Ingestion Throughput: 20K events/second
Segment Availability: 95%
```

Observing these metrics guides performance tuning efforts, addressing bottlenecks through recalibrated configurations and resource adjustments.

Future-Proofing with Scalability

Preparing for future growth involves strategies that ensure Druid scales seamlessly with data and query demand changes. This may involve infrastructural adjustments or optimization of existing configurations.

Elastic Scaling

Integrate cloud services or container orchestration platforms for resource scalability that matches demand fluctuations. Automation enforces policies that align resources dynamically with ingestion and query loads.

Component Configurations

Scaling the capacities of individual Druid components relative to their operational workloads ensures balanced system performance:

```
{
  "druid.indexer.fork.property.druid.processing.numThreads": 4,
  "druid.broker.http.numProcessingThreads": 16
}
```

Adjusting 'numThreads' across ingest and broker tasks maintains fluid task execution, preventing resource wastage or shortages.

Optimizing ingestion and query processes in Apache Druid profoundly impacts the efficacy of the entire analytics pipeline. By implementing thoughtful schema design, parallel task processing, strategic caching, and monitoring-driven tuning, Druid deployments achieve high-performance analytics with minimal latency. These optimized processes facilitate rapid, reliable decision-making, positioning Druid as a powerful platform for real-time data analytics that adapts in magnitude with evolving business needs.

7.7 Dealing with Bottlenecks

In any complex system like Apache Druid, bottlenecks can arise that impede data throughput and query performance. Identifying, diagnosing, and resolving these bottlenecks are vital for maintaining the robustness and efficiency of the data analytics platform. This section explores common performance bottlenecks in Druid deployments and presents strategies and techniques to diagnose and resolve these issues, optimizing performance and ensuring continuous operational fidelity.

Bottlenecks in Druid can manifest at various stages, from data ingestion to query execution. Identifying the nature and location of bottlenecks is the first step in addressing them effectively.

- **Data Ingestion Bottlenecks**

Ingestion bottlenecks may appear in scenarios where data flow from source systems into Druid is slower than expected. It could result from network bandwidth limitations, inadequate task configuration, or resource insufficiencies.

- **Symptoms:**

  - Ingestion task delays or failures
  - Accumulating backlog in streaming pipelines (e.g., Kafka topics)
  - High ingestion latency

- **Query Execution Bottlenecks**

Query bottlenecks typically emerge when Druid cannot efficiently handle incoming query loads, often due to misconfigured query paths or overloaded resources.

- **Symptoms:**

  - Increased query latency
  - High historical node CPU utilization
  - Timeouts or incomplete query results

- **Resource Contention Bottlenecks**

These arise when multiple processes compete for the same resources, leading to system underperformance. Examples include concurrent ingestion, querying tasks vying for CPU, I/O, or memory resources.

- **Symptoms:**

  - Resource utilization (CPU, Memory, Disk) consistently near capacity
  - Frequent garbage collection leading to latency spikes
  - Slow task execution despite available capacity

Diagnosing bottlenecks requires a systematic approach, utilizing Druid's built-in tools and external monitoring solutions to pinpoint the exact cause.

- **Monitoring and Metrics**

Leverage the full range of Druid's metrics infrastructure to gather actionable insights on cluster performance.

```
curl -X GET http://<coordinator-host>:8081/druid/coordinator/v1/metrics
```

This endpoint returns comprehensive metrics that correlate with system workloads, revealing potential bottlenecks through fluctuations or anomalies in the performance data.

- **Log Analysis**

Analyze server logs for patterns or error messages indicative of resource bottlenecks or configuration issues:

```
tail -f var/sv/log/druid/*.log
```

Consolidating logs across node types (Broker, Historical, MiddleManager) offers a holistic view of events leading to preferred operational states.

- **Configuration Review**

Review current configurations against best practices, ensuring they align with workload requirements and system capacity.

```
{
  "druid.processing.buffer.sizeBytes": "512MB",
  "druid.processing.numThreads": "7"
}
```

Check these settings across nodes to confirm proper allocation to ingestion and query tasks relative to available hardware capabilities.

Once identified and diagnosed, resolving bottlenecks involves using targeted strategies to mitigate or eliminate performance-limiting factors.

- **Optimizing Data Ingestion**

For ingestion bottlenecks, enhance parallel task execution by adjusting tuning configurations:

```
{
  "tuningConfig": {
    "maxNumTasks": 20,
    "ingestionRate": "20000"
  }
}
```

Increase the number of concurrent tasks in 'maxNumTasks' allowing higher ingestion throughput. Adjusting 'ingestionRate' also ensures that sources do not overwhelm the system with excess data.

- **Query Path and Process Tuning**

Address query bottlenecks by optimizing query execution pathways and index structures:

- Implement efficient indexing strategies tailored to reduce query execution times.

- Utilize result-level and segment-level caching to lower redundant query processing overhead:

```
"druid.query.cache.useCache": true,
"druid.query.cache.populateCache": true
```

- **Mitigating Resource Contention**

Allocate and isolate resources strategically to mitigate contention, adjusting thread numerations and buffer allocations:

```
{
  "druid.worker.capacity": 12,
  "druid.processing.buffer.sizeBytes": "1GB"
}
```

Raising the 'worker.capacity' enhances task throughput capabilities for nodes, balancing concurrency with stability.

For intricate deployments with complex bottleneck scenarios, consider advanced strategies that extend beyond immediate reactive measures.

- **Auto-Scaling Integration**

Integrate with cloud management tools and automate provisioning of additional resources during peak demand, ensuring seamless adjustments:

```
{
  "autoScaling": {
    "type": "kubernetes",
    "minNodes": 5,
    "maxNodes": 15
  }
}
```

Auto-scaling dynamically adjusts cluster size, accommodating rising queries or ingestion demands while maintaining performance targets.

- **Algorithm and Model Tuning**

For applications involving predictive analytics or machine learning workflows, tuning the algorithms or models themselves can alleviate bottlenecks caused by complex calculations or data handling.

Regularly review algorithm and model effectiveness, incorporating parallel computation techniques and efficient data structure utilization.

- **Load Distribution Policies**

Implement strategic load distribution policies across segments and nodes to even out imbalance. Balancing rules assist in non-intrusively redistributing tasks and resources.

In Apache Druid, bottlenecks represent challenges but also opportunities for enhancement and optimization. By actively identifying, diagnosing, and resolving these constraints, organizations can maintain swift, accurate data processing aligned with real-time analytic demands. These insights ensure that Druid remains an effective, scalable platform, supporting advanced analytics and delivering value-driven insights without interruption. Continuous tuning and adjustment, based on methodical data-driven approaches, reinforce Druid's role as a cornerstone analytics tool in modern data architecture.

Chapter 8

Monitoring and Troubleshooting Druid

This chapter focuses on the tools and practices essential for monitoring and troubleshooting Apache Druid environments. It covers setting up various monitoring tools and frameworks, such as Grafana, to track vital performance metrics like query execution times and resource utilization. The chapter also explains configuring alerts to detect and address system issues proactively. Readers will learn to analyze logs for insights, navigate common troubleshooting scenarios, and apply advanced debugging techniques. Methods for investigating performance degradation and ensuring system stability and reliability are also detailed to support effective operational management.

8.1 Setting Up Monitoring Tools

Effective monitoring of a Druid cluster is essential to ensure operational efficiency and to quickly diagnose and troubleshoot issues. This section delves into the selection and setup of various monitoring tools and frameworks that are well-suited for providing comprehensive insights into the operation of Apache Druid. Notable among these are Apache Superset, Grafana, and various open-source monitoring solutions. Understanding how to configure these tools to accurately monitor Druid performance is crucial to maintaining a healthy and performant cluster.

Apache Superset is a modern data exploration and visualization tool that has proven to be invaluable for monitoring Druid clusters. It integrates seamlessly with Druid, allowing users to create dashboards that visualize real-time data. Its key strengths lie in its ability to handle complex queries and provide operational insights with relative ease.

To set up Apache Superset for monitoring a Druid cluster, it is important to first ensure that Superset is configured to connect to the Druid broker node. This involves modifying the Superset configuration file to add details of the Druid data source. The configuration typically includes specifying the Druid broker's hostname or IP address, the port number, and any necessary authentication credentials.

```
# Superset Configurations
SQLALCHEMY_DATABASE_URI = 'sqlite:////path/to/superset.db'
DRUID_TZ = 'UTC'

# Connecting to Druid
DRUID_IS_ACTIVE = True
DRUID_DATASOURCE_NAME = 'my_druid_datasource'
DRUID_HOST = 'druid_broker_host_ip'
DRUID_PORT = 8082
```

In this example, the DRUID_HOST and DRUID_PORT settings ensure that Superset can communicate with the Druid broker, facilitating query execution and data retrieval.

Grafana is another powerful tool for visualizing system metrics and has extensive support for integrating with Druid. It provides a flexible and dynamic interface for creating interactive dashboards with detailed visualizations of Druid metrics.

Setting up Grafana involves configuring a Druid data source within Grafana itself. This configuration requires the inclusion of Druid's endpoint URL and potentially other authentication-related details depending on the security configuration of the Druid cluster. Below is an illustrative configuration guide when setting up Grafana to connect with Druid:

```json
{
  "name": "DruidDataSource",
  "type": "druid",
  "url": "http://druid_broker:8082",
  "access": "proxy",
  "basicAuth": false,
  "jsonData": {
    "tlsSkipVerify": true
  }
}
```

This configuration snippet sets Grafana to interact with the Druid broker over HTTP, using default ports and skipping TLS verification, which may be tightened according to the security policies of the organization.

One advantageous feature of Grafana is its alerting capabilities, which allow users to set custom thresholds and notifications for various Druid metrics. This proactive approach enables administrators to address potential issues before they escalate into critical failures.

Apart from Apache Superset and Grafana, several open-source monitoring solutions like Prometheus and ELK Stack (Elasticsearch, Logstash, and Kibana) are prevalent due to their robust capabilities and extensive community support.

The integration of **Prometheus** with Druid generally involves using an HTTP API to scrape metrics directly from Druid processes. Druid processes expose metrics over HTTP endpoints, which Prometheus scrapes at regular intervals. The following is an example configuration for integrating Prometheus with Druid:

```yaml
scrape_configs:
  - job_name: 'druid-metrics'
    scrape_interval: 15s
    static_configs:
      - targets: ['druid_broker:8081', 'druid_historical:8083', 'druid_coordinator:8081']
```

This setup specifies that Prometheus should periodically scrape metrics from Druid broker, historical, and coordinator nodes, drawing valuable data that can be used for performance monitoring and alerts.

The **ELK Stack** offers a powerful centralized logging solution for analyzing Druid's operation logs. Elasticsearch serves as the engine for storing and searching through log data, while Kibana provides visualization tools for exploring these logs.

213

Configuring the ELK Stack involves setting up Logstash to parse and ingest logs from Druid nodes into Elasticsearch, followed by crafting Kibana dashboards to visualize and analyze this data. Consider the following fragment for Logstash configuration:

```
input {
  file {
    path => "/var/log/druid/*.log"
    start_position => "beginning"
  }
}

filter {
  grok {
    match => { "message" => "%{TIMESTAMP_ISO8601:timestamp} - %{
        LOGLEVEL:loglevel} - %{DATA:process} - %{GREEDYDATA:logmessage}"
      }
  }
}

output {
  elasticsearch {
    hosts => ["localhost:9200"]
    index => "druid-logs-%{+YYYY.MM.dd}"
  }
}
```

The above configuration snippet enables Logstash to read Druid logs, parse them using pattern matching, and then forward the structured data to Elasticsearch for storage and subsequent analysis.

For system administrators and data engineers, the selection of one or a combination of these tools depends on several factors including the scale of the Druid deployment, prevailing infrastructure, specific monitoring requirements, existing tool chains, and budget constraints. Once the monitoring tools are appropriately configured, they provide extensive visibility into the system's performance, enabling efficient troubleshooting as well as preemptive identification and mitigation of performance bottlenecks and system failures.

Deploying these solutions in a scaled environment may necessitate additional considerations such as high availability, load balancing, and redundancy to ensure that monitoring solutions do not become a single point of failure. Moreover, periodically reviewing and updating monitoring tools and practices helps in accommodating the evolving metrics and operational nuances introduced by newer Druid versions and associated ecosystem changes.

Overall, effectively setting up and integrating monitoring tools with Apache Druid fosters a resilient data processing environment that benefits from early detection of potential issues, efficient resource utilization, and enhanced operational insight, all of which are pivotal to maintaining Druid's performance and reliability.

8.2 Understanding Druid Metrics

Comprehending Druid metrics is fundamental to effectively monitoring and optimizing a Druid cluster. These metrics provide invaluable insights into query performance, node health, and resource utilization, which are critical for ensuring optimum performance and timely identification of potential issues. Druid exposes a wide array of metrics that are accessible via its metrics endpoints, which can be aggregated, visualized, and analyzed using various monitoring tools such as Grafana, Prometheus, or custom scripts. This section elaborates on the primary categories of Druid metrics, illustrating how each contributes to the monitoring strategy.

Druid metrics are broadly categorized into query performance metrics, system and resource usage metrics, and other process-specific metrics. Each metric can provide keen insights into various aspects of your Druid cluster's health and performance:

Query Performance Metrics are pivotal in assessing the efficiency of query execution within the Druid environment. These metrics reveal details such as query time, latency, throughput, and typical query patterns. Important metrics in this category include:

- query/time: Denotes the time taken to execute queries, often measured in milliseconds. High query times can indicate processing bottlenecks or under-provisioned resources.

- query/count: Tracks the total number of queries processed, which can help understand the load patterns on the Druid cluster over time.

A typical approach to monitor these metrics is using a tool like Grafana, which could graph the query/time over time to help spot trends or anomalies. Below is an example configuration for Grafana to create such a visualization:

```
{
  "type": "graph",
  "targets": [
    {
      "expr": "sum(rate(druid_query_time{job=\"druid\"}[5m]))",
      "legendFormat": "{{query}}",
      "refId": "A"
    }
  ],
  "title": "Druid Query Time",
  "x-axis": {
    "mode": "time"
  }
}
```

The above snippet configures a Grafana dashboard to display the aggregated query time collected via Prometheus, grouped by individual query executions. This provides a visual affordance to easily identify spikes in query execution time that may warrant further investigation.

Node Health Metrics are critical for ensuring that each component of the Druid cluster is functioning optimally. System administrators rely on these metrics to remain aware of the availability and health of individual nodes. Key metrics include:

- jvm/mem/used: Reports on the memory currently used by the Java Virtual Machine (JVM) on which a Druid process is running.

- jvm/gc/count: Represents the count of garbage collection events, giving insights into how often memory is being reclaimed, indicating memory pressure.

- jvm/gc/time: Indicates the time taken for garbage collection, which can affect overall node performance if prolonged or frequent.

- task/success/count and task/failure/count: These track the number of successful or failed tasks executed by the indexers and middle managers.

By monitoring memory usage and garbage collection, administrators can optimize the JVM settings, ensuring efficient resource utilization and minimizing performance degradation. Here's an example script that you might use for custom alerting based on JVM memory usage:

```
import requests

def check_jvm_memory_usage():
    response = requests.get('http://druid_node_host:8081/druid/v2/metrics')
    metrics = response.json()
    jvm_memory_used = metrics.get('jvm/mem/used', 0)

    if jvm_memory_used > JVM_MEMORY_THRESHOLD:
        send_alert("JVM Memory Usage Exceeded", "Current memory usage: {}".
            format(jvm_memory_used))

def send_alert(subject, message):
    # send email or pager alert
    print(f"Alert: {subject} - {message}")

check_jvm_memory_usage()
```

This Python script fetches the current JVM memory usage from a Druid node and then checks if it exceeds a predefined threshold. If so, an alert is generated, which could be an email or a notification sent to a monitoring dashboard.

Resource Utilization Metrics are crucial for performance tuning and capacity planning. They help identify whether nodes are over- or under-utilized, aiding in decision-making regarding scaling or resource reallocation. Key metrics here encompass:

- sys/cpu: CPU usage statistics, which indicate the processor usage by Druid processes.

- sys/disk: Disk I/O operations data, which can aid in diagnosing read/write bottlenecks.

- sys/network: Network throughput metrics, crucial for understanding bandwidth usage, especially in distributed Druid deployments.

Analyzing these metrics requires understanding the baseline performance norms so that deviations can be quickly captured and investigated. For example, sustained high CPU or disk usage might prompt a need for scaling or re-architecting the cluster for better performance distribution.

217

Collecting and analyzing these metrics over time allows teams to make data-driven decisions regarding both immediate operational adjustments and longer-term architectural changes. The aggregation of these statistics through tools like Prometheus, storing them in time-series databases, and analyzing them using Grafana or similar tools enables point-in-time analysis, trend recognition, and event correlation, all critical to maintaining operational excellence.

Beyond these general metrics, Druid also provides **Process-Specific Metrics** that are valuable for understanding the role-specific performance of distinct Druid components such as brokers, overlords, middle managers, historical nodes, and coordinators. For instance, the coordinator exposes:

- segment/loadQueue/count: Indicates the number of segments queued for loading onto historical nodes, which helps in assessing data replication mechanics.

- segment/underReplicated/count: Alerts users to segments that are not adequately replicated, potentially highlighting risks to data availability due to hardware failure.

Each Druid process interacts differently with data and queries, thus a keen understanding of these metrics is necessary to ensure that the integration of Druid into a data ecosystem is optimized not just at a cluster-wide level but also at a node-specific and role-specific level.

Proactively evaluating these Druid metrics helps cluster administrators enforce quality of service (QoS) commitments, ensure compliance with operational expectations, and perform robust failure analyses post-issue identification. Researchers or analysts using Druid as a core data engine gain by having predictable and reliable data delivery mechanisms that are both performant and transparent.

Understanding and leveraging these extensive metrics are imperative for advanced deployments of Druid in production environments, and they also serve as key performance indicators for routine DR (Disaster Recovery) testing and validation scenarios. To capitalize on the benefits offered by these metrics, effective workflows should be in place to analyze, react, and adapt based on metric data, turning insights into actionable operational strategies.

8.3 Configuring Alerts and Notifications

Configuring alerts and notifications is an indispensable facet of monitoring a Druid cluster, offering the capacity to promptly identify and react to operational anomalies. This proactive measure is vital for maintaining system health and ensuring that performance expectations are consistently met. This section comprehensively explores strategies to configure alerts and notifications, tailoring them to Druid environments for enhanced responsiveness and reliability.

At the heart of configuring alerts and notifications is the understanding of what constitutes a significant event or anomaly within your Druid cluster. These events could include deviations from expected query response times, excessive resource consumption, node failures, or any metric that diverges from established norms.

One of the primary tools employed in setting up alerts for Druid is **Grafana**, due to its compatibility with various data sources and its sophisticated alerting capabilities. Grafana's alerting mechanism can be configured to set thresholds for any metrics of interest, triggering alerts when those thresholds are breached.

Creating Alerts in Grafana:

To create an alert in Grafana, begin by setting up a panel that visualizes the metric you are interested in monitoring. Configure an alert by following these general steps:

- **Select the Panel:** Choose a panel that displays the relevant metric, such as query time or CPU usage.

- **Define Alert Conditions:** Specify the conditions under which an alert should be triggered. For instance, an alert could be set for when query time exceeds a certain threshold for more than five minutes.

- **Set up Notification Channels:** Configure where notifications should be sent—email, Slack, PagerDuty, or a webhook URL.

- **Test and Save:** Check that alerts are working as expected by running tests. Adjust configurations until you are satisfied with the alert setup.

219

Here is an example of a Grafana alert configuration for monitoring 'query/time' metrics:

```
{
  "conditions": [
    {
      "evaluator": {
        "params": [1000],
        "type": "gt"
      },
      "operator": {
        "type": "and"
      },
      "query": {
        "params": [
          "A",
          "5m",
          "now"
        ]
      },
      "reducer": {
        "params": [],
        "type": "avg"
      },
      "type": "query"
    }
  ],
  "executionErrorState": "alerting",
  "frequency": "1m",
  "handler": 1,
  "name": "High Query Time Alert",
  "noDataState": "no_data",
  "notifications": [
    {
      "uid": "your_notification_channel_id"
    }
  ]
}
```

This configuration sets up an alert condition where the alert fires if the average query time exceeds 1000 milliseconds over a window of five minutes, notifying the specified channel.

Beyond Grafana, **Prometheus Alertmanager** serves as a powerful tool for handling alerts. It routes alerts generated by Prometheus to various endpoints, managing group silencing and inhibitions which is beneficial in dealing with ephemeral or non-actionable alert conditions.

Configuring Alerts with Prometheus:

To configure Prometheus Alertmanager with Druid, one has to define rules for alerting in a 'rules.yml' file and point Prometheus to use this file. Here is an illustrative example:

```
groups:
- name: druid-alerts
  rules:
  - alert: HighJVMHeapUsage
    expr: (jvm_memory_used_bytes/jvm_memory_max_bytes) > 0.85
    for: 10m
    annotations:
      summary: "High JVM Heap Usage on {{ $labels.instance }}"
      description: "JVM Heap usage is above 85\% for more than 10 minutes."
```

In this YAML configuration, an alert titled 'HighJVMHeapUsage' is triggered if the JVM heap usage exceeds 85% for a duration of 10 minutes. Such alerts might highlight memory management issues, necessitating immediate attention to potentially increase heap size or examine memory consumption patterns.

Prometheus Alertmanager further supports deduplication, grouping of alerts, and dynamically silencing alerts during deployments. Notifications through Alertmanager can be delivered across multiple channels like Slack, email, PagerDuty, or any arbitrary webhook.

Integrating with Other Notification Systems:

While Grafana and Prometheus provide robust alert and notification frameworks, Druid environments may also be integrated with external notification systems or services tailored for operational needs. For example, implementing a custom notification via a script that posts to a monitoring dashboard or logging system can be accomplished with relative ease:

```python
import requests

def send_custom_alert(subject, message):
    payload = {
        'subject': subject,
        'message': message
    }
    response = requests.post("https://my_custom_webhook.com/notify", json=
        payload)
    if response.status_code == 200:
        print("Alert sent successfully.")
    else:
        print("Failed to send alert.")

# Example usage
send_custom_alert("High Query Latency", "Query time has exceeded threshold.")
```

Such scripts enable greater customization and flexibility in how notifications are routed and presented to engineers and system operators.

Best Practices in Alert Configuration:

- **Avoid Alert Overload:** Carefully define alert thresholds to minimize false positives, which can desensitize operators to alerts or cause alert fatigue.

- **Dynamically Scale Alerts:** Use dynamic baselines if available metrics fluctuate naturally, setting alerts based on deviations from rolling averages rather than hardcoded thresholds.

- **Contextual Alerts:** Ensure that alerts provide actionable context, including potential causes and recommended actions when possible. This involves enhancing alert payloads with annotations that guide immediate diagnostic steps.

- **Testing and Refinement:** Regularly test alerts and adjust configurations to capture true positives while reducing noise. This could include retrospective analysis of alerts to refine thresholds and conditions.

By effectively configuring alerts and notifications, stakeholders can maintain high service levels and reliability across their Druid environments, proactively manage risks, and address operational anomalies before they affect user-facing services or data integrity. This proactive maintenance ensures that Druid remains responsive, performant, and reliable under varying load conditions and in the face of infrastructure changes.

8.4   Analyzing Logs for Insights

Logs are an essential component of monitoring and troubleshooting within any complex system such as a Druid cluster. These logs provide a comprehensive record of the system's activities, capturing critical events, errors, and performance metrics. Analyzing logs affords insights into system behaviors, aids in anomaly detection, and facilitates the investigation of issues. This section explores the methodologies and best practices for analyzing Druid logs to glean actionable insights.

Understanding the logging infrastructure within Druid is the first step in leveraging the power of logs. Druid follows a multi-tiered logging system where each node type—brokers, historicals, middle managers, coordinators, and overlords—produces its own logs in distinct roles. These logs can range from task execution binaries, query processing details, exception traces, to garbage collection and system health messages.

Log Collection and Aggregation:

To effectively analyze logs, it's imperative to set up a centralized log collection system. Tools such as the Elastic Stack (Elasticsearch, Logstash, Kibana), Fluentd, or open-source solutions like Graylog are commonly used for this purpose. These solutions generally involve forwarding logs from each Druid node to a central location, where they can be processed and stored for subsequent querying and visualization.

Consider a basic example using Logstash for log forwarding and processing in conjunction with Druid:

```
input {
  file {
    path => "/var/log/druid/*.log"
    start_position => "beginning"
    sincedb_path => "/dev/null"
    codec => "json"
  }
}

filter {
  grok {
    match => { "message" => "%{TIMESTAMP_ISO8601:timestamp} %{
        LOGLEVEL:loglevel} %{JAVACLASS:class} - %{GREEDYDATA:logmessage
        }" }
  }

  date {
    match => ["timestamp", "ISO8601"]
  }
}

output {
  elasticsearch {
    hosts => ["localhost:9200"]
    index => "druid-logs-%{+YYYY.MM.dd}"
  }
  stdout { codec => rubydebug }
}
```

223

This Logstash configuration specifies that Druid logs, typically structured as JSON, are read, parsed, and sent to an Elasticsearch cluster for storage. Grok patterns are used to parse log entries into structured formats based on timestamp, log level, and other custom schemas.

Log Analysis Techniques:

- Pattern Recognition: Leveraging regular expressions and machine learning techniques, patterns in log files can be identified. Repeated error patterns or anomalies in logs can signal systemic issues. This approach involves comparing current log patterns against historical baselines.

- Correlation and Contextual Analysis: Correlate logs from different systems or components. Aggregating logs from broker nodes with those from historical nodes may reveal complex interdependencies affecting performance. Contextual associations, such as correlating query logs with failure logs, facilitate identifying root causes of failures.

- Trend Analysis: Historical log data, when visualized as time series plots, can provide insights into periodic trends and anomalies. Identifying trends in logging behavior such as increasing frequency of a specific log entry can provide early warnings of potential system degradation.

- Anomaly Detection: Implement anomaly detection using unsupervised learning approaches. Examples include clustering (k-means, DBSCAN) for unexpected log entry classification or using statistical methods to establish thresholds beyond which anomalies are flagged.

Here's a Python script employing basic natural language processing for extracting entities and anomalies from logs:

```python
import re
from collections import Counter
from sklearn.feature_extraction.text import TfidfVectorizer
from sklearn.cluster import KMeans

# Sample log data
logs = [
    'INFO 2023-10-10T10:00:00 druid.query.QueryRunner - Query complete Jks82',
```

```
        'ERROR 2023-10-10T10:05:00 druid.segment.SegmentLoader - Error loading
            segment A12',
        'WARN 2023-10-10T10:10:00 druid.cache.Cache - Cache miss for key X1'
]

# Simple regex-based entity extraction
pattern = re.compile(r"(INFO|ERROR|WARN) (\d+-\d+-\d+T\d+:\d+:\d+) (\S+)
    - (.+)")
entities = [pattern.match(log).groups() for log in logs if pattern.match(log)]

entity_counter = Counter([entity[0] for entity in entities])
print(f"Log Levels Distribution: {entity_counter}")

# TF-IDF Vectorization and Clustering for Anomaly Detection
vectorizer = TfidfVectorizer(stop_words='english')
X = vectorizer.fit_transform([entity[3] for entity in entities])
num_clusters = 2
km = KMeans(n_clusters=num_clusters)
km.fit(X)

# Output cluster analysis
clusters = km.labels_.tolist()
print(f"Cluster Assignments: {clusters}")
```

In this script, basic entity extraction is performed on log messages, along with clustering that can help identify anomalous log messages by analyzing the term frequency-inverse document frequency (TF-IDF) across log entries to detect outliers or notable divergence from standard entries.

Common Log-based Insights:

- Resource Exhaustion: Through patterns of increasingly frequent garbage collection events or OutOfMemory errors in jvm logs, one can deduce memory leaks or insufficient heap configuration.

- Performance Bottlenecks: Logs showing excessive query times interlinked with system metrics logs indicating high CPU or I/O wait times suggest resource-bound performance constraints.

- Operational Anomalies: Sudden influxes in error logs, particularly when associated with task execution or data ingestion pipelines, can indicate operational issues such as network partitioning or data corruption.

- Security Breaches: Unauthorized access attempts, typically identifiable in the auth logs, flagged by unusual patterns or accesses from abnormal IP addresses.

- Application Errors: Recurring errors in application-level logs may suggest bugs or necessitate application-level debugging where exception stack traces offer pointers to problem areas.

Channels like Kibana, with customizable dashboards, amplify the ability to visualize log trends and synthesize insights rapidly, supporting scripted reports and real-time dashboards to showcase critical aspects of log behavior.

Best Practices in Log Management:

- Employ Rotations and Archiving: Implement log rotation to manage disk usage and archive critical logs for long-term storage and compliance purposes.

- Log Levels Management: Use appropriate logging levels (DEBUG, INFO, WARN, ERROR, CRITICAL) to ensure log volume is manageable and each entry's importance is preserved.

- Ensure Log Consistency: Establish consistent logging formats across nodes for easier parsing and analysis and harmonize time zones for temporal correlation.

- Securing Logs: Implement access controls and encryption for logs containing sensitive information to comply with data protection regulations and to avoid leaks.

Analyzing logs in Druid can transform raw operational data into actionable intelligence, playing a mission-critical role in maintaining cluster stability, performance, and security. The methodologies outlined will empower operators not only to detect and diagnose issues promptly but also to gain comprehensive oversight of their infrastructure's historical and real-time behavior.

8.5 Common Troubleshooting Scenarios

Operating an Apache Druid cluster entails addressing a variety of challenges that administrators might face during deployment, scaling, or routine operations. Recognizing common troubleshooting scenarios and understanding their resolutions is essential for maintaining cluster health and ensuring consistent performance. In this section, we explore typical issues encountered in Druid environments, along with systematic approaches to diagnosing and resolving them.

Scenario 1: Query Performance Issues

One of the most common challenges in Druid environments involves suboptimal query performance, which can manifest as increased response times or timeouts. Query performance degradation often results from several factors including inefficient resource utilization, suboptimal query design, or data layout configurations.

Diagnosis and Resolution:

- **Examine Query Metrics:** Analyze the 'query/failed', 'query/time', and 'query/wait/time' metrics to identify trends and irregularities. An uptick in 'query/wait/time' may suggest resource contention.

- **Profile Slow Queries:** Use the built-in Druid query profiler or view the broker logs, which may include debug information detailing query execution phases. Capture the most time-intensive parts of the query plan.

- **Optimize Segment Utilization:** Over-segmentation may lead to high I/O wait times. Use compaction tasks to merge smaller segments into larger ones where appropriate, balancing between segment size and query parallelism.

```
{
  "type": "compact",
  "dataSource": "my_data_source",
  "interval": "2023-01-01/2023-01-31",
  "tuningConfig": {
    "targetCompactionSizeBytes": 500000000
  },
  "granularitySpec": {
    "segmentGranularity": "day"
  }
}
```

- **Enhance Query Filters:** Use indexed columns for high-cardinality filters to accelerate query processing. Additionally,

227

evaluate if time-based partitioning could benefit temporal queries.

Scenario 2: Data Ingestion Failures

Data ingestion issues often arise due to misconfigurations in input source definitions, file formats, or schema mismatches, leading to incomplete or failed ingestion tasks.

Diagnosis and Resolution:

- **Review Task Logs:** Inspect middle manager logs for errors pertaining to task failures. Common issues include incorrect paths or formats, schema drift, or insufficient permissions.

- **Validate Ingestion Specs:** Check JSON ingestion specification files for structural correctness. A frequent issue is a mismatch between the data types declared in the ingestion spec and the actual data.

- **Data Format Issues:** Ensure input formats are correctly declared. For instance, mismatched CSV delimiters or incorrect JSON parsers can cause ingestion tasks to fail unexpectedly.

```
{
  "type": "index_parallel",
  "spec": {
    "ioConfig": {
      "type": "index_parallel",
      "inputSource": {
        "type": "local",
        "baseDir": "/path/to/data",
        "filter": "*.csv"
      },
      "inputFormat": {
        "type": "csv",
        "columns": ["timestamp", "metric1", "metric2"],
        "findColumnsFromHeader": true
      }
    }
  }
}
```

- **Capacity Constraints:** Monitor resource allocation for ingestion tasks—insufficient 'worker' or 'thread' resources can curtail task execution. Adjust these in the middle manager configuration as necessary.

Scenario 3: Historical Node Overload

Occasionally, historical nodes may become overloaded due to excessive segment requests or data skews, resulting in degraded retrieval performance or node failures.

Diagnosis and Resolution:

- **Load Queue Observations:** Analyze 'segment/loadQueue/count' and 'segment/memoryUsed' metrics to ascertain if historical nodes are struggling to maintain segment objectives.

- **Redistribute Load:** Use Druid's Coordinator console to rebalance segments across available historical nodes.

- **Tune Segment Cache:** Evaluate 'druid.server.maxSize' and 'druid.server.http.numConnections', scaling up server capacities or redistributing segments to distribute the load more evenly.

- **Horizontal Scaling:** Consider scaling out historical nodes, increasing processing bandwidth, especially if the resource utilization remains consistently high.

Scenario 4: Node Communication Failures

Communication failures between Druid nodes could manifest due to network partition issues, incorrectly configured node communication ports, or service discovery problems.

Diagnosis and Resolution:

- **Network Diagnostics:** Verify basic network connectivity and latency among nodes using tools like 'ping' or 'traceroute'. Inspect firewall rules ensuring permissive Druid node traffic.

- **Zookeeper Issues:** Druid relies significantly on Apache Zookeeper. Ensure that Zookeeper nodes are accessible and properly cocooning the expected paths necessary for service discovery. 'zk' logs are invaluable for this analysis.

229

- **Port Configuration:** Double-check port numbers in configuration settings ('druid.port', 'druid.service.curd') corresponding to the respective node type. These ports must not conflict with other running services.

```
"zk": {
  "druid.zk.service.host": "zookeeper_host:2181",
  "druid.zk.paths.base": "/druid/base"
}
```

Scenario 5: Memory and Garbage Collection Issues

Memory bottlenecks or excessive garbage collection can lead to significant performance degradation, potentially leading to mid-query failures.

Diagnosis and Resolution:

- **Monitor JVM Memory:** Leverage metrics like 'jvm/mem/-max' and 'jvm/gc/time' to gauge memory suitability and GC overhead at runtime.

- **Tweak JVM Options:** Based on GC analysis from logs, tune JVM options such as heap size ('-Xms' and '-Xmx') and GC algorithms (e.g., G1 GC or ZGC).

- **Garbage Collection Logs:** Analyze garbage collection logs regularly to detect anomalies or repeated full GCs indicating inefficient memory utilization.

Overcoming these scenarios involves not just knowing potential issues but also applying understanding of performance patterns and system limits. Building robust troubleshooting skills in Druid often requires familiarity with underlying logs, metric dashboards, task and segment management consoles, and the natural architecture and flow of the Druid ecosystem. By developing an efficient strategy to diagnose issues early and comprehensively, administrators can better ensure that their Druid installations continuously deliver the intended high-performance outcomes.

8.6 Debugging and Resolution Techniques

For maintaining the high performance and reliability of an Apache Druid cluster, it is imperative to have robust debugging and resolution techniques at hand. This section provides a comprehensive examination of effective strategies and methodologies for debugging common and complex issues that emerge in Druid environments. Utilizing these approaches ensures that users can swiftly identify discrepancies and implement resolutions without significant downtime or performance degradation.

Debugging in Druid is multi-faceted, encompassing everything from query optimization issues to configuration misalignments and suboptimal hardware utilization. The ability to effectively isolate and resolve these issues requires a combination of log analysis, performance metrics interpretations, and strategic interventions at both software and hardware levels.

1. Systematic Debugging Approach

A consistent debugging framework or process can help structure thoughts, track issues, and document findings, improving resolution times and reducing recurrence. The basic steps in a systematic debugging approach can include:

- Reproduce the Issue: Ensure the problem is repeatable to reliably examine the symptoms and confirm a solution.

- Hypothesize Potential Causes: Based on symptoms, form hypotheses for potential root causes, which will drive your investigation.

- Gather Diagnostic Data: Collect logs, metrics, and system states that illuminate the issue context.

- Isolate the Problem: Narrow down subsystems involved, whether it is a particular node type or a specific query type in Druid.

- Implement and Test Solutions: Apply changes one at a time to address hypothesized root causes and evaluate outcomes.

- Document Findings: Keep a record of the issue, its diagnosis, and resolution for future references.

2. Log-based Debugging Techniques

Proper log analysis is often the starting point for debugging in Druid. Logs document operational data, exceptions, and trace events critical to identifying root causes.

- Log Level Management: Adjust log levels to ensure details (e.g., DEBUG level) relevant to the issue are captured without inundation of too much information. For deeper insights, temporarily escalate the log level to capture detailed outputs specific to problematic nodes or operations.

```
druid.common.config={}
druid.logging.logLevel=debug # Temporarily set for deeper investigation,
    remember to change back to info/warn level.
```

- Exception Stack Traces: Focus on stack traces in error logs which highlight Java exception failures or uncaught runtime anomalies. This provides clues about where failures occur and potential dependencies involved.

- Comprehensive Log Analysis Tools: Utilize log analysis tools like Elasticsearch and Kibana for pattern recognition or anomaly detection across massive log datasets. Creating dashboards to visualize logs can help spot recurring issues or failure states.

3. Metrics-driven Debugging Approach

Metrics expose system behavior over time, enabling administrators to identify performance bottlenecks or anomalous trends:

- Real-time Monitoring: By integrating Prometheus with Druid, monitor JVM memory usage ('jvm/mem/used'), CPU loads ('sys/cpu'), and query times ('query/time') with dashboards that can alert you when thresholds are breached.

- Historical Analysis: Leverage historical metrics to detect when an issue first arose which could relate to system updates, workload changes, or configuration adjustments.

4. Query Optimization Techniques

Suboptimal query performance is a frequent focal point during debugging. Common methods for addressing these involve:

- Query Execution Analysis: Employ Druid's native query logs or tools to measure query execution times, capture complex query plans, and evaluate their efficiency.

- Data Layout Improvements: Optimize data segment structure and partitioning. Horizontal query distribution can be improved by refining segment granularity to suit workload characteristics.

- Leverage Caches: Ensuring optimal use of 'cache' and 'result-caching' can considerably enhance repeated query throughput.

```
{
    "druid.broker.cache.useCache": true,
    "druid.broker.cache.populateCache": true,
    "druid.broker.cache.unCacheable": ["groupBy", "select"]
}
```

- Utilize Indices: Enhance the utilization of secondary indices for columns most frequently filtered or grouped upon. The use of bitmap indices optimizes filter operations on high-cardinality columns.

5. Configuration and Resource Allocation Debugging

Irregularities in configuration and resource allocations often result in subpar performance or stability issues:

- Validate Configuration Files: Ensure configurations (e.g., 'runtime.properties') reflect resource capacities and application requirements. Validate properties using automated linting tools to detect common errors or misconfigurations.

- Resource Monitoring: Assess the resource distribution across the cluster using monitoring solutions to determine if vertical or horizontal scaling is required, or if load balancing strategies should be adjusted.

6. Deep Dive into JVM Tuning

Java applications like Druid rely on the JVM heap configurations and garbage collection settings for resource efficiency:

- Heap Memory Adjustments: Tailor '-Xmx' and '-Xms' settings to alleviate memory pressure and to prevent GC thrashing.

- GC Logs and Analysis: Regularly review garbage collection logs to identify whether frequent full GCs contribute to performance degradation and adjust objectives or GC algorithms as necessary.

```
# Enables GC Logs for further analysis
-Dcom.sun.management.jmxremote
-XX:+PrintGCDetails
-XX:+PrintGCTimeStamps
-XX:+UseG1GC
-XX:MaxGCPauseMillis=200
```

Incorporating these debugging and resolution techniques into routine cluster management can greatly reduce downtime and ensure a more robust performance baseline for Druid. Regularly updating skill sets around log analysis tools, performance monitoring environments, and systems architecture will not only equip teams in supporting dynamic workloads but also in forecasting resource requirements and potential scaling strategies. Through these practices, system administrators can foster a responsive, resilient, and high-performing Druid installation.

8.7 Performance Degradation Investigations

Performance degradation in Apache Druid can manifest through increased query latencies, resource bottlenecks, or system stalling, impacting the overall efficiency of real-time data analytics. Identifying and addressing these performance issues is crucial for maintaining a responsive and robust Druid cluster. This section provides a comprehensive exploration into the methodologies for investigating performance degradation, with actionable insights for diagnosis and optimization.

Delving into performance degradation involves analyzing various components of the Druid architecture to understand where and why bottlenecks are occurring. This requires a detailed look at both cluster-wide and node-specific metrics, configurations, and query strategies.

1. Identifying Symptoms of Performance Degradation

The first step in performance degradation investigations is recognizing symptoms that indicate an existing issue. Typical symptoms include:

- **Elevated Query Latency**: Queries take longer to complete than usual, which can result in unmet SLAs for real-time analytics.

- **Increased Error Rates**: Higher instances of timeouts or failures in query execution.

- **Resource Saturation**: Consistent high utilization of CPU, memory, or I/O resources across nodes.

- **Lag in Data Refresh**: Data ingestion backlogs leading to stale or incomplete datasets.

Quick detection involves configuring monitoring tools like Grafana or Prometheus with alerting capabilities to ensure any deviations from normal performance metrics are immediately flagged.

2. Analyzing Query Performance

A substantial portion of performance issues in Druid can be traced back to inefficient query patterns. Investigating these involves:

- **Query Profiling**: Use Druid's query metrics ('query/time', 'query/cpu/milliseconds') to assess and compare query execution performance over time. Additionally, use the 'EXPLAIN PLAN' feature for visibility into query execution paths.

```
curl -X POST 'http://druid-broker:8082/druid/v2/?pretty' -H 'Content-Type:
    application/json' -d '{
  "query": {
    "queryType": "groupBy",
    "dataSource": "my_datasource",
```

```
    "dimensions": ["dim1", "dim2"],
    "granularity": "day",
    "intervals": ["2023-01-01/2023-01-31"]
  }
}'
```

This sample query execution can be analyzed further for bottlenecks using brokers' logs that detail time spent in various query stages.

- **Query Optimization**: Use indexing strategies judiciously. Incorporate bitmap and sketch indices for high-cardinality columns to expedite filters. Opt for optimized query plans, including combining smaller segments into larger ones tactically.

3. Resource Utilization and Configuration Management

Resource inefficiencies often stem from misconfiguration or the uneven distribution of resources:

- **Evaluate Hardware Utilization**: Utilize druid.monitoring extensions to gather and visualize CPU, I/O, and memory checks. Flag nodes consistently running near their resource limits and consider vertical scaling or load redistribution.

- **Tune Configuration**: Assess configurations in runtime.properties emphasizing memory allocation (druid.processing.buffer.sizeBytes, druid.server.maxSize) to ensure they match current load requirements and hardware capabilities.

```
druid.processing.buffer.sizeBytes=500MB
druid.server.maxSize=200GB
```

- **Optimize JVM Parameters**: JVM flags such as -Xms, -Xmx, and GC tuning parameters (-XX:+UseG1GC, -XX:MaxGCPauseMillis) should be optimized according to profiling insights to prevent frequent GC cycles contributing to latency.

236

4. Segment Management and Optimization

Effective segment management is key to improved data retrieval speeds and throughput:

- **Segment Size and Granularity**: Assess segment sizes using segment/size and segment/count metrics. Smaller segments might increase parallelism but can also cause overhead; conversely, overly large segments can strain memory and I/O.

- **Automate Compaction**: Implement automatic data compaction tasks to consolidate small segments, reducing segment load time (segment/loadQueue/size).

```
{
  "type": "compact",
  "dataSource": "sample_data_source",
  "tuningConfig": {
    "type": "index_parallel",
    "maxRowsInMemory": 1000,
    "targetCompactionSizeBytes": 100000000
  }
}
```

5. Investigating Node and Service Failures

Service or node failures can exacerbate performance woes, underscoring the need for diagnostics in these areas:

- **Check Node Logs**: Detailed inspection of node logs (historical, broker, middleManager logs) for abnormal shutdowns, which can reveal underlying issues such as heap exhaustion or I/O contention.

- **Zookeeper Monitoring**: As Druid uses Apache Zookeeper for coordination tasks, ensure Zookeeper instances are stable and responsive. Fluctuations here can cause wider coordination delays within the cluster.

6. Utilizing Advanced Monitoring Tools

Leverage tools such as Datadog, New Relic, or custom dashboards in Grafana to aggregate and visualize more complex scenarios, facilitating drilldowns into historical data correlations.

237

- **Statistical Analysis and Predictive Monitoring**: Using machine learning models or statistical methods to forecast trends from historical data, potentially preventing incidents before they manifest fully.

Performance degradation investigations rely heavily on proactive monitoring, structured diagnostic approaches, and strategic tuning of both configuration and query processes. It's beneficial to continuously iterate on monitoring setups, fine-tune system parameters, and create feedback loops where insights derived from diagnostics inform future system designs and operational strategies. Understanding these techniques, and practicing their application in an iterative manner, ultimately empowers administrators to uphold the high-performance mandates of their Druid clusters.

Chapter 9

Integrating Druid with Other Systems

This chapter explores the integration of Apache Druid with various external systems and data sources to extend its capabilities. It provides guidance on connecting Druid to data sources such as cloud storage services, databases, and streaming platforms like Apache Kafka for real-time data ingestion. The use of Druid with Hadoop and Spark for batch processing and with BI tools like Tableau for data visualization is discussed. Additionally, it examines the interoperability with REST APIs for seamless external interactions and offers strategies for building custom applications leveraging Druid. Considerations for deployment in multi-cloud environments are also outlined to address integration challenges effectively.

9.1 Connecting Druid to Data Sources

Apache Druid's strength as a real-time analytics database comes from its ability to efficiently ingest, index, and query a wide array of data sources. The process of connecting Druid to multiple data avenues, such as cloud storage, relational databases, and streaming platforms, involves understanding the plethora of connectors and ingestion capabilities that Druid offers. This section delves into the nitty-gritty of facilitating this integration, ensuring robust data flow for high-performance analytics.

- Druid's architecture supports several types of ingestions, primarily categorized as batch and real-time ingestion.

- Batch ingestion involves processing a large volume of static data tables often found in cloud storage or databases, whereas real-time ingestion focuses on dynamically flowing data streams, commonly sourced from platforms such as Apache Kafka or AWS Kinesis.

- This dual ingestion capability allows Druid to serve a vast range of analytical scenarios.

- Cloud storage is often the preferred choice for enterprises due to its scalability, reliability, and cost-effectiveness.

- Druid can integrate seamlessly with cloud storage solutions such as Amazon S3, Google Cloud Storage, and Microsoft Azure Blob Storage.

- The ability to leverage these services for batch ingestion requires configuring Druid's external data sources section in its configuration files.

To ingest data from Amazon S3, the configuration may look like:

```
{
  "type": "index_parallel",
  "spec": {
    "dataSchema": {
      "dataSource": "example-datasource",
      "parser": {
        "type": "string",
        "parseSpec": {
          "format": "json",
          "dimensionsSpec": {
            "dimensions": ["dim1", "dim2", "dim3"]
          }
        }
      }
    }
```

```
  },
  "ioConfig": {
    "type": "index_parallel",
    "inputSource": {
      "type": "s3",
      "bucket": "my-bucket",
      "prefix": "data/prefix/",
      "objectMapper": {
        "type": "default"
      }
    },
    "inputFormat": {
      "type": "json"
    }
  },
  "tuningConfig": {
    "type": "index_parallel"
  }
 }
}
```

In this configuration, the inputSource specifies an S3 bucket and a prefix under which the data files reside. The inputFormat can vary between JSON, CSV, or any other supported format depending on the nature of the data. Security and IAM roles need to be correctly configured to allow Druid access to these resources securely.

For many organizations, vital business data resides within relational databases such as MySQL, PostgreSQL, or Oracle. Druid's native ingestion capabilities allow for seamless integration with these sources using JDBC connectors. The diversity of relational database support allows for extensive flexibility in managing data ingestion workflows.

Below is a JDBC ingestion task example for ingesting data from a PostgreSQL database:

```
{
  "type": "index_parallel",
  "spec": {
    "ioConfig": {
      "type": "index_parallel",
      "inputSource": {
        "type": "jdbc",
        "connectorConfig": {
          "createTables": false,
          "connectURI": "jdbc:postgresql://host:port/database",
          "user": "db_user",
          "password": "db_password"
        },
        "table": "example_table",
        "columns": ["column1", "column2", "column3"],
      },
```

```
    "inputFormat": {
      "type": "tsv"
    }
  },
  "tuningConfig": {
    "type": "index_parallel"
  },
  "dataSchema": {
    "dataSource": "database-datasource",
    "granularitySpec": {
      "type": "uniform",
      "segmentGranularity": "DAY",
      "queryGranularity": "HOUR",
      "rollup": true
    }
  }
 }
}
```

This ingestion configuration initializes a JDBC connection and specifies the table from which data is extracted. Note that Druid requires
the necessary database drivers to be available within its runtime environment.

The need for real-time streaming data ingestion is crucial in many modern applications, where event-driven architecture forms the backbone
of operations. Apache Kafka and AWS Kinesis are among the many
supported streaming platforms that enable Druid to ingest data with
minimal latency.

For Kafka, configuring a real-time ingestion involves setting up a supervisor task that can dynamically monitor and consume records:

```
{
  "type": "kafka",
  "dataSchema": {
    "dataSource": "kafka-ds",
    "parser": {
      "type": "string",
      "parseSpec": {
        "format": "json",
        "dimensionsSpec": {
          "dimensions": ["event_time", "event_type", "value"]
        }
      }
    }
  },
  "ioConfig": {
    "topic": "events-topic",
    "consumerProperties": {
      "bootstrap.servers": "kafka-broker:9092"
    }
  },
```

```
"tuningConfig": {
  "maxRowsInMemory": 10000,
  "intermediatePersistPeriod": "PT1M"
}
}
```

The consumerProperties field specifies Kafka's broker details, and data schema configurations need to match the message format used in Kafka topics. Druid's Kafka indexing service ensures fault tolerance and high throughput, crucial for mission-critical real-time analytics.

Druid's data processing capabilities are bolstered by its support for diverse data formats including JSON, CSV, Avro, and Parquet. Each format has benefits depending on the data characteristics, and Druid's configuration for ingestion can handle transformations necessary for optimized querying.

To ingest data in Avro format from Google Cloud Storage, the configuration is modified similarly as follows:

```
{
  "type": "index_parallel",
  "spec": {
    "ioConfig": {
      "type": "index_parallel",
      "inputSource": {
        "type": "google",
        "bucket": "my-bucket",
        "prefix": "data-files/",
      },
      "inputFormat": {
        "type": "avro_ocf"
      }
    },
    "dataSchema": {
      "dataSource": "avro-datasource",
      "parser": {
        "type": "avroStream",
        "parseSpec": {
          "format": "avro",
          "dimensionsSpec": {
            "dimensions": ["id", "name", "timestamp"]
          }
        }
      }
    }
  }
}
```

For Avro-encoded data, inputFormat is adjusted accordingly to represent Avro object container format. This versatility allows analysts to choose a format that best suits their storage and operational constraints.

During ingestion, Druid enables extensive data transformation and enrichment through the use of its supported expression language, accommodating complex operations from simple calculations to advanced transformations. This makes it possible to reshape data directly as it enters Druid, avoiding post-ingestion modifications.

An example of an inline data transformation is as follows:

```
{
  "type": "index_parallel",
  "spec": {
    "dataSchema": {
      "dataSource": "transform-datasource",
      "parser": {
        "type": "string",
        "parseSpec": {
          "format": "json",
          "dimensionsSpec": {
            "dimensions": ["newField"],
            "transformSpec": {
              "transforms": [
                {
                  "type": "expression",
                  "name": "newField",
                  "expression": "concat(name, '_transformed')"
                }
              ]
            }
          }
        }
      }
    },
    "ioConfig": {
      "type": "index_parallel",
      "inputSource": {
        "type": "http",
        "uris": ["http://data-source-url"]
      }
    }
  }
}
```

In this instance, the transformSpec employs an expression transform operation, concatenating a suffix to each value in the 'name' field, demonstrating how ingest-time transformations enhance analytical capabilities.

Connecting Druid effectively to a wide array of data sources unleashes its full potential in delivering real-time and batch analytics. By closely aligning these ingestion strategies with organizational data architecture, Druid becomes more than an analytical engine; it transitions into a pivotal piece of the big data ecosystem.

9.2 Integrating with Apache Kafka

Apache Kafka is a distributed streaming platform used for building real-time data pipelines and streaming applications. It is renowned for its horizontal scalability, high-throughput, and fault-tolerant architecture, making it an ideal choice for real-time analytics. Integrating Apache Druid with Kafka leverages these strengths, enabling seamless ingestion of event streams into Druid for analysis. The integration can be divided into configuring Kafka topics, understanding Druid's Kafka indexing service, and administering the ingestion processes effectively.

Understanding Kafka Topics

At the core of Kafka's architecture are topics, which are categories or feeds to which records are published. Each topic can support multiple consumers, allowing data to be distributed efficiently across various applications. The key features of Kafka topics, such as partitioning and replication, dictate how data is stored and accessed. When integrating with Druid, it is crucial to set up these topics considering the data volume and ingestion rate to optimize performance.

For each topic, data is broken down into partitions, with each partition acting as a sequential log of records. The degree of partitioning is a critical factor in balancing load across consumer services like Druid's Kafka indexing tasks. More partitions facilitate greater concurrency in consumption but require more sophisticated management of read offsets and data order preservation.

Connecting Druid with Kafka

Druid's Kafka indexing service is designed to connect directly to Kafka topics, listening and consuming messages as they are published. This service operates using a supervisor-task model where supervisors oversee the creation and management of ingestion tasks.

A basic Kafka ingestion task configuration is shown below:

```
{
```

```
"type": "kafka",
"dataSchema": {
  "dataSource": "kafka-source",
  "parser": {
    "type": "string",
    "parseSpec": {
      "format": "json",
      "dimensionsSpec": {
        "dimensions": ["event_time", "user_id", "user_action"]
      }
    }
  },
  "granularitySpec": {
    "type": "uniform",
    "segmentGranularity": "hour",
    "queryGranularity": "minute"
  }
},
"ioConfig": {
  "topic": "events-topic",
  "replicas": 3,
  "taskCount": 3,
  "useEarliestOffset": true,
  "consumerProperties": {
    "bootstrap.servers": "kafka-broker:9092"
  }
},
"tuningConfig": {
  "maxRowsInMemory": 10000,
  "intermediatePersistPeriod": "PT10M",
  "logParseExceptions": true
}
}
```

This configuration specifies a Kafka topic (events-topic) that Druid will consume from. The dataSchema outlines the structure of the data, with a focus on the format and dimensions expected. The granularity specification assists in optimizing how Druid partitions data over its timeline.

Tuning the Ingestion Process

Fine-tuning the Kafka ingestion process is essential for achieving optimal resource allocation and query performance. Several parameters in the configuration file impact how ingestion happens, potentially affecting latency, memory usage, and fault tolerance.

- taskCount: Determines how many Kafka indexing tasks will be spawned to consume from the partitions concurrently. A higher value can enhance throughput but requires sufficient infrastructure to support these tasks.

- replicas: Defines the number of task replicas that are maintained. Replication ensures that even if one task fails, there are others available to continue ingestion without data loss.

- useEarliestOffset: This parameter controls whether tasks start consumption from the earliest available record in a partition or from the latest, impacting the starting point of data history analysis.

- maxRowsInMemory: Limits the number of rows buffered in-memory before they are persisted to segment files. This has implications on memory usage and data throughput.

- intermediatePersistPeriod: Dictates how frequently intermediate data is persisted to disk to prevent data loss. This not only aids in disaster recovery but also facilitates eventual consistency in data analysis.

Handling Data Transformations and Enrichments

Druid's ingestion from Kafka not only supports basic data extraction but also allows for inline transformations using an expression language. This capability is invaluable for enriching data streams before they are made available for analysis.

An example of an inline transformation with enhanced specifications could be:

```
{
  "type": "kafka",
  "dataSchema": {
    "dataSource": "kafka-transformed-source",
    "parser": {
      "type": "string",
      "parseSpec": {
        "format": "json",
        "dimensionsSpec": {
          "dimensions": ["user_id", "event_type", "new_metric"],
          "transformSpec": {
            "transforms": [
              {
                "type": "expression",
                "name": "new_metric",
                "expression": "if(user_action == 'click', metrics + 1, metrics)"
              }
            ]
          }
        }
      }
    },
```

```
    "metricsSpec": [
      {
        "type": "count",
        "name": "total_count"
      }
    ]
  }
},
"granularitySpec": {
  "type": "uniform",
  "segmentGranularity": "day",
  "queryGranularity": "minute"
}
},
"ioConfig": {
  "topic": "enriched-events",
  "replicas": 2,
  "taskCount": 5,
  "useEarliestOffset": false,
  "consumerProperties": {
    "bootstrap.servers": "kafka-cluster:9092"
  }
},
"tuningConfig": {
  "maxRowsInMemory": 8000,
  "intermediatePersistPeriod": "PT5M",
  "logParseExceptions": true
}
}
```

In this scenario, each ingested record undergoes a transformation where a new field, new_metric, is calculated conditionally. This pre-processing of data aids in specifically targeting the analytics needed for particular use cases without the need for post-ingestion adjustment.

Managing Schema Evolution

The dynamic and evolving nature of business requirements often necessitates adjustments in data schemas over time. Druid handles schema evolution by allowing dimensional additions transparently since each segment retains its schema metadata. However, proper forward planning is indispensable to ensure changes in the Kafka event schema do not introduce inconsistencies or lead to the reprocessing of large volumes of historical data.

Implementing a message versioning system can aid in this process, where newer versions of events encapsulate new fields and potentially deprecate obsolete ones. Implementing a deserialization process that accounts for message versions ensures that older data remains compatible with current analysis demands.

Monitoring and Optimization Practices

Monitoring the integration pipelines is crucial for detecting bottlenecks and ensuring the reliable delivery of analytics. The synergy of Druid and Kafka benefits substantially from tooling such as Kafka's own suite of lag monitoring utilities, aligning them with Druid's metrics-related queries for a holistic view of the ecosystem's performance.

Moreover, optimizing Kafka broker configurations around data retention and log segment sizes can better align with Druid's ingestion cycles, preventing overburdened topics and ensuring timely data availability.

Through this integration, Druid surpasses mere data consumption, evolving into an agile, scalable analytical platform adept at handling the demands of real-time data environments. Proper configurations, combined with best practices, allow leveraging of both platforms' strengths, ensuring swift, accurate, and actionable insights.

9.3   Using Druid with Hadoop and Spark

The integration of Druid with big data processing frameworks such as Hadoop and Spark enhances its capability to fulfill comprehensive ETL (Extract, Transform, Load) scenarios and complex analytical queries. While Druid serves as a real-time analytics database, Hadoop and Spark enable large-scale data processing and transformation. By leveraging the power of these tools together, organizations can orchestrate sophisticated data workflows, promoting effectively optimized analytical pipelines.

Integrating with Hadoop for Batch Processing

Hadoop is a versatile framework designed for the distributed storage and processing of large datasets using its high-throughput HDFS (Hadoop Distributed File System) and MapReduce programming model. Druid harnesses these capabilities for batch ingestion, where historical data directories are processed to create queryable segments.

Druid offers a specific Hadoop-based ingestion method that employs Hadoop's capabilities to perform tasks like data preparation, transfor-

249

mation, schema validation, and ingestion into Druid segments. This is particularly advantageous when dealing with extensive data stored in HDFS.

Configuring Hadoop Batch Ingestion

For batch ingestion, a Hadoop-based ingestion task is created to define the source, schema, and input format, as shown in the YAML configuration file example below:

```
{
  "type": "hadoop",
  "dataSchema": {
    "dataSource": "hadoop-datasource",
    "parser": {
      "type": "string",
      "parseSpec": {
        "format": "json",
        "dimensionsSpec": {
          "dimensions": ["time", "category", "action", "value"]
        }
      }
    },
    "granularitySpec": {
      "segmentGranularity": "DAY",
      "queryGranularity": "HOUR",
      "intervals": ["2022-01-01/2023-01-01"]
    }
  },
  "ioConfig": {
    "inputSpec": {
      "type": "hdfs",
      "paths": "/user/hive/warehouse/events/"
    }
  },
  "tuningConfig": {
    "type": "hadoop",
    "jobProperties": {
      "mapreduce.job.reduces": "2"
    }
  }
}
```

The task executes within the Hadoop ecosystem, leveraging its native parallel processing. The inputSpec specifies HDFS directories containing data files, while jobProperties can customize job settings such as the number of reduce tasks. Hadoop's robust fault tolerance ensures reliable ingestion processing, redistributing workloads upon any task failures.

Integrating with Spark for In-Memory Processing

Apache Spark is an open-source analytics engine designed for large-scale data processing, excelling in its in-memory computing capabilities. Integrating Druid with Spark combines the fast query performance of Druid with Spark's powerful ETL and data processing functionalities, optimizing overall data pipeline efficiency.

Spark can be utilized to enrich data, conduct complex transformations, or prepare datasets precisely before ingestion into Druid. With Spark's dynamic Resilient Distributed Datasets (RDDs) and DataFrame API, analytics teams can tackle large-scale data transformations with ease.

Spark-Druid Connector

To facilitate this integration, the Spark-Druid connector is employed, allowing Spark to write data directly into Druid. It partners Spark's analytical prowess with Druid's storage optimization for rapid insights.

The following Scala example illustrates using the connector for writing DataFrames to Druid:

```
import org.apache.spark.sql.SparkSession
import org.apache.druid.spark.DruidDataFrameWriter

val spark = SparkSession.builder
  .appName("Spark Druid Integration")
  .master("local[*]")
  .getOrCreate()

val df = spark.read.json("hdfs://path/to/json/files")

df.write
  .format("org.apache.druid.spark")
  .option("druidDataSource", "spark-druid-datasource")
  .option("druidBroker", "broker-host:8082")
  .save()
```

In this example, a Spark DataFrame is created from JSON files stored in HDFS, which is then written to a Druid data source using options to specify the Druid broker and target data source name. This approach simplifies the process of ingesting transformed datasets directly from Spark, enriching Druid's analytical capacities.

Managing Workloads and Scaling Computational Resources

Synergizing Druid with Hadoop and Spark facilitates the distribution of workloads between components designed for specific functions, optimizing resource utilization and improving process efficiency. Hadoop and Spark handle the initial data stages like extraction and transforma-

251

tion, while Druid excels at storing and querying the results.

The ability to orchestrate and run tasks on Spark and Hadoop cluster managers such as YARN (Yet Another Resource Negotiator) or Kubernetes allows for scaling workloads elastically. This helps enterprises align computational resources according to demand peaks, ensuring cost-effective and sustainable operations.

Security Considerations

When integrating with frameworks like Hadoop and Spark, maintaining a robust security posture is of paramount importance. Implementing Kerberos authentication ensures secure service-level communication across distributed clusters. Additionally, fine-grained access controls can restrict access to data and resources, complementing encryption protocols for data at rest and in transit.

Advanced Techniques for Data Transformation

Combining Druid with the advanced data processing capabilities of Hadoop and Spark opens up avenues for sophisticated data transformation and enrichment that are operationally significant. For instance, time-series data can undergo normalization, aggregation by window functions, or derived metric creations while traversing through Spark workflows, resulting in prepared datasets tailored for high-impact Druid visualizations.

Given Spark's ability to handle complex computational models, supporting machine learning workloads through its MLlib library, companies are empowered to deploy data science models into ETL processes, making predictions part of real-time analytical dashboards powered by Druid.

Use Cases and Practical Applications

Industries across finance, telecommunications, and e-commerce often harness the combined powers of Druid, Hadoop, and Spark for various practical applications, including:

- *Real-time Fraud Detection in Finance*: Using Spark for feature engineering, ML models can be deployed for fraud prediction before data is loaded into Druid for immediate visualization and monitoring.

- *Network Performance Monitoring in Telecommunications*: Hadoop processes call detail records (CDR) to produce meaningful network performance metrics, which are then ingested by Druid, facilitating real-time dashboards that make performance metrics comprehensible at a glance.

- *Recommendation Systems in E-Commerce*: Processing click-stream data through Spark for customer behavior analysis affords insights that, once processed into Druid, render dynamic recommendation systems efficient and responsive.

By combining expertise in these big data frameworks and leveraging their individual strengths, organizations are equipped to surmount the challenges associated with large-scale, complex data environments, paving the way for holistic, end-to-end data solutions in fast-paced digital landscapes.

9.4 Leveraging Druid with BI Tools

Integrating Apache Druid with Business Intelligence (BI) tools is instrumental in unlocking the full potential of data analytics and visualization. Druid's efficiency in managing large datasets with low-latency query performance complements popular BI platforms' capabilities, such as Tableau, Looker, and Power BI. These platforms enhance data exploration and visualization, turning raw data stored in Druid into actionable insights. This section explores best practices and strategies for effectively combining Druid's backend processing strengths with BI tools' rich frontend capabilities.

Understanding the importance of BI tools is crucial in contemporary data-driven decision-making processes. They offer interactive dashboards, real-time reporting, and advanced visualizations that aid stakeholders in interpreting complex data sets with ease. BI tools provide invaluable insights into trends, patterns, and anomalies, empowering organizations to make informed strategic choices.

Druid's powerful data aggregation, fast query response times, and real-time ingestion capabilities significantly bolster BI tools' analytical performance. This synergy allows users to interact with data more fluidly, fostering a more insightful, exploration-driven analytical environment.

Integrating Druid with Tableau   Tableau is a widely-used BI tool known for its intuitive drag-and-drop interface and robust data visualization features. Connecting Druid with Tableau transforms how data is visualized, enabling the creation of dynamic, interactive dashboards that reflect real-time data changes almost instantaneously.

Connecting Tableau to Druid   Tableau connects to Druid via JDBC (Java Database Connectivity) or through REST APIs for optimum data flow. Upon establishing this connection, Tableau acts as a gateway, seamlessly fetching data from Druid and rendering it for visualization.

Creating a JDBC connection involves the following configuration:

- **Download JDBC Driver**: Obtain the Druid JDBC driver and install it within Tableau.

- **Configure Datasource**: Within Tableau, choose Connect and select More > Other Databases (JDBC).

- **Connection Configuration**: Input the JDBC database URL, driver class, and credential details.

Example JDBC URL for Druid:

```
jdbc:avatica:remote:url=http://druid-broker-host:8082/druid/v2/sql/avatica/
```

Creating Dashboards   Once configured, Tableau enables the build-up of visual dashboards where users can apply filters, aggregates, and compute metrics on-the-fly. Users can leverage Tableau's extensive visualization options, including heat maps, scatter plots, and more, for rich, visual storytelling based on the dynamic data retrieved from Druid.

Table extracts can be constructed to understand sales velocity across different regions by combining time-series data and geographic data for dynamic spatial analytics, enhancing insights into market trends.

Optimizing Performance Druid's segment and index functionalities provide significant optimization in query response times. To capitalize on this when linked with BI tools, follow these practices:

- **Reduce Query Complexity**: BI tools often allow users to create complex queries. However, to keep performance optimal, encourage the use of simple, aggregated queries.

- **Use Granular Segments**: Ensure data is segmented optimally in Druid to align with the dimensionality and time-frames common to your BI questions.

- **Index Appropriately**: Utilize bitmap indexes in Druid to improve lookup performance on high-cardinality dimensions.

Integrating time partitioned datasets enables BI users to slice data by different periods easily, leading to quick insights despite extensive data volumes.

Integrating Druid with Looker Looker provides a modern BI solution focused on in-depth data exploration and integrated analytics workflows. Its LookML model enables complex data modeling capabilities, defining relationships and transformations directly related to Druid's data structure.

Enabling Looker-Druid Connection To establish a backend connection between Looker and Druid:

- **JDBC Driver Setup**: Similar to Tableau, install the JDBC driver and configure it within Looker.

- **Connection Details**: Setup the connection in Looker using the JDBC details, specifying server hostname and credentials.

- **Modeling with LookML**: Customize data models using LookML files to determine dimensions and measures reflective of Druid's data architecture.

Looker provides extensive caching mechanisms which, when combined with Druid's incremental data updates, ensure the latest datasets are always available for query by Looker, while intelligently managing loads on Druid itself for performance.

Using Power BI with Druid Microsoft Power BI's integration with Druid focuses on data analytics, enabling robust reporting and prototyping capabilities. This integration facilitates seamless data import and modeling, with custom visual components empowering stakeholders to explore complex scenarios visually.

Power BI-Druid Integration Connecting Power BI to Druid involves direct querying via ODBC or embedding data import mechanisms. Power BI's query editor can transform and clean data for analytical tasks.

- **ODBC Configuration**: Install and configure ODBC drivers for Druid, ensuring connectivity settings align with Druid broker configurations.

- **Direct Query Access**: Enable querying capabilities via Data Connectors for real-time data access, conforming to live data refresh requirements.

With Power BI, dashboard authors can embed Druid-managed data models, creating interactive reports where data integrity is maintained from source ingestion in Druid to end-user visualization.

Best Practices for Integrating BI Tools with Druid Implementing BI tools alongside Druid necessitates the adoption of best practices to leverage both platforms efficiently. Key practices include:

- **Data Governance and Quality**: Regularly audit and validate data ingested into Druid to ensure integrity and accuracy in BI visualizations.

256

- **Training and End-User Enablement**: Foster a culture of data literacy. Train users on effectively using BI tools and interpreting advanced visualizations, powering analytical literacy across the organization.

- **Metric Standardization**: Define and standardize metrics and KPIs within the organization to ensure uniformity in BI reporting.

- **Regular Performance Reviews**: Monitor and optimize BI tool queries frequently to minimize load on Druid clusters and maintain seamless user experiences.

Adopting these approaches enhances operational efficiency, ensuring that business users derive the maximum possible value from real-time and batch analytics facilitated through Druid and complementary BI technologies.

Analytical Workflows and Automation Modern BI ecosystems thrive on automation and streamlined analytics delivery. Coupling Druid's high-performance data ingestion and querying capabilities with automated workflows in BI tools enables scheduling of updates, alerts, and reports, anticipating stakeholders' needs.

With Druid's architectural support for multi-tenancy, and by harnessing BI tools' alert generation mechanisms, businesses enable proactive analytics strategies. These strategies allow for continuous monitoring, detecting anomalies immediately, and taking corrective measures without manual intervention.

Druid's interoperability with BI tools underpins a strategic advantage in the data-driven landscape, capturing not only the speed and depth of analytic insights but also the cognitive capacities of every decision-maker involved. Leveraging these integrations effectively positions enterprises at the frontier of predictive analytics and data innovation.

9.5 Interoperability with REST APIs

Apache Druid's design philosophy strongly supports interoperability, enabling seamless integration with various external systems through REST APIs. REST APIs offer a standardized way for applications to interact programmatically with Druid, facilitating operations ranging from data ingestion and query execution to administrative tasks. This section elaborates on Druid's REST API capabilities, emphasizing its role in building robust data workflows and the nuances of employing Druid's API for maximum efficiency.

Overview of Druid's REST APIs

REST (Representational State Transfer) APIs are a set of web standards enabling communication between clients and servers using HTTP methods. Druid exposes several REST endpoints that cover essential operations such as data ingestion, querying, and cluster management. These APIs emphasize simplicity and stateless communication, allowing developers to interact with Druid through straightforward HTTP requests.

Druid's API schema is organized primarily around three core functionalities:

1. **Ingestion**: APIs that assist in submitting, monitoring, and managing data ingestion tasks. 2. **Querying**: APIs that facilitate the execution of Druid's native and SQL queries for obtaining analytical results. 3. **Cluster Management**: APIs for managing cluster operations such as viewing task statuses and modifying configurations.

Using APIs for Data Ingestion

Data ingestion through REST APIs enables real-time and batch data loading into Druid. By leveraging these capabilities, developers can automate ingestion workflows, ensuring timely data availability for analysis.

Submitting Ingestion Tasks

Ingestion into Druid typically involves submitting a task specification in JSON format to the /druid/indexer/v1/task endpoint. Here is a basic example of a POST request to submit an ingestion task:

```
POST /druid/indexer/v1/task
Content-Type: application/json

{
  "type": "index_parallel",
  "spec": {
    "dataSchema": {
      "dataSource": "example_data",
      "parser": {
        "type": "string",
        "parseSpec": {
          "format": "json",
          "dimensionsSpec": {
            "dimensions": ["dim1", "dim2", "dim3"]
          }
        }
      },
      "granularitySpec": {
        "type": "uniform",
        "segmentGranularity": "hour",
        "queryGranularity": "minute"
      }
    },
    "ioConfig": {
      "type": "index_parallel",
      "inputSource": {
        "type": "http",
        "uris": ["http://data-source-url"]
      },
      "inputFormat": {
        "type": "json"
      }
    }
  }
}
```

This request configures an ingestion task to pull data from a specified HTTP source. The use of such API-based ingestion allows dynamic task submissions responsive to event triggers, ensuring that Druid's datasets remain current.

Monitoring and Managing Tasks

The progress and status of ingestion tasks can be tracked using endpoints like:

- /druid/indexer/v1/task/{taskId}/status: Retrieve task status. - /druid/indexer/v1/task/{taskId}: GET request to fetch metadata about a task.

Polling these endpoints allows applications to verify execution success or failure, providing input for handling task retries or alert notifications programmatically. This continuous feedback loop enhances operational confidence regarding data pipeline resilience.

Executing Queries via APIs

Druid's REST API supports querying through JSON-based native queries or standard SQL, accommodating various analytical use cases. Users can construct powerful analytic queries and send them to:

- /druid/v2/: Endpoint for native queries. - /druid/v2/sql/: Endpoint for SQL-based queries.

Native Query Execution

Native queries provide low-level access to Druid's powerful analytical capabilities, allowing explicit definition of data aggregation, filtering, and transformation processes.

An example of a groupBy query request:

```
POST /druid/v2/
Content-Type: application/json

{
  "queryType": "groupBy",
  "dataSource": "example_data",
  "dimensions": ["dim1", "dim2"],
  "granularity": "day",
  "aggregations": [
    { "type": "longSum", "name": "total_value", "fieldName": "value" }
  ],
  "intervals": ["2023-01-01T00:00:00.000Z/2023-01-31T00:00:00.000Z"]
}
```

This query aggregates the total 'value' for each combination of dimensions 'dim1' and 'dim2' within the specified interval. These native queries unleash the full potential of Druid's query execution engine, tailored for high-complexity, low-latency analytical tasks.

SQL Query Interface

SQL queries provide a familiar syntax, allowing users to leverage Druid's analytical power without deep diving into its native query language. An SQL request example using POST:

```
POST /druid/v2/sql/
Content-Type: application/json

{
  "query": "SELECT dim1, SUM(value) AS total_value FROM example_data
    WHERE __time >= TIMESTAMP '2023-01-01' AND __time <
    TIMESTAMP '2023-01-31' GROUP BY dim1"
}
```

The SQL interface simplifies complex query construction by using established relational syntaxes, easing the adaptation for operators accustomed to traditional database systems.

Cluster Management via APIs

Druid's REST APIs facilitate administrative oversight and configuration management of clusters, extending capabilities to automate operations and enhance cluster resilience. Administrative endpoints include:

- /druid/coordinator/v1/: Oversee management tasks, such as segment-related operations. - /druid/indexer/v1/workers: View worker nodes and load distribution.

An essential management operation includes the use of APIs for automatic scaling. Developers can script the opening and decommissioning of nodes in response to demand fluctuations, optimizing resource usage without manual intervention.

Enhancing Security and Authentication

Interfacing with Druid's REST APIs necessitates securing communication channels and implementing robust authentication mechanisms. Enabling SSL/TLS encryption is crucial to safeguarding data in transit, preventing interception or unauthorized data access.

Druid supports various authentication schemes, configurable through extensions. Commonly deployed options include:

- **Basic Authentication**: Simple to implement but less secure due to plaintext credential transmission unless combined with TLS. - **Kerberos**: For enhanced security in enterprise environments, providing mutual authentication and encrypted communication.

Implementing role-based access control (RBAC) enables granular permission assignment, ensuring users can only perform operations necessary for their role. This minimizes risk exposure by restricting API access to sensitive functionality.

Practical Applications and Use Cases

Druid's REST APIs empower diverse data interaction scenarios. Some practical applications include:

- *Custom ETL Pipelines*: Automate ETL tasks by triggering ingestion tasks through REST APIs, ensuring synchronized data updates in Druid. - *Real-Time Analytics Dashboards*: Develop real-time dashboards that execute Druid queries via APIs, dynamically updating analytics views for stakeholders. - *Monitoring and Alerts*: Utilize task status APIs for proactive monitoring, automatically alerting upon task failures or anomalies. - *Data Driven Workflows*: Generate domain-specific workflows where analytics results trigger further processing or decision-making tasks across interconnected systems.

Best Practices for API Integration

Successful integration of Druid's REST APIs requires adherence to several best practices:

- **Efficient Rate Limiting**: Implementing rate limitation policies helps protect Druid clusters from overwhelming request loads, maintaining operational integrity. - **Asynchronous Task Processing**: Design APIs to handle tasks asynchronously, reducing client-side latency and enhancing user experiences. - **Robust Error Handling**: Employ comprehensive error-checking and retry mechanisms to recover gracefully from unexpected responses. - **API Versioning Compatibility**: Account for potential changes in API versions to accommodate evolving frameworks while maintaining backward compatibility.

Apache Druid's REST APIs facilitate integrative, high-performance data operations across diverse systems. By strategically implementing these APIs, organizations can engineer flexible, powerful solutions that unlock the extensive analytical capabilities inherent within Druid's framework.

9.6 Building Custom Applications with Druid

In the evolving landscape of data analytics, the ability to build custom applications using Apache Druid provides a formidable advantage. Custom applications enable organizations to tailor analytics capabilities to their specific needs, addressing unique business challenges with precision and efficiency. Druid's architecture and functionality are conducive to such customizations, supporting high performance, real-time data ingestion, and complex queries. This section explores how developers can leverage Druid to construct applications that provide dynamic analytics results tailored to specialized requirements.

Custom applications powered by Druid allow organizations to move beyond out-of-the-box analytics, creating tailor-made solutions that integrate seamlessly with existing workflows. Designing these solutions begins with understanding business needs and identifying metrics that drive insights.

- **Identify Core Analytical Needs**: Before developing, it's crucial to define the specific metrics, insights, and goals the application should achieve. This involves collaborating with stakeholders to map business objectives to analytical measures.

263

- **Define Data Architecture**: Outline the data architecture, focusing on how data will be ingested into Druid and structured to support the application's analytics. This includes defining schemas and ensuring that the data model aligns with analytical goals.

- **Draft User Interface Specification**: The UI is central to user interaction. Define how users will engage with the application, specifying dashboards, visualization components, and interactivity features that underpin user experience.

Building custom applications with Druid involves integrating its core components into the broader tech stack. This integration enables the creation of applications that maximize the utility of Druid's capabilities.

RESTful API Utilization

Druid provides REST APIs that can be harnessed for application development, facilitating ingestion, querying, and managing tasks programmatically. A typical application architecture could employ these APIs to dynamically fetch data or trigger processing tasks.

```
// Example of a Node.js function to query Druid's REST API

const axios = require('axios');

async function queryDruid() {
  try {
    const response = await axios.post('http://druid-broker:8082/druid/v2/sql/', {
      query: "SELECT dim1, SUM(value) AS total_value FROM example_data
          GROUP BY dim1"
    });
    console.log(response.data);
  } catch (error) {
    console.error('Error querying Druid:', error);
  }
}

queryDruid();
```

This Node.js snippet demonstrates how simple it is to integrate Druid queries into applications, showcasing the potential for dynamically generated insights served to end-users.

Druid in a Microservices Architecture

Within microservices, Druid acts as a potent analytics engine, serving lightweight services dedicated to specific analytical tasks.

- **Data Service**: A microservice dedicated to serving data from Druid, managing authentication, query construction, and response formatting.

- **Ingestion Scheduler**: Handles ingestion tasks submission, controlling data flow based on application requirements and external triggers.

- **Query Engine**: Uses Druid's SQL capabilities to interpret business logic into queries that fetch tailored insights, optimizing for performance and context relevance.

Implementing Real-time and Batch Data Processing

A critical aspect of custom analytics applications is the ability to handle both real-time and batch data. Druid's native capabilities cater to both ingestion types, ensuring applications can provide up-to-date and comprehensive analytics.

Real-time Processing

Applications can leverage Druid's real-time ingestion capabilities to serve dashboards that refresh in near real-time, allowing for live monitoring of metrics.

```
// Example Kafka ingestion task definition to handle real-time data

{
  "type": "kafka",
  "dataSchema": {
    "dataSource": "real_time_source",
    "parser": {
      "type": "string",
      "parseSpec": {
        "format": "json",
        "dimensionsSpec": {
          "dimensions": ["event_time", "type", "value"]
```

```
      }
     }
   },
   "granularitySpec": {
     "type": "uniform",
     "segmentGranularity": "minute",
     "queryGranularity": "minute"
   }
  },
  "ioConfig": {
   "topic": "events",
   "replicas": 1,
   "taskCount": 4,
   "consumerProperties": {
     "bootstrap.servers": "kafka-broker:9092"
   }
  }
}
```

By setting up dedicated Kafka ingestion tasks, applications can react swiftly to incoming data changes, ensuring they remain relevant and timely.

Batch Processing

When dealing with historical data or integrating periodic data dumps, batch processing steps in to maintain a comprehensive data context.

- Configure typical Hadoop-based batch ingestion tasks for efficient processing of historical data.

- Utilize Apache Spark to preprocess and transform data before ingestion into Druid, creating value-added datasets ready for analysis.

```
// Spark transformation pipeline for batch processing

val df = spark.read.json("hdfs:///data-dir/historical.json")
val processedDf = df.groupBy("category").agg(sum("value").alias("total_value"))

processedDf.write.format("org.apache.druid.spark").option("druidDataSource", "
    batch_data_source").save()
```

Enhancing User Experience with Interactivity and Visualization

As an application front-end is crafted, enhancing user interaction through meaningful visuals is crucial. Druid's quick response times to queries empower rich visualizations, ensuring seamless user experiences.

- **Interactive Dashboards**: Use frontend libraries like React.js or Vue.js coupled with visualization tools like D3.js or Chart.js to create interactive dashboards.

- **Data-driven Alerts**: Implement alert systems based on threshold parameter monitoring within Druid data, coupling analytical insights with proactive operational actions.

```
// React component for rendering a line chart using D3.js

import React, { useEffect } from 'react';
import * as d3 from 'd3';

const LineChart = ({ data }) => {
  useEffect(() => {
    const svg = d3.select("svg").attr("width", 500).attr("height", 300);
    const xScale = d3.scaleTime().domain(d3.extent(data, d => d.date)).range([0,
        500]);
    const yScale = d3.scaleLinear().domain([0, d3.max(data, d => d.value)]).range
        ([300, 0]);

    svg.append("g").attr("transform", "translate(0,300)").call(d3.axisBottom(xScale));
    svg.append("g").call(d3.axisLeft(yScale));

    svg.append("path").datum(data).attr("fill", "none").attr("stroke", "steelblue").attr
        ("stroke-width", 1.5)
      .attr("d", d3.line().x(d => xScale(d.date)).y(d => yScale(d.value)));
  }, [data]);

  return <svg />;
};

export default LineChart;
```

This snippet charts a dynamic line visualization, representing analytics outputs that change in response to updates from Druid.

Security and Scalability Considerations

While power and flexibility are core advantages of Druid for custom applications, implementing security and scaling strategies is vital:

- **Authentication**: Employ OAuth or JWT tokens for secure data requests, ensuring proper authorization checks before query execution.

- **Rate Limiting**: Maintain system integrity by instituting rate limits, preventing API abuse and ensuring fair workload distribution.

- **Scalable Infrastructure**: Deploy Druid nodes across scalable environments such as Kubernetes or cloud services, catering to varying operational loads.

Empowering Data Science and Machine Learning

Integrating machine learning workflows with Druid enables predictive analytics. Custom applications can harness Spark MLlib for model training using historical data and deploy those models to predict future trends.

- **Preprocessing**: Spark can be used to clean and transform data sets prior to ingestion into Druid.

- **Model Training**: Train models on historical data stashed in Druid segments; Apache Spark can inherently enhance predictive insights when paired with Druid data.

```
// Example Spark ML pipeline for predictive modeling

import org.apache.spark.ml.Pipeline
import org.apache.spark.ml.feature.VectorAssembler
import org.apache.spark.ml.regression.LinearRegression

val assembler = new VectorAssembler().setInputCols(Array("feature1", "feature2")).
    setOutputCol("features")
val lr = new LinearRegression().setLabelCol("label").setFeaturesCol("features")

val pipeline = new Pipeline().setStages(Array(assembler, lr))
val model = pipeline.fit(trainingData)
```

```
// Use the model to predict on new data
val predictions = model.transform(newData)
```

Custom applications designed around Druid ensure that a holistic data narrative is continuously available, providing every stakeholder with intuitively accessible and actionable insights.

9.7 Considerations for Multi-Cloud Environments

In today's digital landscape, adopting a multi-cloud strategy offers a significant advantage by enhancing flexibility, resilience, and innovation potential for enterprises. Apache Druid's capability to adapt to diverse cloud infrastructures makes it an ideal candidate for deployment across multi-cloud environments. However, managing Druid within a multi-cloud architecture introduces distinct considerations, challenges, and strategic opportunities that must be carefully addressed to ensure seamless operations and optimal performance.

A multi-cloud strategy involves utilizing cloud services from more than one provider, such as AWS, Azure, and Google Cloud Platform (GCP), and combining them to suit an organization's specific business goals and technical requirements.

- **Benefits of Multi-Cloud:**

    - **Redundancy and Disaster Recovery:** By diversifying cloud investments, businesses can achieve higher availability and failover capability.

    - **Avoiding Vendor Lock-In:** Using multiple providers prevents reliance on a single vendor, fostering negotiation leverage and diversity in technological solutions.

    - **Optimizing Workloads:** Different providers excel in various services; multi-cloud allows leveraging specialized capabilities, such as machine learning, storage, and compute.

- **Challenges:**

- **Complexity in Management:** Managing resources and data across multiple clouds requires sophisticated orchestration strategies.

- **Data Consistency and Integration:** Ensuring consistent data states and synchronization between cloud systems is complex yet crucial.

- **Security and Compliance:** Security protocols must span across providers, and compliance requirements can differ per jurisdiction.

The deployment of Druid in such an environment must consider these complexities, ensuring that the integrity, performance, and scalability of analytics operations are maintained.

Effective deployment begins with careful planning of infrastructure architecture across chosen cloud platforms. Key considerations include:

- **Network Configuration:** Ensure efficient networking with low-latency, high-bandwidth links between different cloud resources. Employ VPNs or dedicated connections like AWS Direct Connect, Azure ExpressRoute, and Google Cloud Interconnect.

- **Resource Distribution:** Appropriately distribute Druid components (historical nodes, brokers, middle managers) across clouds to support redundancy and load balancing.

```
// Terraform configuration for provisioning Druid clusters across multi-cloud

provider "aws" {
  region = "us-west-2"
}

provider "google" {
  region = "us-central1"
}

resource "aws_instance" "druid_hist" {
  ami = "ami-0c28cdf5668b670c1"
  instance_type = "t2.medium"
  count = 3 // Deploy in AWS for fast EBS access
}

resource "google_compute_instance" "druid_broker" {
  name = "druid-broker-instance"
  machine_type = "n1-standard-1"
```

```
  count = 2 // Spread broker responsibilities over GCP zones
}
```

Using Terraform to define infrastructure as code facilitates orchestrating multi-cloud deployments. Instances are detailed for relevant services across AWS and GCP, showcasing how resources can be methodically assigned.

Data management gains complexity in multi-cloud environments, necessitating effective strategies for handling data storage.

- **Multi-Region Buckets:** For cloud storage (e.g., S3, Azure Blob, Google Cloud Storage), prefer multi-region buckets for increased data availability and durability.

- **Database Bridging:** Use cross-cloud database connectors and dataflow tools like Apache Nifi or cloud-native solutions to bridge data pipelines.

Druid's architecture, with its segment storage capabilities, can leverage distinct storage formats in each cloud for optimized access:

```
// Sample configuration for mixed storage path

{
  "deepStorage": {
    "type": "hdfs",
    "path": "s3://my-druid-bucket/segments"
  },
  "backupStorage": {
    "type": "google",
    "path": "gs://my-backup-bucket/segments"
  }
}
```

Such configurations illustrate using S3 for primary storage while maintaining Google Cloud as a backup repository, ensuring robust data redundancy protocols.

Ensuring that all deployed components across clouds remain compatible and interconnected is crucial for maintaining a unified Druid experience:

- **Interoperability:** Use open APIs and platform-independent services when possible to circumvent proprietary bottlenecks.

271

- **Consistent Monitoring:** Employ tools like Prometheus and Grafana that work uniformly across clouds for real-time systems monitoring, ensuring that metrics and alerts offer a cohesive operational view.

```
// Example Docker Compose file for running a monitoring stack

version: "3"
services:
  prometheus:
    image: prom/prometheus
    volumes:
      - ./prometheus.yml:/etc/prometheus/prometheus.yml
    ports:
      - "9090:9090"
    networks:
      - multi-cloud

  grafana:
    image: grafana/grafana
    ports:
      - "3000:3000"
    networks:
      - multi-cloud

networks:
  multi-cloud:
    driver: bridge
```

This deployment exemplifies how cloud-agnostic monitoring stacks can be configured using Docker, offering consistent metrics collection and UI operation across differing platforms.

Aligning performance and cost efficiency across multi-cloud deployments is essential for sustainable operations:

- **Auto-Scaling:** Deploy auto-scaling groups to adjust resource allocation in response to real-time demand, supported by metrics from pipelines.

- **Spot Instances:** Utilize spot or preemptible instances for cost-effective compute resource provisioning where feasible.

- **Cross-Cloud Task Scheduling:** Define a task scheduler, such as Apache Airflow, for orchestrating complex workflows that span multiple clouds, optimizing task latency and execution.

```
// Example configuration snippet for 'Airflows DruidOperator

from airflow.contrib.operators.druid_operator import DruidOperator

druid_task = DruidOperator(
    task_id='druid_ingestion',
    json_index_file='path/to/json',
    druid_ingest_conn_id='druid_webserver',
    dag=dag
)
```

Integrating Apache Airflow empowers scheduled and conditional execution of tasks, fostering efficiency in managing pipeline dependencies across clouds.

A uniformly strong security posture through consistent policy implementation is vital:

- **Unified Security Policies:** Ensure cloud security measures apply equitably, adopting a Zero Trust approach.

- **Encryption Standards:** Maintain data encryption at rest and in transit across all cloud storage and networking.

- **Audit Trails:** Continuously audit access and operations over unified logs with solutions like AWS CloudTrail or GCP Cloud Audit Logs combined with SIEM systems.

Implementing security controls consistently across cloud services improves overall compliance with rigorous data sovereignty and privacy standards like GDPR or CCPA.

As cloud services evolve, the role of multi-cloud environments will continue to grow, coalescing flexibility, power, and innovation potential. By effectively navigating the complexities outlined, organizations can ensure that their Druid deployments maximize operational impact, delivering consistent analytics capabilities across global, multi-cloud infrastructure landscapes. Continued innovation in inter-cloud operability tools and practices promises an even more seamless future for managing big data analytics in increasingly distributed architectures.

Chapter 10

Security and Best Practices in Druid

This chapter provides a comprehensive guide to implementing security measures and best practices within Apache Druid environments. It covers mechanisms for configuring authentication and authorization to secure data access and manage user roles and permissions. Strategies for encrypting data at rest and in transit are discussed to ensure data protection. The chapter also details configuring network security, including firewall settings and secure inter-node communication. Techniques for auditing and monitoring access provide visibility into user activities, while considerations for adhering to industry regulations like GDPR and HIPAA ensure compliance. Implementing robust security policies is emphasized to maintain data integrity and privacy.

10.1 Authentication and Authorization in Druid

In Apache Druid, robust mechanisms for authentication and authorization are pivotal for securing access to the clusters, ensuring that only authenticated and authorized users can access or manipulate data. This section delves into the components and configurations integral to implementing these security measures effectively.

Druid supports authentication through a variety of mechanisms, enabling the use of internal basic authentication or integration with existing security infrastructures such as LDAP, OAuth, or Kerberos. For authorization, Druid leverages role-based access control (RBAC), allowing for granular permissions management. These security features together help enforce the principle of least privilege, providing users with only those privileges necessary for their roles.

The authentication process in Druid begins with user identity verification. When a user attempts to access the Druid cluster, their credentials must be authenticated against the configured authentication schemes. Basic authentication in Druid requires the use of username and password combinations which are verified against stored credentials within Druid's internal metadata store. The configuration of this system is handled through a JSON-based configuration file, ensuring easy setup and management.

```
{
  "type" : "basic",
  "basic" : {
    "passwordProvider" : {
      "type" : "config",
      "userName" : "druid_system",
      "password" : "password123"
    }
  }
}
```

The above configuration sets up a basic authentication provider where user credentials are supplied in a clear-text fashion for simplicity. However, in production environments, it is advisable to use more secure methods such as hashed passwords, facilitated by Druid's extensible authentication framework.

Druid allows integration with LDAP for authentication, providing centralized management of user identities, especially beneficial in large organizational environments. The LDAP integration requires setting up a connection to your LDAP server and specifying details such as base DN, search filter, and connection credentials. Here is an illustrative example of setting up LDAP authentication:

```
{
  "type" : "ldap",
  "ldap" : {
    "url" : "ldap://ldap.yourcompany.com:389",
    "userDnSearchFilter" : "(uid={username})",
    "baseDn" : "ou=users,dc=yourcompany,dc=com",
    "bindDn" : "cn=read-only-admin,dc=yourcompany,dc=com",
    "bindPassword" : "bindPassword"
  }
}
```

This configuration connects to an LDAP server to authenticate users trying to access the Druid cluster. The support for LDAP ensures that user credentials are not locally stored in the Druid system but rather managed externally, reducing the risk of unauthorized access.

For applications requiring single sign-on (SSO), OAuth and Kerberos provide comprehensive solutions. Druid's OAuth extension facilitates integration with OAuth providers like Google, GitHub, or Okta. This method leverages OAuth tokens which are supplied by the identity provider (IdP), significantly enhancing security as user credentials are not directly handled by Druid.

Authorization in Druid is configured via role-based access control (RBAC). This involves defining roles corresponding to the organizational needs and assigning these roles to users. Each role has specific permissions that determine what the role's members can view or manipulate within the Druid environment. Here is an example of setting up RBAC in Druid:

```
{
  "roles" : [
    {
      "name" : "ADMIN",
      "permissions" : [
        { "resource" : "datasource", "action" : "read", "scope" : "*" },
        { "resource" : "datasource", "action" : "write", "scope" : "*" }
      ]
    },
    {
      "name" : "ANALYST",
```

```
    "permissions" : [
      { "resource" : "datasource", "action" : "read", "scope" : "*" }
    ]
  }
 ]
}
```

In this configuration, the "ADMIN" role is granted both read and write access to all datasources, while the "ANALYST" role has read-only access. This clear division ensures strict adherence to data governance policies.

Druid's security model is flexible, supporting the configuration of permissions at various levels - entire clusters, individual nodes, or specific datasources - enabling detailed control over who can access what within the system. Furthermore, these permissions can be dynamically adjusted to accommodate evolving needs without requiring a system shutdown or restart.

In practice, implementing a comprehensive security posture in Druid involves combining these authentication and authorization configurations with rigorous policy enforcement, regular audits, and monitoring. For instance, enabling logging and tracking of authentication failures can help quickly identify and react to unauthorized access attempts.

```
{
  "druid" : {
    "auth" : {
      "logAuthenticationFailures" : "true"
    }
  }
}
```

This configuration ensures that any failed attempts to authenticate are logged, providing insights that can be crucial for forensic investigations or compliance monitoring.

Additionally, Druid's security infrastructure can be extended through custom extensions. Developers can create plugins to integrate proprietary identity management systems or bespoke authorization mechanisms, showcasing the system's adaptability to diverse enterprise requirements.

Through careful planning and implementation, Druid administrators can capitalize on these authentication and authorization features to establish a secure environment that protects sensitive data, supports organizational compliance, and builds user trust in the system. The adaptation of authentication methods and authorization models to the specific security policies and technical capabilities of the organization is essential to the establishment of a sound data governance framework within Apache Druid environments.

10.2 Data Encryption and Secure Transfers

Ensuring the protection of sensitive data is a paramount concern within any data management system. In Apache Druid, data encryption and secure transfers are critical components in guaranteeing data confidentiality and integrity. This section explores best practices for encrypting data at rest and in transit within Druid, detailing configurations and methodologies that enhance security against unauthorized access and data breaches.

Data encryption is the process of converting data into a coded format, rendering it unreadable to anyone who does not possess the decryption key. In Druid, encryption can be applied to data at rest, such as segments stored in deep storage, and data in transit, which includes the data being transferred between client applications and Druid, as well as between Druid nodes.

- **Encryption at Rest**

Data at rest refers to data stored in persistent storage. In Druid, this typically relates to segments stored in deep storage options like Amazon S3, HDFS, or the local file system. To protect this data, it is vital to encrypt it so that even if unauthorized actors gain access to the storage media, they cannot make sense of the data without the decryption keys.

Encryption at rest in Druid is generally managed through the underlying storage system's capabilities. For instance, Amazon S3 provides server-side encryption (SSE) options, such as using Amazon S3-managed keys (SSE-S3), AWS Key Management Service (AWS KMS) managed keys (SSE-KMS), or customer-provided keys (SSE-C).

279

To enable SSE for S3 in Druid, the configuration in the conf/druid/_-common/common.runtime.properties file is essential. Here is a snippet illustrating the setup:

```
druid.storage.type=s3
druid.storage.aws.sseAlgorithm=AES256
druid.storage.bucket=your-druid-bucket
druid.storage.baseKeyPath=druid/segments
```

This sets up server-side encryption using AES-256, an industry-standard encryption algorithm, ensuring that the Druid segments stored in S3 are encrypted. Likewise, other storage systems, such as HDFS, can also be configured to encrypt data using their native encryption capabilities.

In addition to native storage encryption, Druid can employ application-level encryption where encryption is applied within the application logic before the data is written to deep storage. This involves utilizing custom Druid extensions that encrypt data upon serialization and decrypt it upon deserialization.

- **Encryption in Transit**

Data in transit is susceptible to interception, making encryption during transmission vital to secure communication. In Druid, data moves in transit when communicated over networks between client applications, between nodes within the Druid cluster, and between Druid and external storage systems.

Druid utilizes TLS/SSL protocols to encrypt data in transit. The Transport Layer Security (TLS) protocol ensures that data sent over the network is accessed securely. To implement TLS in Druid, certificates must be obtained and configured on all nodes within the cluster. Below is an example configuration for enabling TLS on a Druid broker node:

```
druid.server.https.enabled=true
druid.server.https.port=8282
druid.server.https.keyStorePath=/path/to/keystore.jks
druid.server.https.keyStorePassword=changeit
druid.server.https.certAlias=druid
```

In this setup, HTTPS is enabled on port 8282, and the Java Keystore (JKS) format is used to store the certificate and private key required for TLS encryption. The keyStorePath points to the location of the keystore file, and keyStorePassword denotes the password to access the keystore. The certAlias specifies the alias name of the credential that the server uses for SSL.

Certificates can be self-signed or obtained from trusted Certificate Authorities (CAs). Generally, certificates from trusted CAs provide additional verification and mitigate man-in-the-middle attacks. Secure connections between Druid nodes help prevent data tampering and eavesdropping.

- **Key Management**

A central component of any encryption strategy is key management. Keys used for both encrypting and decrypting data must be managed securely to ensure data safety. Effective key management includes generating strong keys, storing them securely, having access control policies, and employing regular key rotation to minimize risks.

For instance, when using AWS KMS for managing encryption keys in S3, IAM policies should be configured to control who can access or manage the keys. These keys must be rotated at regular intervals as part of a comprehensive key lifecycle management process.

- **Performance Considerations**

While encryption significantly enhances security, it introduces additional processing overhead. The encryption and decryption processes can increase CPU and memory usage, impacting system performance. In light of this, careful evaluation and optimization should be performed. It's important to balance security requirements with acceptable performance levels.

Druid architects can mitigate performance impacts through hardware acceleration features available in many modern processors or by offloading encryption tasks to specialized hardware security modules (HSMs) which are optimized for encryption-related operations.

- **Conclusion and Best Practices**

Implementing encryption and secure transfer protocols within Druid forms a critical line of defense against unauthorized access to sensitive data. By encrypting data at rest and in transit using strong algorithms and secure key management practices, organizations can ensure data integrity and confidentiality.

Security configurations should be validated and audited regularly. Security measures should be part of an organization's larger information security governance policy, reflecting changes in security regulations and best practices to remain compliant with standards such as GDPR, HIPAA, or PCI-DSS.

Ultimately, the implementation of data encryption and secure transfers within Druid requires a strategic approach combining technical configuration with sound security policy planning to establish a resilient and secure data environment.

10.3 Configuring Network Security

Network security in Apache Druid is essential to ensure that data flowing within the cluster and externally to clients is safeguarded from potential threats. Proper configuration of network security involves setting up firewalls, implementing VPNs, securing inter-node communication, and controlling access to the network endpoints. This section elaborates on the methodologies and configurations necessary to build a robust network security model for Druid environments.

Firewalls and Port Management

Firewalls play a central role in network security by controlling incoming and outgoing network traffic based on predetermined security rules. In the context of a Druid cluster, firewalls are utilized to restrict access to specific ports and IP addresses, ensuring that only authorized clients and services can communicate with the cluster.

Each Druid service, such as broker, coordinator, historical, and overlord, listens on specific ports for client requests and intra-cluster communication. Configuring firewalls to allow traffic on these ports only from trusted IP addresses significantly reduces the attack surface. For example, in a Linux-based environment using iptables, firewall rules can be set up as follows:

```
# Allow SSH from trusted IP only
```

```
iptables -A INPUT -p tcp --dport 22 -s 192.168.1.100 -j ACCEPT

# Allow Druid Broker service
iptables -A INPUT -p tcp --dport 8082 -s 192.168.1.0/24 -j ACCEPT

# Allow Druid Coordinator service
iptables -A INPUT -p tcp --dport 8081 -s 192.168.1.0/24 -j ACCEPT

# Allow Established Connections
iptables -A INPUT -m conntrack --ctstate ESTABLISHED,RELATED -j ACCEPT

# Drop all other traffic
iptables -A INPUT -j DROP
```

This configuration permits SSH access from IP 192.168.1.100, allows Druid Broker and Coordinator service access from the trusted subnet 192.168.1.0/24, and drops all other network traffic, helping to keep the system focused and secure.

Virtual Private Networks (VPNs)

VPNs enable secure remote access to the Druid cluster by encrypting data traffic between remote clients and the Druid network. Through encryption and tunneling, VPNs protect data integrity and confidentiality even over public networks.

By integrating VPN solutions like OpenVPN or strongSwan (an IPsec-based VPN), organizations can create secure connections between remote users and Druid clusters, ensuring that data remains protected at all times. A simplified example of configuring OpenVPN on a Linux server is shown below:

```
port 1194
proto udp
dev tun
ca /etc/openvpn/ca.crt
cert /etc/openvpn/server.crt
key /etc/openvpn/server.key
dh /etc/openvpn/dh.pem
server 10.8.0.0 255.255.255.0
push "route 10.0.0.0 255.255.255.0"
keepalive 10 120
comp-lzo
persist-key
persist-tun
status openvpn-status.log
verb 3
```

The configuration specifies UDP for communication protocol, a dedicated tunnel interface (dev tun), along with certificate paths. Importantly, the push "route ..." directive configures client-side routing, ensuring that traffic is directed through the VPN to the Druid services.

Securing Inter-node Communication

In a Druid cluster, multiple nodes (servers) collaborate to provide data ingestion, storage, and querying functionality. Securing communication between these nodes is critical to prevent interception or tampering by unauthorized entities.

TLS/SSL provides encryption for data in transit between Druid nodes. As mentioned previously, it involves setting up SSL on each Druid node using certificates. Additionally, mutual TLS (mTLS) can be configured where both client and server verify each other's certificates, adding an extra layer of security.

For example, enabling SSL with mutual authentication on a Druid historical node:

```
druid.server.https.enabled=true
druid.server.https.port=8281
druid.server.https.keyStorePath=/path/to/historical-keystore.jks
druid.server.https.keyStorePassword=druidKeystorePass
druid.server.https.trustStorePath=/path/to/historical-truststore.jks
druid.server.https.trustStorePassword=druidTrustStorePass
druid.server.https.clientAuth=want
```

This configuration establishes an SSL-enabled server with mutual authentication, requiring that connecting clients also provide valid certificates.

Network Monitoring and Incident Response

The deployment of network monitoring tools offers real-time insights into the traffic patterns and potentially suspicious activities occurring within the network. Tools such as Zabbix, Prometheus, or Splunk can be used in conjunction with Druid to gather logs and metrics, identifying potential threats through anomaly detection methods.

Network monitoring solutions should be integrated with incident response plans, defining steps to take in response to detected security incidents, such as isolating impacted network segments, analyzing threat vectors, and implementing corrective measures.

Zero Trust Architecture

Embracing a Zero Trust network security model provides an adaptive, integral solution that assumes breach and continuously verifies each request's legitimacy. Zero Trust leverages identity-based authentication and context-aware security policies to ensure that only the right people, devices, and applications can access Druid resources.

Implementing Zero Trust involves integrating with identity and access management systems (IAM), endpoint security solutions, and enforcing micro-segmentation. Moreover, setting up continuous monitoring and automated threat detection further distills this approach.

Conclusion and Best Practices

Configuring network security for Apache Druid requires a multifaceted approach that incorporates firewalls, VPNs, TLS/SSL, network monitoring, and potentially adopting a Zero Trust framework. Implementing these measures demands collaboration between network administrators, security experts, and Druid architects to ensure a holistic, secure environment.

Security configurations are not immutable; they should be periodically reviewed and updated to adapt to evolving security landscapes, threat models, and organizational policies. Regular penetration testing and auditing of network configurations help verify their effectiveness and identify opportunities for refinement. Collectively, these practices ascertain that Druid networks remain resilient to contemporary cyber threats, safeguarding data integrity and availability.

10.4 Auditing and Monitoring Access

The practice of auditing and monitoring access within Apache Druid is essential to maintain visibility over user activities and establish accountability for data actions. Auditing and monitoring serve as key components of a comprehensive security posture by allowing organizations to detect unauthorized access attempts, ensure compliance with regulatory requirements, and identify areas for improvement in data governance. This section provides an in-depth exploration of techniques for auditing and monitoring access within Druid and presents methods to leverage these practices effectively.

Logging and Audit Trails

Druid's comprehensive logging framework is foundational to its auditing capabilities. Every significant action performed by users and the system is recorded in logs, forming an audit trail. Audit trails are essential for tracking user activities and analyzing the historical usage patterns within the Druid system. They contribute significantly to both operational and security audits, facilitating investigations and enabling post-incident analysis.

Druid uses different log levels: DEBUG, INFO, WARN, and ERROR, to categorize events by their significance. For audit purposes, the INFO level is typically used for recording normative business events, whereas the DEBUG level may capture more detailed diagnostic information. The configuration for logging levels is managed via properties within the log4j2.xml configuration file:

```
<Configuration status="warn">
  <Appenders>
    <Console name="Console" target="SYSTEM_OUT">
      <PatternLayout pattern="%d{ISO8601} [%t] %-5p %c{1} - %msg%n"/>
    </Console>
  </Appenders>

  <Loggers>
    <!-- Log everything at INFO level -->
    <Root level="info">
      <AppenderRef ref="Console"/>
    </Root>

    <!-- Example: Custom logging level for specific classes -->
    <Logger name="org.apache.druid.server.metrics" level="debug">
      <AppenderRef ref="Console"/>
    </Logger>
  </Loggers>
</Configuration>
```

This XML configuration sets the global log level to INFO, ensuring all pertinent activities are captured in the logs. The granularity of events logged can be adjusted as needed by customizing the logger settings.

Enabling Audit Logs

Beyond standard logs, specialized audit log functionality in Druid captures critical security-related events such as configuration changes, permissions modifications, and data access operations. Audit logs are stored in the metadata database, making them easy to query and analyze to derive insights into security and operational aspects.

To enable audit logging within Druid, the appropriate configuration

286

must be specified in the common.runtime.properties file:

```
# Enables audit logging
druid.audit.logging.enabled=true

# Configures the metastorage type
druid.metadata.storage.type=mysql

# Connection details for audit logs
druid.metadata.storage.connector.connectURI=jdbc:mysql://metadata-db-server/druid
druid.metadata.storage.connector.user=druid
druid.metadata.storage.connector.password=secret
```

This setup activates audit logging and directs audit records to a MySQL metadata store. Configuring proper access controls for the metadata store is crucial to ensure that audit logs remain tamper-proof and accessible only to authorized personnel.

Monitoring Tools and Techniques

Monitoring access requires effective tools and technologies that can observe patterns and detect anomalies. Druid integrates well with monitoring and alerting solutions such as Apache Kafka, Prometheus, and Grafana for real-time visibility and responsive alerting:

- **Prometheus and Grafana:** Prometheus can scrape and store time-series data collected from Druid metrics exporters. Grafana then visualizes this data with dashboards, offering a clear insight into Druid's operational metrics and security events. This combination facilitates proactive monitoring and can alert on unusual activity such as spikes in query frequency or unauthorized access attempts.

- **Apache Kafka:** By configuring Druid to emit operational metrics and logs into Kafka topics, administrators can create a flexible, scalable platform for consuming, processing, and analyzing log data. This architecture supports the building of advanced monitoring pipelines, integrating with systems like Splunk to harness sophisticated log analysis and visualization features.

```
# Enable metrics emission
druid.emitter=parametrized
druid.emitter.parametrized.recipient.kafkaproducer.bootstrap.servers=kafka-broker
    :9092
druid.emitter.parametrized.recipient.kafkaproducer.topic=druid-metrics
```

Visual tools and log analysis systems enable correlating data from various sources to personalize monitoring based on organizational requirements and can massively reduce the time between issue detection and resolution.

Behavioral Anomaly Detection and Alerts

Auditing and monitoring systems can be augmented with anomaly detection algorithms that observe usage patterns and highlight deviations that may indicate potential security incidents or misuse. Machine learning models can be trained using historical usage data to determine baseline behaviors, enabling the detection of anomalies from these baselines.

For instance, machine-learning-based solutions can track user login attempts, query volumes, and access patterns, raising alerts if any activity deviates notably from established norms. Implementing such solutions complements traditional monitoring tools and heightens the overall security stance.

User Activity Auditing

In addition to system-level auditing, user activity audits enhance visibility over how data within the Druid ecosystem is utilized. User-centric audits can identify which users queried or modified specific datasets, providing accountability and assisting in fair usage enforcement.

Scheduled reports can be generated from audit logs or metadata SQL queries, summarizing user activity and highlighting accesses that necessitate further investigation.

Compliance and Reporting

Many organizations must comply with industry regulations like GDPR, HIPAA, or PCI DSS. These regulations often require stringent auditing measures, including detailed record maintenance of data access, reporting capabilities, and secure log retention.

Ensuring compliance involves a well-documented policy on data retention, access controls, and regular security audits to demonstrate adherence to regulatory mandates. Reporting tools integrated with Druid can automate compliance reports generation, easing the burden on operations teams and maintaining operational efficiency.

Conclusion and Best Practices

Auditing and monitoring access in Druid are pillars for building a secure and responsible data environment. By implementing logging, applying rigorous monitoring tools, incorporating anomaly detection, and maintaining compliance, enterprises can ensure the security integrity of their data assets.

As organizations continue to evolve and expand their Druid implementations, the auditing and monitoring solutions must also be scalable and adaptable to new data payloads, user bases, and compliance requirements. Regular reviews, updates to security policies, and the integration of emerging technologies will aid in achieving a robust, future-proof auditing and monitoring framework.

10.5 Managing User Roles and Permissions

Managing user roles and permissions in Apache Druid is pivotal for implementing an effective access control strategy, which helps enforce the principle of least privilege and ensures that users have the necessary permissions aligned with their job functions. This section explores how to manage user roles and permissions within Druid, detailing the configuration and best practices to maintain a secure, compliant, and efficient access control environment.

Role-Based Access Control (RBAC)

Druid utilizes a Role-Based Access Control model, wherein roles are defined with specific permissions, and users are assigned to these roles. This model simplifies management by allowing administrators to assign roles to users instead of configuring permissions individually. RBAC provides a scalable way to manage complex permission structures, especially in large organizations with many users.

In Druid, roles can define permissions to access specific datasets (datasources), as well as administrative capabilities like managing indexing tasks or viewing system status. Here is an example configuration illustrating how roles can be set up in Druid's security model:

```
{
  "roles": [
    {
      "name": "DATA-SCIENTIST",
      "permissions": [
        {"resource": "datasource", "action": "read", "scope": "data-scientist-datasource
          "},
        {"resource": "task", "action": "read", "scope": "*"}
      ]
    },
    {
      "name": "SYSTEM-ADMIN",
      "permissions": [
        {"resource": "datasource", "action": "read", "scope": "*"},
        {"resource": "datasource", "action": "write", "scope": "*"},
        {"resource": "task", "action": "write", "scope": "*"},
        {"resource": "status", "action": "read", "scope": "*"}
      ]
    }
  ]
}
```

In the above configuration example, the DATA-SCIENTIST role allows read access to a specific datasource, while the SYSTEM-ADMIN role grants broader permissions to perform administrative tasks across datasources and system statuses.

Defining Permissions

Permissions are specific actions that can be performed on a resource, and they form the core elements of RBAC. In Druid, permissions are defined across various resource types such as datasources, tasks, server status, and more. These permissions can be categorized into actions such as read, write, and submitTask, among others. Granularly defining these permissions ensures that access is appropriately restricted.

Creating and Managing Users

User management is integral to implementing RBAC. Users are declared and associated with roles; thus, their privileges are inherited from the roles they belong to. In Druid, users are managed through the security APIs or a user management console if available. Creating a user typically involves specifying the username, credentials, and role associations:

```
{
  "users": [
    {
      "name": "jdoe",
      "credentials": "hashed_password_or_token",
```

```
    "roles": ["DATA-SCIENTIST"]
  },
  {
    "name": "admin",
    "credentials": "hashed_password_or_token",
    "roles": ["SYSTEM-ADMIN"]
  }
  ]
}
```

From the example above, user jdoe is associated with the DATA-SCIENTIST role, while admin holds the SYSTEM-ADMIN role. User credentials should be handled with secured hash techniques to prevent unauthorized access.

Dynamic Role Management

Druid offers flexibility in modifying role definitions on the fly. This is particularly useful as organizations evolve and users change roles or responsibilities. Role adjustments can be performed in response to audits or regular security reviews to realign permissions.

Dynamic role management can be facilitated through RESTful APIs, providing a programmatic way to interact with the security configurations. APIs allow adding, modifying, or deleting roles and permissions without impacting service availability, offering agility in access management.

Permission Auditing and Review Processes

Regular auditing of roles and their assigned permissions is a critical component of maintaining a secure environment. Ensuring that unused roles are pruned and that permissions mapped to roles accurately reflect job requirements helps minimize security risks.

Periodic reviews of roles and permissions allow organizations to ensure compliance with policies such as GDPR, HIPAA, or internal security directives. Automated scripts or built-in tools can facilitate the auditing process, flagging any discrepancies or aberrations.

Implementing Least Privilege Principle

The principle of least privilege dictates that users should only have access to the information and resources required for their legitimate purposes. Implementing this principle requires careful analysis and assignment of permissions.

Limit excessive authorization by creating fine-grained roles and specific permissions. Review historical user activity and adjust roles based on actual user requirements. By aligning permissions very closely with functional duties and responsibilities, organizations can significantly lower the risk of accidental or malicious data breaches.

Handling Role Hierarchies and Inheritance

In some environments, roles need to be structured in a hierarchical manner to reflect organizational structures or responsibilities. In Druid, although it does not directly support hierarchical roles, you can effectively simulate this by using composite roles, where roles are combinations of existing roles to encapsulate a higher level of permission aggregation.

Integrating with Identity Management Systems

While Druid provides its authentication and role management capabilities, integrating with external identity and access management (IAM) systems can significantly simplify user management. Systems such as LDAP, Active Directory, or OAuth can centralize identity management, enabling single sign-on (SSO) functionality and enhancing security by offering strong, federated authentication mechanisms.

The integration with IAM systems allows roles and permissions within Druid to be synchronized with corporate policy configurations, ensuring consistent security postures across all organizational boundaries.

Conclusion and Best Practices

Effectively managing user roles and permissions in Druid is essential for maintaining data security and achieving operational efficiency. Establishing a disciplined RBAC policy, periodically reviewing and auditing roles, and ensuring a principle of least privilege are fundamental components of a robust access control strategy.

Continuous education and training of administrative staff on security best practices contribute to the overall security resilience, as does incorporating feedback from users on access challenges—it fosters a security culture that values diligence and responsibility.

By implementing a thoughtful and considerate permissions model complemented by rigorous auditing and compliance checks, Druid administrators can ensure that their environment is not only secure but also flexible enough to adapt to ongoing organizational needs.

10.6 Implementing Security Policies

The implementation of robust security policies in Apache Druid is essential for safeguarding data integrity, confidentiality, and availability. Security policies serve as the framework through which organizations can apply prophylactic measures, manage risk, and address compliance requirements. This section delves into strategies and best practices for developing and enforcing security policies within Druid environments, providing essential details on policy creation, implementation, and maintenance.

Understanding Security Policies

Security policies are formalized sets of rules and practices that govern how an organization's sensitive data and resources are managed, protected, and distributed. These policies ensure that security measures align with organizational goals and compliance mandates while addressing potential security risks.

Key components of effective security policies in Druid involve:

- **Data Access Controls:** Define who has access to what data and under what conditions, often implemented via Role-Based Access Control (RBAC).

- **Authentication Measures:** Establish protocols for verifying the identity of users and services accessing the system.

- **Data Protection:** Include encryption strategies to safeguard data at rest and in transit.

- **Monitoring and Audit Mechanisms:** Outline practices for logging, monitoring, and reviewing user and system activities.

- **Incident Response:** Detail procedures for responding to and recovering from security incidents.

Creating a Security Policy Framework

Developing a security policy framework involves organizing security objectives into comprehensive and actionable plans. A structured framework typically encompasses the following stages:

1. **Assessment of Current Environment:** Begin by understanding the existing security landscape within your Druid deployment. This involves identifying critical data assets, current vulnerabilities, compliance requirements, and existing security controls.

2. **Policy Development:** Based on the assessment, draft policies that address identified risks and compliance needs. Ensure these policies include clear objectives and are realistic and enforceable.

3. **Stakeholder Engagement:** Involve a wide range of stakeholders, from IT security to business operations, ensuring that policies align with business processes and requirements. Engagement encourages policy adoption and compliance across the board.

4. **Implementation:** Enforce policies using Druid's built-in security features, third-party tools, and integrations such as firewalls, access controls, and identity management systems. Automation tools can help maintain policy consistency and reduce the risk of human error.

5. **Monitoring and Maintenance:** After implementation, continuously monitor for policy adherence, effectiveness, and gaps. Regularly review and update policies to ensure they remain relevant against evolving threats and organizational changes.

Incorporating Best Practices into Security Policies

To establish and uphold effective security policies in Druid, the following best practices should be integrated:

- **Use Principle of Least Privilege:** Grant users and systems only the access necessary to perform their tasks, minimizing the potential damage from inadvertent actions or compromises.

- **Adopt Defense-in-Depth Approach:** Layer multiple security measures (e.g., encryption, network segmentation, and endpoint protection) to protect against breaches. If one line of defense is compromised, other layers still protect the system.

- **Regular Security Audits:** Conduct audits frequently to evaluate the effectiveness of security measures and identify areas for improvement. Utilization of third-party security audits can provide unbiased scrutiny of policy adherence.

- **Comprehensive Training:** Develop robust training programs for employees and system administrators to ensure awareness and compliance with security practices. Training reduces human error, which is often a significant factor in security incidents.

- **Log Retention and Analysis:** Implement detailed logging of access, changes, and anomalies. Retain logs as dictated by compliance requirements and analyze them regularly for signs of unauthorized access or anomalies.

- **Backup and Recovery Plans:** Ensure that data backup procedures are included in security policies, with clear recovery protocols for major incidents. Regularly test backup restoration processes to guarantee data availability and integrity.

Implementing Security Policies using Druid's Features

Druid functionalities offer a range of options for security policy implementation. Below, we explore specific implementations aligned with modern security practices:

1. **Authentication and Authorization:** Druid's extensible architecture allows integration with authentication frameworks such as LDAP, Kerberos, and OAuth. Configuring these integrations involves specifying connection details, binding parameters, and security controls that align with internal authentication policies.

```
{
    "type" : "ldap",
    "url" : "ldap://secure-ldap.example.com:636",
    "userDnSearchFilter" : "(uid={username})",
    "baseDn" : "ou=users,dc=example,dc=com",
```

```
"bindDn" : "cn=admin,dc=example,dc=com",
"bindPassword" : "strongLDAPPassword"
}
```

2. **Data Encryption:** Implementing TLS/SSL ensures that all data in transit within the network is encrypted. Employ configurations for Druid nodes that establish secure communication channels, verified using server certificates.

```
druid.server.https.enabled=true
druid.server.https.port=8443
druid.server.https.keyStorePath=/path/to/keystore.jks
druid.server.https.keyStorePassword=keystorePassword
```

3. **Monitoring and Logging:** Use Druid's built-in logging capabilities to enforce logging policies. Setting appropriate log levels ensures necessary details are captured while avoiding data overload.

```xml
<Configuration status="warn">
  <Appenders>
    <File name="File" fileName="logs/druid-system.log">
      <PatternLayout pattern="%d [%t] %-5level: %msg%n"/>
    </File>
  </Appenders>
  <Loggers>
    <Root level="info">
      <AppenderRef ref="File"/>
    </Root>
  </Loggers>
</Configuration>
```

4. **Role and Permission Management:** Utilize Druid's RBAC model to develop role definitions and assign permissions that faithfully represent security policies, implementing controls for data access and system management.

```json
{
  "roles": [
    {
      "name": "REPORT-VIEWER",
      "permissions": [
        {"resource": "datasource", "action": "read", "scope": "monthly-
            reports"}
      ]
    },
    {
      "name": "DATA-ADMIN",
      "permissions": [
        {"resource": "datasource", "action": "write", "scope": "*"},
```

```
            {"resource": "status", "action": "read", "scope": "*"}
          ]
        }
      ]
    }
```

Monitoring Compliance with Security Policies

Ensuring compliance requires continuous monitoring and periodic reviews:

- **Automated Monitoring Tools:** Leverage automation tools to monitor adherence to security policies and to detect violations promptly.

- **Compliance Dashboards:** Deploy dashboards to visualize compliance metrics and identify areas needing attention. Tools like Grafana can provide the necessary visualization capabilities to track compliance over time.

- **Third-Party Audits:** Utilize periodic audits by external professionals to ensure objectivity in evaluating policy compliance. Audits assess the practical enforcement of security measures outlined in policies.

Evolving Security Policies

Security policies are not static and should evolve to address emerging threats, new technologies, and changes in regulation. Emphasize agility in policy-making, ensuring an adaptive security posture:

- **Regular Policy Reviews:** Incorporate regular review cycles to update policies, aligning them with current business processes and threat landscapes.

- **Feedback Mechanisms:** Establish channels for receiving feedback on policy effectiveness from stakeholders, enabling continuous improvement.

Conclusion and Best Practices

Implementing comprehensive security policies in Apache Druid is an ongoing process requiring diligence, collaboration, and foresight. By structuring robust, adaptable policies, employing best practices, and leveraging Druid's versatile features, organizations can safeguard their data assets against threats and comply with regulatory demands. The adoption of a proactive, layered security strategy ensures that security remains a cornerstone of Druid operations, safeguarding the organization's objectives and data assets.

10.7 Staying Compliant with Regulations

In data management and analytics, compliance with industry regulations is integral to maintaining trust with customers, partners, and stakeholders. Apache Druid, being a powerful analytical database, often stores and processes sensitive data, necessitating strict adherence to regulatory standards such as the General Data Protection Regulation (GDPR), Health Insurance Portability and Accountability Act (HIPAA), and SOC 2, among others. This section discusses strategies for leveraging Druid to remain compliant with these regulations, focusing on data security, privacy, access control, and auditing.

Understanding Regulatory Requirements

To effectively implement compliance within Druid environments, it is crucial to first understand the specific requirements of relevant regulations:

- **GDPR:** Focuses on data protection and privacy for individuals within the European Union. Requirements include data minimization, informed consent for data processing, data breach notifications, and ensuring data subject rights such as access, correction, and erasure.

- **HIPAA:** Pertains to the protection of health information within the United States, emphasizing the need for confidentiality, integrity, and availability of electronic protected health information (ePHI).

- **SOC 2:** Centers on service organizations and their information systems, underpinned by trust services criteria like security, availability, processing integrity, confidentiality, and privacy.

Each of these regulations imposes specific mandates for data handling, protection, and transparency in operations, which organizations using Druid must carefully address.

Implementing Data Encryption

Data encryption is a fundamental requirement across most regulations to protect data at rest and in transit. Druid supports encryption mechanisms allowing secure data management:

- **Data at Rest:** Leveraging the encryption capabilities of underlying storage systems, such as Amazon S3 SSE-KMS or HDFS, ensures that data stored within Druid remains secure. Coupling this with Druid's internal data handling through strong encryption algorithms like AES-256 contributes to meeting encryption requirements.

```
{
  "type":"s3",
  "s3": {
    "bucket": "druid-data-bucket",
    "baseKey": "druid/segments",
    "kmsKeyId": "arn:aws:kms:us-east-1:123456789012:key/abcd1234-a123
      -456a-a12b-a123b4cd56ef"
  }
}
```

- **Data in Transit:** Configure Druid to use TLS, ensuring that all data transfers between nodes and client interactions are encrypted, thus meeting compliance through secure transmission protocols.

```
druid.server.https.enabled=true
druid.server.https.port=8280
druid.server.https.keyStorePath=/path/to/.keystore
druid.server.https.keyStorePassword=keystore-password
```

Enforcing Access Controls

Access control mechanisms are essential for ensuring that only authorized users can access sensitive data. Druid's RBAC features allow granular management of permissions and roles:

- **Role Definition and User Provisioning:** Define roles that align with job functions and responsibilities. Assign users to these roles carefully, ensuring necessary access is provided while maintaining least privilege principles.

```
{
    "roles": [
        {
            "name": "COMPLIANCE-OFFICER",
            "permissions": [
                {"resource": "audit", "action": "read", "scope": "*"},
                {"resource": "datasource", "action": "read", "scope": "sensitive-data
                    "}
            ]
        }
    ]
}
```

- **Integration with IAM Systems:** Leverage LDAP or OAuth to manage user identities and access controls consistently, ensuring synchronization with broader organizational access policies.

Privacy by Design and Data Minimization

Regulations often require that systems are designed with privacy in mind (Privacy by Design). Implement privacy-centric features in Druid:

- **Data Minimization:** Limit data collection and storage to only that which is necessary for analytical purposes. Implement data lifecycle management policies to ensure timely de-identification or deletion of data.

- **Pseudonymization:** Apply data anonymization techniques, such as masking or pseudonymization, where feasible, to protect identities within datasets.

Auditing and Reporting

Comprehensive logging and auditing mechanisms are obligatory for compliance, providing transparency and accountability across operations:

- **Audit Trails:** Ensure audit logs capture access events, data queries, system changes, and security incidents. Securely store these logs for future reference and compliance audits.

```
<AuditLogsConfiguration>
  <LogDestination>audit-logs.db</LogDestination>
  <EnableDetailedLogs>true</EnableDetailedLogs>
</AuditLogsConfiguration>
```

- **Automated Reporting:** Implement automated tools to generate compliance reports on a regular basis. These reports should summarize compliance status, incidents, and provide actionable insights.

Responding to Data Breaches

Regulations necessitate prompt response mechanisms for data breaches:

- **Incident Response Plans:** Develop and regularly update incident response plans which detail steps for identifying, containing, and mitigating breaches.

- **Breach Notifications:** Ensure processes are in place for timely notifications to regulators and affected parties, as specified by regulatory mandates.

Training and Awareness

Maintain an organizational culture of compliance through regular training programs. Equip employees with the knowledge of regulations and responsibilities regarding data protection and privacy. Training should include:

- **Policy Understanding:** Ensure comprehensive understanding of internal and external policies related to data protection among all employees.

- **System Use Protocols:** Educate users on correct use protocols, emphasizing secure data handling, timely reporting of incidents, and maintaining confidentiality.

Regular Reviews and Updates

As regulations evolve, so too must the practices in place within Druid:

- **Regular Compliance Audits:** Conduct thorough internal audits to review compliance with established policies. Address findings proactively to bridge any gaps.

- **Policy Adaptation:** Adapt security and privacy policies to respond to new regulatory requirements or changes in the operational environment.

- **Engagement with Legal Advisors:** Consult with legal advisors specializing in data protection laws to validate ongoing compliance and preemptively address potential regulatory changes.

Conclusion and Best Practices

Remaining compliant with regulations such as GDPR, HIPAA, and SOC 2 while leveraging Apache Druid requires strategic planning, robust implementation of security measures, and continuous adaptation to changing legal landscapes. By emphasizing encryption, access control, data privacy, auditing, and employee training, organizations can achieve compliance, mitigate risks, and build user trust in the handling of sensitive data. Adhering to these practices not only fulfills legal obligations but serves as a cornerstone of an ethical data strategy, fostering operational excellence and sustainable business practices.

www.ingramcontent.com/pod-product-compliance
Lightning Source LLC
LaVergne TN
LVHW051434050326
832903LV00030BD/3076